HERE IS a unique collection of skewer recipes from every part of the world for imaginative and delicious meat, seafood and vegetable dishes. There are even some ideas for skewered fruit desserts. Inspired by the famous dishes of her Greek ancestors, the author has gathered together a treasury of superb yet easy-to-prepare skewer recipes from all the interesting cuisines of the world. You will find Korean Beef San Juk, with a rich garlic-soy sauce; Japanese Kushi Yaki, seasoned with ginger and sherry; Polynesian Chicken Kebobs; Russian Lamb Shashlik; Greek-style Fish Kebobs with garlic and lemon; and a whole range of other exciting dishes. In addition to these international favorites, the author has created many memorable recipes of her own. And all of them are quick to prepare for satisfying family meals and exciting but relaxed entertaining.

In addition to the wide variety of recipes for main dishes, the book offers sauces, side dishes, salads and desserts to round out the meal. Also, there are

(continued on back flap)

(continued from front flap)

party plans and menus that make entertaining as much fun for the hostess as for her guests. A special section on cooking methods gives full directions for skewer cooking indoors as well as outdoors so that you can enjoy these wonderful dishes all year round. For everyone interested in good food, here is a book that will introduce you to a whole new world of eating pleasure.

Skewer Cooking Around the World

GEORGIA CHEOPELAS

SIMON AND SCHUSTER · NEW YORK

Designed by Eve Metz
Manufactured in the United States of America

1 2 3 4 5 6 7 8 9 10

Library of Congress Cataloging in Publication Data

Cheopelas, Georgia.
    Skewer cooking around the world.

    1. Skewer cookery.   I. Title.
TX834.C47   641.5′9   74-12457
ISBN 0-671-21802-6

ACKNOWLEDGMENTS

When I began this book, I simply did not anticipate the vast scope of the time-consuming—indeed, emotionally consuming—task ahead of me. And so I learned even more about patience. Being patient, however, was possible only because the people who worked with me—who trusted and encouraged me—made that possible. For their support through the tasting and testing of several manuscript revisions, I am deeply grateful to:

Mom, Dad. Teddie.

Nancy Gadbois and your family—Phil, David, Greg and the T's.

Also Diane Brown; Carole Stanton; David Burns; John Stiefel; Dot and Dick Lovell.

In addition, I would like to acknowledge all the organizations I contacted in my early research stages—the foreign consulates and embassies, food trade associations, food manufacturers and the many restaurants throughout the country. Whether by phone, letter or a visit, everyone was very generous in providing information.

I appreciate, too, Pat Read's initial enthusiasm. And I am particularly appreciative of Diane Harris, who helped me to see the manuscript and guided me through to publication.

To those of you who directly or indirectly assisted me in completing these pages, Thank you!

TO MY MOTHER AND FATHER
for their agape,
for their daily living examples
of what happiness is all about

TO MY SISTER, TEDDIE,
for her cooperation and encouragement.
Having the friendship of a sister like
mine is something I treasure

CONTENTS

AN INTRODUCTION   11

PART ONE: This Is Skewer Cooking   15
  1. About Skewer Cooking Today   17
  2. Methods of Cooking   22
  3. The Indispensable Seasonings   28

PART TWO: Now for the Recipes   35
  4. Beef   37
  5. Ground Beef   73
  6. Veal   88
  7. Lamb   97
  8. Fresh Pork and Ham   121
  9. Variety Meats   144
10. Sausage   153
11. Poultry   168
12. Shellfish and Fish   188
13. Vegetables, Fruits, Cheese   208
14. Mixed Meats   238

15. Sauces   258
16. Suggested Accompaniments   275

PART THREE: And Here Are Entertaining Ideas   299
17. Menus   301
18. Parties   324

INDEX   337

AN INTRODUCTION

One of my main reasons for wanting to write a cookbook was this: I've always felt that food is a means of communication, a very important means—often more important than words. I simply wanted to suggest this somehow between two covers.

It shouldn't be difficult to highlight the point that food is a communication tool by an analogy with words. With food, just as in conversation, it's not what you serve but the way you serve. Your attitude and the way you set a table or arrange food on a plate tell perceptive people how you feel about yourself and them. Everyone can't be a great chef. That, in my opinion, requires an innate talent. You either have the natural feel to use ingredients starting from scratch to create gems consistently or, like most, you patiently sharpen your culinary skills, never quite achieving perfection but having enough rewarding winners to make continued efforts worthwhile. I am often surprised at how simply prepared and attractively presented food can evoke such a favorable response in guests. Of course, if the food comes near to tasting extraordinary according to the standards of culinary experts, so much the better. What I'm essentially trying to reinforce here is this: there's more to food than its use in appealing to the taste buds, in satisfying hunger, in supplying nutrients; and eating should be more than a mere habit.

Maybe these little, obvious things tend to become obscure because we sometimes take food for granted. (Although I should add that with the present realities of food shortages and soaring prices, probably fewer of us are doing that today or will be doing that tomorrow.) Anyway, I do know that it would be much nicer if eating were dictated not so much by the hour as by the heart. Food is an enormously expressive medium for communicating thought, feeling and care . . . for self-expression . . . for sharing. That's the attitude, it seems to me, by which we should serve food more often—as if it were a gift.

Now, you ask, what does all this have to do with my idea of skewer cooking for a cookbook? It provided my vantage point. I became immensely intrigued with the *ways* in which kebobs could be served—the limitless possibilities for expression; the aesthetics, the satisfaction to be derived from food preparation and presentation. However, I never took seriously the idea of writing a book on skewer cooking until I couldn't find a book that treated this subject exclusively. I suppose it was the challenge. Certainly, an all-persuasive reason was the versatility of skewer cooking. Especially today —our way of life characterized as it is by many alternative life styles coupled with the wide range of preferences for food and seasonings—kebobs seem one good answer to the entertaining problem of how to please many at one time.

So I plunged into my commitment confidently, dauntlessly and in a way, naively. I researched to pinpoint consumer food preferences in the States, analyzed information and recipes on kebobs and studied favorite dishes and seasonings characteristic of the various cuisines. With that background, plus my personal experience traveling throughout the States and observing people in all walks of life, I began to create and develop my version of kebob recipes for this book. You will note that recipes such as German Sauerbraten Kebobs, page 46, Greek Orange Beef Kebobs, page 39, Lamb Kebobs Scandinavian, page 113, or Flank Steak Kebobs Oriental, page 61, will appear unusual to those of you who are familiar with the traditional kebobs of these areas. Also, since I've been exposed to Greek cooking most of my life, I wanted to share with you a few favorite recipes adapted from this cuisine, a little something extra, you might say.

No doubt you are curious about my credentials for writing a cookbook. And I want you to know them. My professional experience in the cooking field is far from extensive. That is, I haven't earned my living working in test kitchens of food manufacturers or trade associations. Nor have I spent years creating and cooking great dishes. But I have been exposed in a sense to a teacher—yes, to my mother, who I think has a feel for cooking and who encouraged and tolerated my experimenting (some people might have called it messing) with kitchen adventures as a youngster. And although I've earned a degree in home economics, my core curriculum was General, not Foods. (I hope you're still with me.)

It's people. I don't know of anyone genuinely interested in people who doesn't have an acute interest in food—that is, in the psychological implications of food. My background is in the field of marketing communications—public relations, advertising, education. I'm a generalist and therefore can't claim expertise in any one subject, like cooking. This book couldn't appeal to the purist. It's for the practical, for you who want something different and simple, using available foods from the supermarket. You should know, too, my recipes were tested by a home economist, a major in foods. It was a joy working with someone of Nancy's rare earnestness and sincerity. We became friends.

And that's how I hope you respond to this book. Make it your friend. Turn to it at leisure or at a time of need when you want to serve a gift.

Do be receptive—to recipes, to the menus, and to the party suggestions—and dare those which seem different to you, or follow the familiar. But do get involved. It's fun. Just look at what can be speared and cooked on a skewer. Look at the methods of cooking—not only outdoors over coals but indoors. Broil, bake and yes, braise, too; even no cooking at all. Enhance precooked foods or leftovers by simply spearing on a skewer and serving. And the size of meat chunks used for kebobs does mean fast cooking. But perhaps of most interest, it is a convenient way to cook. You can prepare sauces, thread meats on skewers, do almost everything in advance. Let me invite you to experience the following pages and hope that you, too, will come to savor the many pleasures of skewer cooking.

Your enjoyment is the objective of this book.

PART ONE

This Is
Skewer Cooking

1 · ABOUT SKEWER COOKING TODAY

HOW TO SERVE KEBOBS
Skewers: From Swords to Implements to Flatware

At the very heart of skewer cooking is—the skewer. If you were to omit the skewer—perhaps cook small chunks of food without it, or cook small chunks with it but then remove before serving—there would be a void, either way. In the first case, the taste would be inferior to that achieved by cooking foods close to one another; and in the second, the appearance would be much less striking than it could be. At this point, I suspect you're a little puzzled. As for using a skewer during cooking, you can understand that; after all, this is a cookbook on kebobs. But, you ask, what's this about not removing skewers before serving? Before I get to answering your good question, let's first take a look at the skewer.

Let's go back to its use in cooking yesterday . . . years ago . . . centuries ago. Indeed, I'm inclined to think skewer cooking was perhaps man's first method of cooking. After digging through pages of history, I've this summary to share. Precisely where and when in the Middle East it originated are uncertain. According to some sources it began in Persia when soldiers used their swords to cook chunks of mutton over campfires. Others point to its origin in Arabia near Mesopotamia. Still others say that the herdsmen of Turkey are responsible for creating the first shish kebobs. And its creation is claimed by *all* the Balkan countries. What is certain, however, is the derivation of the words. *"Sis"* (pronounced *shish*) means skewer in Turkish, and "kebob" is from the Arabic *"kebap,"* meaning roasted meat.

It seems plausible to infer that the first skewer—something used to impale and cook several chunks of meat—was the sword. (I'm not discounting the possibility of a stick if we went way, way back to primitive times.) As the idea of cooking meat on a stick, a sword—a *skewer*—spread to many countries throughout the world, the food and seasonings popular in those areas were used. As a result, today we have an extensive selection of skewered dishes which represent nearly every cuisine. Even shish kebob is identified by other names. The Japanese call it "kushi yaki"; Moroccans call it "brochettes"; Spanish—"pinchos"; South Africans—"sosaties"; Indonesians—"satés"—and so on. Also, the skewer itself has taken on every shape and material imaginable.

In the past, because of awkward sizes and unattractive styles, skewers have been limited to use as implements for cooking foods. Today, however, you can use skewers not only for cooking but also for serving. You can, that is, if they've been designed as flatware. By this I mean skewers that are all metal, preferably stainless steel; the handles are designed to enhance table settings and complement appointments; they come in standard sizes (6, 8 and 10 inches) for use with dinnerware for serving appetizers, snacks and main courses; and they can be used with all indoor cooking methods—broiling, baking, braising—and for spearing precooked foods. Note, though, I specified indoors. Remember this: think *short* handles and blades for kebobing indoors, using the skewers to cook and serve as well; think *long* for outdoors (longer than flatware), using skewers only to cook food and removing them before serving.

At this point you're probably wondering—and rightly—how does one eat from a skewer? Since I've an aversion to rigid rules of etiquette, I'll tell you what I do and then you decide what's going to be your way. I never remove food from the skewer all at once, except for sandwiches or in some recipes where I have so indicated. Basically, the food is removed and eaten a piece at a time. The food remaining on the skewer makes a more attractive arrangement than would chunks of meat scattered at random on a plate. It's also a good idea to have the host or hostess begin eating first to set an example for this procedure. One thing more: I store skewers point down in a skewer holder (a decorative tumbler) placed on a counter near the range. Yes, if I had tots around, I'd make a special point of keeping skewer points away from their reach.

Kebobs on the Menu

You can feature kebobs on the menu in one of two ways. The first way is "strictly skewered," with every course from appetizer to dessert kebobed. Think of this as a skewer-tasting event. Object: to taste not only different foods but also different methods of skewer cooking. This informal type of menu adapts perfectly to both small and large groups. The second way to feature kebobs on the menu is more common. Here the kebobs appear either as the entree for lunch or dinner or as the main attraction of an appetizer or snack assortment. Or, serve them as an accompaniment—a dessert, or a side dish of vegetables or fruits. Unless the menu is designed as "strictly skewered," I'd avoid placing kebobs in more than two courses. And if serving more than two kebobs per person, have a skewer stand (or tall tumbler) nearby for disposal of used skewers, which should be inserted point down.

You ask now, is there a way to estimate portions per serving? All I can provide is a guide. In the introductions to some meat sections, you'll find an approximate number of servings per pound of boneless meat. That's one help. The other is: *Think pairs!* Generally, two 8-inch or 10-inch kebobs provide an adequate portion for a main dish— and for snacks and appetizers, at least two 6-inch ones. How you thread foods on a skewer also has a bearing on what determines a satisfying serving. If, for instance, you're threading nothing but meat, often one kebob is ample. Needless to say, forecasting the size of appetites can baffle even the experienced. That's why I prefer to overestimate the amount of food needed rather than underestimate, allowing for at least one, preferably two kebobs extra. And for eating outdoors—plan extra extras! I feel safer that way—and leftover kebobs don't taste bad, really.

Three Styles of Serving

TABLE SERVICE

Informal . . . semiformal . . . formal. Table service lends itself nicely to all three of these moods, and whatever the occasion, kebobs on the menu do too. Place them on serving platters, or on individual plates for each setting, or serve in one of my favorite ways—which is to place them uncooked on an open-hearth broiler on top of a cart adjacent to the table. Invite guests to cook the kebobs of their choice, or recruit an assistant to help oversee the timing of the kebobs. These suggestions are worth every consideration—especially when you're serving those who appreciate having their meat cooked exactly so. Another feature: cooking on the cart helps to stimulate pleasant conversation.

SELF-SERVICE STYLE

The buffet is the best way to serve many people at one time. And since all your guests help themselves to food by going to a table, it also would seem extremely conducive to sociability. However, buffet service alone is not always sufficient to stimulate interaction. The food that makes up the menu and the way it's served are really what counts. This is one reason fondue became phenomenally popular: there's action at the table. Guests are involved in *doing* something—lingering at the table huddled around the pot rubbing elbows. And kebobs offer this same kind of involvement.

Kebobs can be assembled in a ready-to-cook assortment or they can be created by guests. On a table arrange 6-, 8- and 10-inch skewers; platters with chunks of meat, vegetables and fruits; and bowls or cups with various seasoned sauces.

Provide portable appliances nearby and, if desired, a few hibachis outdoors.

LAP STYLE

Convenience! That's really the only way to describe this method, in which the traffic pattern is virtually direct from kitchen to wherever guests are seated. And lap-style service seems to be increasing in popularity, if for no other reason than space. Kebobs are especially well suited to this style, since many kinds can be served without a knife. Serve kebobs lap-style for appetizers, snacks, perhaps first course and sometimes dessert. In fact, this is my old standby. Why? It seems appropriate anytime, whether guests come invited or drop by unexpectedly; it's easy on me for serving; and it's undeniably attractive in an unpretentious way: two 6-inch kebobs on a decorative tray, handles matching on both skewer and fork—and a giant-size, colorful napkin.

One final point: these styles of serving aren't mutually exclusive. For something different, leisurely, and informal, combine all three of them to serve one meal. This should take three to four hours, or the span of a visit. (For suggestions see Chapter 18.)

Now to the inevitable question: Should you serve kebobs flambé? Flaming swords, I think, belong in restaurants, which have the facilities to present them with a flourish—a flourish appropriate for the dining-out kind of setting. For home entertaining, this seems garish, and there's hazard if you're inexperienced in the art. Certainly you could achieve a formal flair (if that's your objective) without serving ignited kebobs at the table. But this is only my opinion. Serve —always—in a style that reflects your personality and experience and fits harmoniously with the occasion and the persons you intend to please.

2 · METHODS OF COOKING

The basic methods of skewer cooking are these: indoors—broiling, baking, braising; and outdoors—grilling. In this section, you'll find basic instructions for skewer-cooking all foods. For information pertinent to specific items, review the preface material to each recipe section. Note, too, that my emphasis throughout the book is essentially on cooking kebobs indoors—the area I believe more often overlooked. Yet I see no reason why the dishes whose recipes indicate "Broil" couldn't be grilled over coals or why portable appliances couldn't be taken outdoors.

BROILING

For selecting meat to broil, the single most important consideration is this: select the naturally tender or that which has been tenderized. Why? Broiling is a dry-heat method of cooking, which doesn't increase tenderness. As for the technique of broiling and use of equipment, a number of considerations emerge. Because of the wide variety of ranges and broiling units in use today, it's impossible to establish a precise standard for broiling time that's useful to everyone. Refer to broiling timetables as a very approximate guide. Both my tester and I used the gas ranges available to us in our homes. Make your adjustments attuned to your equipment—gas, electric or other; old, new; oven and broiler in one or separate compartments; precision-calibrated, consistently unreliable, idiosyncratic—whatever. If you have an electric range and I've indicated a low broiling temperature in one of my recipes—let's say, 425°—then leave the indicator on BROIL, but move the rack farther from heating element.

Should you start the broiler cold or preheat? People in the utility business take the position that preheating is not essential; in fact, they don't recommend it for ranges with separate broiling compartments such as those below the oven. Many, however, consider it a good idea when meats are to be broiled rare. Here the pan with the grid is removed and the broiler compartment preheated about 4 to 5 minutes. Since cold meat on a cold grid surface prevents sticking, no one advises preheating the broiler pan and grid.

In the past, I preheated the broiler compartment habitually, until I learned it's actually a waste of fuel. The food is not cooked by the heat from the compartment but by the heat source, and this source—flame or element—heats instantly. Also, the new ranges in particular have burners and elements that generate heat extra fast. The best advice is to follow manufacturer's directions with individual equipment. My recipes were tested starting with a cold broiler.

Next, how should you place kebobs in a range broiler? The ways are many. Place kebobs directly on the grid, greasing lightly if you wish, or place first on a separate pan. You could use the shish kebober cook sets—inexpensive all-metal cookware ensembles with skewers suspended on a frame. Place these directly on grid or use a cookie sheet as an underliner to catch drippings. Then there is what I call the homemade shish kebober, which is this: use a pan at least 1 inch deep and arrange 8- and 10-inch skewers on it so that handles and tips protrude over the edge, thereby achieving the principle of the suspended skewer, which facilitates uniform cooking. If using 6-inch skewers for appetizers and snacks, place a long metal skewer, about 18 inches, lengthwise down the center of the pan and arrange the kebobs alternately on each side. If your pan were about 15 × 10½ × 1 inches, it would accommodate approximately twenty 6-inch kebobs, ten on each side.

For some meats—particularly beef—portable broilers in

my opinion provide for juiciness unattainable with other equipment. These appliances come closed or open, the latter perhaps more familiar as open hearth and, what's now becoming popular, the electric hibachi. Since these provide smokeless, spatterless cooking, cook on them anywhere an outlet is convenient. Although some units come with a separate shish kebob attachment that operates as a rotisserie, I still much prefer placing kebobs directly on the grid. But this is truly a matter of personal preference.

Another type of broiling—pan broiling, sometimes referred to as griddle broiling—is cooking kebobs on a griddle on top of the range or on one of the many portable appliances. Although additional fat is not required, I usually grease the griddle lightly. Use this method for quickly searing kebobs of raw meats and for heating the ready-to-eat varieties. You could, if preferred, use a heavy aluminum or cast-iron griddle, although I'm satisfied with the results from the lightweight metals coated with a nonstick surface. To give you an idea, an 11-inch-square griddle accommodates five to six 8- to 10-inch kebobs or seven to eight 6-inch ones.

BAKING

Like broiling, baking is a dry-heat method of cooking which requires the use of naturally tender or tenderized meats. Unlike broiling, however, baking involves cooking by indirect heat. Its advantages? For kebobs it seems better than broiling when you're using a baste with a good deal of sugar and when meats must be cooked well done. Actually, in many of the recipes where I've indicated "Broil," you could also bake; of course, you'd need to increase the cooking time to allow for the lower temperatures and indirect heat. Place kebobs in a baking pan, lined with foil if you wish, or use the shish kebober cooking ideas suggested under Broiling, page 22. The recipes indicating "Bake" in this book have been tested with a preheated oven.

BRAISING

Although braising, a moist-heat method of cooking, suggests that thrifty, tough cuts also can be skewer-cooked, this is not why I braise them. My reason is flavor and moistness. I cook even the very tender cuts this way. However, braising is the best alternative when you're cooking kebobs with meats that must be well done, have little marbleization of fat, or contain an abundance of connective tissue.

There is one requisite for braising kebobs so obvious I'm actually almost afraid to mention it: the fit. Skewers must fit into the skillet. With the 6-inch skewers, there is usually no problem: that is, the standard 10-inch skillet (round or square shape) accommodates them fine. If, however, you're using 8-inch skewers, you'll need either a 12-inch round skillet or a 10-inch square one. When braising kebobs, always cover unless otherwise indicated in recipes. And, of course, the skewer blade as well as the handle must be metal or of another fire-resistant material. Scoop skillet sauce over kebobs, and if the liquid evaporates too quickly, just add more of the predominant liquid ingredient from the skillet sauce. As for turning kebobs, here is my advice: do not as I do, but as I say—unless you have thermotolerant fingers. Please, grab the skewer handles and turn the kebobs with the assistance of tongs. I might also mention that when serving braised kebobs, I frequently have two skillets going at the same time and on occasion even three.

GRILLING

The terms broiling and grilling are often interchanged. They both employ the dry-heat method of cooking food in which one side is exposed to the source of heat. But there is, I've learned, a distinction. With broiling, the direct source of heat comes from the top, whereas with grilling it comes from the bottom. Since this semantic distinction is not taken too seriously, I'm taking author's license here and using the term grilling with reference to cooking kebobs outdoors over a bed of coals. I've also tried to steer clear of the term "barbecue," since it really describes whole hunks of meat on a spit, rather than chunks on a skewer.

Concerning utensils in grilling kebobs, remember one word: long. Skewer handles and blades as well as fire-tending tools all must be long, for the practical reason of preventing burns and splashes on garments. However, when you're grilling over small grills such as the hibachi, the skewers used for indoor cooking are appropriate.

Size of grill; sophistication of grill; lump charcoal or briquets; use of electric starters; amount of ash; ventilation; distance the food is placed from coals—all these factors regulate the amount of heat. The skill necessary to start and control a fire comes from experience—trial and error.

Since I don't have that "feel" for starting a fire, I can't provide very meaningful advice on techniques. Quite frankly, for some inexplicable reason, I dislike this chore immensely. Yet, since there always seem to be fire-starting experts around to give a hand, thus far this hasn't been a problem.

How to use a fire in grilling kebobs successfully is, of course, another matter. First of all, timing is important. Have the fire started well in advance so that when the kebobs are ready for grilling, the coals are not flaming, but glowing. When all the coals have formed a white ash, this is usually a good indication that you've reached the right cooking temperature. Is there a way to gauge temperature? For a very rough idea, place the palm of your hand close to the cooking surface and count slowly. If you can't stand the heat for 1 or 2 counts, the heat, needless to say, is very intense; 4 to 5 counts is usually moderate; and 6 to 8 counts, slow to very slow. To control the heat intensity, lower or raise the grid. Generally, allow 4 to 6 inches from the coals for most kebobs except rare beef, which is seared as close as 1 inch from the coals. For pork, which must be cooked well done, place farther away—about 6 to 8 inches—and cook long and slowly over low to moderate temperatures. Next, consider threading of foods. When cooking kebobs outdoors, I prefer to keep meat and vegetables on separate skewers. Finally, a word on placing kebobs on the grill—and there is quite a choice. Place them directly on the grid, rubbing with suet or oil to prevent the meat from sticking; arrange bricks on the grid and suspend the skewers; wrap the kebobs in aluminum foil; cook on a shish kebob rotisserie unit; or place the filled shish kebob cook set (metal frame with suspended skewers) directly on the grid. Another thought. If you prefer the very natural taste of foods basted only with melted butter yet highlighted with a delicate smoke flavor, try this: during cooking, add to the charcoal a few water-soaked chips of wood such as oak, hickory, apple or cherry.

3 · THE INDISPENSABLE SEASONINGS

Baste . . . Marinade . . . Topping Sauces . . . Dips . . . Skillet Sauces. These are the seasoning mixtures common to skewer cooking. In the recipes I've identified most of them according to use. For example, if the marinade worked best primarily as a marinade, I listed it as such. If, on the other hand, it doubled as a baste, I referred to it as a Marinade-Baste; and if it tripled in use, you'll find Marinade-Baste-Topping Sauce.

Whenever possible, prepare seasoning mixtures from scratch, and wherever practical, insist on fresh ingredients. But there are two other methods of preparation: one, the semi-instant, in which all you add to a prepared mix is a liquid such as lemon juice or vinegar; and two, the instant, the ready-to-use from the bottle or jar.

THE BASTE

The most essential of the seasoning mixtures—at least for broiling, baking, and grilling kebobs—is the baste. It adds flavor, but more importantly, moistness. A thin or thick liquid, it might consist of little fat, no fat or all fat. Seasoned butter sauces—melted butter with spirits or spices—are perhaps the most popular. An exception to the liquid is bacon, which when wrapped around foods on a skewer bastes them by dripping fat during cooking. As for a basting brush, don't discount the idea of purchasing a good thick brush from an art-supply store. It's worth the investment and will last longer, not to mention eliminating the anguish that comes from having a few loose bristles floating in the sauce or on the kebobs. Apply bastes frequently throughout cooking— except when using those containing considerable sugar, which should be applied near the end of cooking to prevent burning.

THE MARINADE

The marinade, it seems to me, is the most misunderstood of the seasoning mixtures. And this undoubtedly stems from association with its original uses: first, as a preservative— a pickling liquid or brine to prevent the spoilage of meat in the days of no refrigeration; and secondly, as a tenderizer —a seasoned liquid in which to soak chunks of tough meat day after day. Today the marinade is definitely used to enhance flavor. There is never a guarantee that a marinade will *tenderize* a piece of meat to a specified degree. Certainly it helps, and particularly when it contains an acid such as fruit juice, wine or even yogurt. But some tough connective tissue—collagen—is not dissolved by acid. Only heat converts it to a gelatin, which incidentally is the reason for using the moist-heat method of cooking for tough cuts. Thus, there is also no guarantee that the longer certain meats marinate, the more tender they will become. In fact, I don't marinate kebob chunks very long at all. The flavor of some ingredients such as acids and herbs—garlic in particular—becomes more pronounced the longer they're left in a marinade, and may overwhelm the taste of the meat. (This may or may not be objectionable, depending on personal preference.) Actually, three to five hours is sufficient for marinating kebob chunks of tender meats and one or two hours for fish and poultry.

To soak kebob chunks, use nonporous containers such as glass and always cover, except of course when you're marinating filled skewers, which would remain uncovered. Turn the chunks several times to expose all sides to the marinade, and fork the tough cuts to help the marinade penetrate more thoroughly. I don't think much of commercial tenderizers, but this too is a matter of personal preference.

I usually marinate at room temperature, unless the food must stand more than three hours, in which case it then goes into the refrigerator. Certain meats—ground round, always —are refrigerated immediately. Refrigerate shellfish and fish if they must stand more than 30 to 40 minutes at room temperature.

Of all the seasoning mixtures, marinades are potentially the most versatile. Some can be used as bastes and others also as a topping sauce, thickened, if desired, by the addition of cornstarch, flour, or egg yolk. And note this: foods soaked in a marinade containing melted butter generally don't need basting. Since melted butter (a fat) loses its liquid property at room temperature, the marinade as it solidifies adheres to the meat chunks and during cooking the meat bastes itself— surprisingly well, in fact. If you wish to use any such remaining marinade as a baste, heat in a saucepan until melted. Don't limit your image of the marinade to the traditional heavily spiced oil and acid mixtures. Yes, many are liquids, but others are thick, such as those having a yogurt base; and there is the nonliquid, too—what's known as a dry marinade, a process of rubbing spices and herbs into meat.

TOPPING SAUCES

If you've dined in restaurants throughout the country and have observed and/or consumed the many preparations of kebobs, you'll have noted that the seasoning mixture most often accompanying skewered dishes is the topping sauce. It is the most sophisticated. I'm referring, of course, to the well-known French sauces such as Bordelaise, Béarnaise, Chasseur, Newburg, Hollandaise, Diable. These often are spread over kebobs just before serving and are sometimes served with ladle and bowl for extra helpings. Although I've never been overly enthusiastic about them (and I'm in the minority here), I've included a few in the section Sauces, page 258. There is another kind of topping sauce that also can be used to top kebobs just before they're placed in the oven to bake. Examples are Plaki, page 203, and Skordalia (Greek garlic), page 264. You can use a different marinade, a different baste, and a different topping sauce, provided they all complement one another; in other words, seem compatible to you.

DIPS

These, the thickest of sauces known to skewer cooking, mainly accompany hot or cold cooked foods served as appetizers or snacks—principally the 6-inch kebobs. Serve in one of two informal ways: one, dunk and roll the kebobs in a bowl containing the dip sauce; or two, remove the chunks from the skewer with a fork and dip each chunk in small cups of one or several dip sauces. A skewer threaded with one meat takes on as many as four or five different tastes depending on the number and kinds of dip sauces. Guacamole and horseradish sauces make excellent dips for Burger Kebobs. And those with a sour cream base complement many meats.

SKILLET SAUCES

This type of sauce used in the braising of kebobs is, in my opinion, the most flavorful of the seasoning mixtures—or more accurately stated, it *becomes* the most flavorful. The drippings from the seared meat, plus the addition of the seasoned skillet sauce, plus the exchange of flavors that occurs when food cooks on a skewer—all add up to extra-full flavor.

A Word on Salt, Spices, and Spirits

SALT

Some people are indifferent toward salt as a seasoning. To me, this subject evokes a picture of my grandparents engaging in a demonstrative discussion rating the culinary skills of relatives. Two titles resounded vividly: "Alatoo," the Greek word for one who saturates food with salt, and "Analatos," one who uses such a scant amount that the food tastes flat. I can't recall the title for the one who adds just the right amount. In any event, what does one do to satisfy different tastes—or tolerances—for salt?

For kebobs, I find this helpful: use salt by all means (unless prohibited medically) and add it lightly (note, I didn't say very lightly). In cooking, generally, one teaspoon is adequate for one pound of meat. Also, be alert to hidden salt. That is, carefully review the recipes, noting those ingredients containing salt, such as bouillon cubes, tomato sauce, soy sauce, and processed meats. Salt added to raw meat acts to draw the juices to the surface, which retards browning. Thus, when broiling kebobs that haven't been marinated, you might want to add salt on the cooked side after turning them once.

SPICES

After salt, it seems natural to consider pepper. A dash of pepper—freshly ground pepper—perks up most meats and nonsweet sauces. Use white pepper whenever black specks seem inaesthetic to you in certain foods. As for red pepper, the color alone should be a warning: add sparingly.

What are spices? The word "spice" includes six categories: *True Spices*—parts of tropical plants such as bark, roots, buds, flowers and the like. Examples are pepper, nutmeg, cinnamon. *Herbs*—the leaves of plants such as oregano, mint, thyme. *Seeds*—just what the name suggests. Examples are cardamom, dill, caraway. *Dehydrated Vegetable Seasonings* —vegetables with more than 90 percent of the water removed. Rehydration brings the original flavor back for use immediately. *Spice Blends*—certain combinations of true spices, herbs, seeds and dehydrated vegetable seasonings. Examples are chili powder, curry powder, and Italian seasonings. And *Spice Salts*—dehydrated vegetables such as onion and celery combined with table salt.

How should you use spices? This question can't be answered as definitively as the one above, since now we're embarking into the area of personal preference. On the one hand, there are households where the use of a variety of seasonings and the willingness to experiment are shared by all. Then, there are those households (perhaps too many) where seasoning is humdrum. In the latter case, kebobs offer a safe way to launch out. You can season each skewer of meat differently, thereby including familiar seasonings along with the new.

Selection aside, there are only a few things to remember for using spices successfully. Heat strengthens them. The ground spices release their flavor more quickly than whole spices. And they do vary in intensity. This means a few pinches of one might be delightfully subtle whereas the same amount of another could be objectionably strong. Add them very gradually and by all means try adventurous combinations. If, for example, you are accustomed to using cinnamon exclusively in cakes, cookies, and breads, don't turn the page and discount the idea because you see it in a recipe for meat. And most important to remember and to practice is this: insist on freshness. The test is simple: sniff. If you have to inhale deeply to capture the aroma, they belong not on the spice rack but in the garbage sack. To maintain freshness, store them in tightly sealed containers in a cool, dry place.

SPIRITS

By spirits I mean any beverage containing alcohol, although technically wine and beer are not distilled spirits. All of them —wine, liquor, liqueurs—give food a characteristic personality not achieved with any other seasoning. Explore! There are really no hard and fast rules about their use. And note how sweet liqueurs spruce up nonsweet dishes, and how the more bitter liquors offset the sweet.

Actually, the question today in cooking is not should you use wine or liquor; rather, it is *which* wine, *which* liquor. I've tried in my recipes to address myself to this question, being as specific as possible. Just as it is of little use to know whether a wine for drinking is simply red or simply white, so it is for cooking. And the taste you like the best is your guide, the rule to follow. For instance, I understand someone established a rule that sweet wine shouldn't be used in cooking meats. For certain dishes I think sweet vermouth is great. The important principle is quality. When cooking, never add a beverage that you wouldn't first drink.

Lastly, when spirits are cooked, alcohol and calories disappear. In fact, you could rank low-calorie cooking as the second reason next to taste for using spirits as freely as salt and pepper. If a sauce is laden with high-calorie ingredients, keep in mind: spirits substitute sensibly.

PART TWO

Now for
the Recipes

4 · BEEF

WHAT TO CONSIDER
BEFORE SKEWER-COOKING BEEF

Certainly it shouldn't surprise you that the largest sum paid by shoppers in supermarkets for a single item is for meat. Nor should it be news that beef is by far the most popular meat in our country. Here, according to the National Food Situation report, is the number of pounds of meat consumed per person in the year 1973: beef, 109.5; pork, 61.6; poultry, 50.1; lamb, 2.6; veal, 1.8. It would seem, at least from these figures, that for those times when you're nonplussed about which meat to kebob for a guest meal, beef is the safest selection.

As for cuts of beef most desirable for skewer cooking, I recommend only those from the loin and rib sections—tender cuts such as tenderloin (filet mignon), rib eye (sometimes called Delmonico) and top sirloin or bone-in sirloin steak. At least for guest meals, I'd never use anything but those, since when entertaining I prefer not to risk unpredictable outcomes. And the fact is: the marination process alone doesn't guarantee tenderization of tough meats.

Although in some markets sirloin tip and sirloin top are both referred to as sirloin, they're not the same, not even similar. Sirloin top, a tender cut, comes from the loin area and can be cooked by dry heat. Sirloin tip, on the other hand —a tougher, less expensive cut—comes from the knuckle of the round and is best cooked by the braising method. However, if from a well-aged CHOICE or PRIME carcass, sirloin tip can at times be acceptably tender when broiled without being tenderized.

Though I've indicated in some recipes top sirloin and in others bone-in sirloin steak, use them interchangeably according to your preference. When selecting the bone-in sirloin steak, I look for the double or long, flat bone in preference to the round or wedge bones. Essentially, the bone-in sirloin steak consists of three parts: top sirloin, bottom sirloin and a portion of the tenderloin. In some markets, the top sirloin can be purchased alone. Although this cut is higher in price per pound than the bone-in steak, it doesn't have the waste of bone and fat, which must be trimmed. As for yield from bone-in steaks, I was unable to arrive at a standard number of cubes of meat per pound, so with every steak that you use, you'll have to expect a few less or a few more cubes than I've indicated.

If you do use round steak, flank and sirloin tip, these will require some tenderizing before broiling. When purchasing round steak, ask for the top and if possible the first cuts in preference to the center ones. To help increase the tenderness of these meats, soak in a marinade at room temperature, occasionally forking and turning. You also could use the process of scoring or the prepared instant meat tenderizers. (For myself, I'd rather chew a little than use the latter method.) If you're contemplating using still tougher meats such as stew meat, chuck, or the bottom or eye of the round, my recommendation is: stick to their use in recipes calling for moist-heat cooking and simply skip the idea of kebobs. For suggestions on skewer-cooking ground beef, see Burger Kebobs, pages 74–86.

Beef kebobs could be baked or braised, but I'm convinced the best methods of cooking are, for the most part, grilling and broiling. To determine the correct broiling time, you'll need to consider the size of the meat chunks in relation to the distance they're placed from source of heat, the broiling temperature; and above all, the individual preferences for doneness—rare, medium rare, medium, or well done. Although it seems to me a downright sin to cook and serve tender steaks well done, I've included this in the broiling guide, since there are a number of others who don't share the same opinion.

Spacing is another factor to consider in broiling beef kebobs. Space kebob chunks farther apart for well done and closer together for rare. Also, for rare, broil beef cubes of about 1½ inches, at a distance of 3 inches or less from source of heat for 6 minutes or less. The idea is to place the meat farther from the source of heat for well done and closer for rare with a charred surface. And since fresh vegetables and fruits obviously will burn when positioned too close to direct heat, you might prefer (when cooking meat to the rare stage) to thread them on separate skewers and place them farther from the heat.

For main-dish servings, allow ⅓ to ½ pound of boneless beef per person and for appetizers and snacks, ¼ to ⅓ pound. Whatever size chunks you use—1, 1½, or 2 inches— keep size consistent on each skewer for even cooking.

Greek Orange Beef Kebobs

BROIL: *Makes 4 10-inch skewers*

This is an adaptation of a Greek lamb dish, Kapama—an adaptation that's far less rich and much quicker to prepare. As for taste, I think it's very interesting for beef. Serve with buttered egg noodles sprinkled with grated Parmesan or Kefalotiri cheese and Greek Salad, page 291.

2 pounds top sirloin cut into 12 to 14 1½-inch cubes	4 pieces lemon peel
8 square pieces thick orange peel	4 bay leaves (optional)
	4 cherry tomatoes (optional)

MARINADE

½ cup tomato sauce	1 teaspoon salt
½ cup orange juice	¼ teaspoon ground cinnamon
¼ cup melted butter	1 clove garlic, minced
¼ cup freshly squeezed lemon juice (about 1 lemon)	2 bay leaves

Two hours in advance: Combine marinade ingredients in a bowl. Add cubes of beef and cover. Let stand at room temperature, turning meat occasionally.

Before serving: Thread meat on skewer alternately with orange and lemon peel, beginning and ending with meat. Allow one bay leaf per skewer. Broil about 4 inches from source of heat for medium rare, 7 to 9 minutes; for medium, 10 or 11 minutes. For well done, broil about 4 to 5 inches from source of heat for 12 to 15 minutes. Turn once about halfway through total broiling time. If you wish, add cherry tomatoes on tips of skewers the last few minutes of broiling.

Pepper Steak Kebobs

BROIL: *Makes 4 10-inch skewers*

Greens! Yellows! Oranges! Reds! Colorful . . . that these kebobs are. And their attraction lasts until the very last bite, at least from my observation. These, especially, should be broiled on a table appliance where everyone can share the sight and tantalizing smell. Serve with browned potatoes, or if you prefer, Instant Potato Balls, page 286, and a fruit salad.

2 pounds top sirloin cut into 12 to 14 1½-inch cubes
3 green peppers cut into 24 pieces
1 jar (4 ounces) whole pimientos cut into 1-inch pieces

1 jar (6 ounces) pickled peppers (the sweet banquet variety of reds and yellows)

MARINADE–BASTE

½ cup salad oil
¼ cup finely chopped onion
2 tablespoons wine vinegar
1 teaspoon chili powder

1 clove garlic, minced
2 peppercorns, crushed
1 teaspoon salt

Two hours in advance: Combine marinade-baste ingredients in a bowl. Add cubes of beef. Cover. Let stand at room temperature, turning meat occasionally.

Before serving: Thread meat on skewer alternately with green pepper, pimiento, and pickled peppers, allowing 6 pieces of green pepper per skewer. Broil about 4 inches from source of heat for medium rare, 7 to 9 minutes; for medium, 10 or 11 minutes. For well done, broil about 4 to 5 inches from source of heat for 12 to 15 minutes. Turn once halfway through total broiling time, and baste often.

Skewered Beef with Hearts of Palm

BROIL: *Makes 3 10-inch skewers*

Serve with a side dish of Wild Rice and Mushrooms, page 290, and on the plate next to the kebobs place asparagus tips with one or two strips of pimiento.

1 pound rib eye steak, cut into 10 to 12 1½-inch cubes
1 can (14 ounces) hearts of palm cut into 1-inch pieces

Green onions (the green part) cut into 3-inch pieces, folded once
Cherry tomatoes (optional)

MARINADE

¼ cup olive oil
3 tablespoons cognac
1 tablespoon minced parsley
1 teaspoon minced onion

¼ teaspoon salt
⅛ teaspoon freshly ground black pepper

BASTE

½ cup melted butter
2 ounces crumbled Roquefort or blue cheese

2 tablespoons cognac

One hour in advance: Combine marinade ingredients in a bowl. Add cubes of beef, toss and coat well. Cover. Let stand at room temperature, stirring occasionally.

Before serving: Thread meat alternately with hearts of palm and onion. Broil about 4 inches from source of heat for medium rare, 7 to 9 minutes; for medium, 10 or 11 minutes. For well done, broil about 4 to 5 inches from source of heat for 12 to 15 minutes. Turn halfway through total broiling time. Combine baste ingredients in a saucepan and heat just until warmed. Baste kebobs with sauce lightly after turning once and generously right before serving.

Variations: Garnish tips of skewers with cherry tomatoes near the end of cooking. If you wish to omit the cheese in the baste, then use melted clarified butter, omit the salt from the marinade, and instead season to taste just before turning kebobs. You could substitute beef tenderloin here, but rib eye is far juicier—it's a matter of taste, really.

Special Beef Souvlakia

BROIL: *Makes 6 10-inch skewers*

The reason I've identified these main-dish kebobs as special is twofold: First, souvlakia (the Greek word for skewered meats) are traditionally prepared with lamb, veal, or pork, not beef; secondly, I'm suggesting that they be served with a first-course dish which I think is special—My Mother's Pastitsio, page 287.

2½ to 3 pounds rib eye steak, top sirloin, or tenderloin cut into 1½-inch cubes—about 22 to 25

12 fresh mushroom caps
12 lemon slices
Salt to taste
6 cherry tomatoes

MARINADE

1 large clove garlic
¼ cup olive oil
¼ cup melted clarified butter
2 tablespoons lemon juice

2 tablespoons dry sherry
¼ teaspoon freshly ground black pepper

BASTES: choice of . . .

or . . .

Garlic Butter	*Anchovy Butter*
⅓ cup melted butter	⅓ cup melted butter
1 tablespoon lemon juice	1 tablespoon lemon juice
1 tablespoon minced parsley	1 tablespoon anchovy paste
¼ teaspoon garlic powder or garlic juice to taste	

One hour in advance: Rub each cube of meat with cut side of garlic. Combine olive oil, clarified butter, lemon juice, dry sherry and pepper and remaining garlic pieces as well. Add cubes of beef. Let stand at room temperature, turning meat occasionally.

Before serving: Thread beef on skewer alternately with mushrooms and lemon slices, allowing 2 mushrooms and 2 lemon slices per skewer. Broil about 4 inches from source of heat for medium rare, 7 to 9 minutes; for medium, about 10 or 11 minutes. For well done, broil about 4 to 5 inches from source of heat for 12 to 15 minutes. Turn once about halfway through total broiling time. Just before turning, season with salt to taste. Garnish tips of skewers with cherry tomatoes near the end of cooking. Baste kebobs with your choice of bastes.

Korean San Juk

BROIL: *Makes 9 6-inch skewers*

As prepared traditionally, San Juk—the Korean version of kebobs—consists of beef, carrots, bean cake, green onions, and mushrooms all threaded on a skewer, then dipped in a sauce of sesame seeds and sesame oil and grilled over coals. In the following adaptation, you'll find that the distinctive flavor of San Juk—which comes from the sesame seeds—is still delightfully retained. Serve as a substantial appetizer or as part of a snack assortment.

1 sirloin steak, 1 inch thick (2 to 3 pounds), trimmed and cut into 1-inch cubes, about 24 to 28
18 whole mushrooms

1 can (8½ ounces) bamboo shoots, sliced
Green onions (the green part) cut into 1-inch pieces (about 36)

MARINADE

6 tablespoons sesame seeds
6 tablespoons soy sauce
5 tablespoons peanut oil
1 tablespoon granulated sugar

1 clove garlic, crushed
2 tablespoons minced onion
¼ teaspoon freshly ground black pepper

Two hours in advance: Heat sesame seeds in skillet until browned, stirring often. Add soy sauce and browned sesame seeds in blender and blend. In a bowl, combine soy sauce and sesame-seed mixture with remaining marinade ingredients. Add cubes of beef and cover. Let stand at room temperature.

Before serving: Thread skewers as follows: mushroom · several bamboo shoots . BEEF . four pieces of onion . BEEF . several bamboo shoots . BEEF . mushroom. Broil about 4 inches from source of heat for medium rare, 6 to 8 minutes; for medium, 9 or 10 minutes. For well done, broil about 4 to 5 inches from source of heat for 11 to 14 minutes. Turn several times during cooking.

Variation: Grill 4 inches above hot glowing coals, turning often, for about 8 to 12 minutes depending on desired degree of doneness.

JAPANESE KUSHI YAKI

The seasoning that characterizes Kushi Yaki—the Japanese version of kebobs—is the same as that of Teriyaki. Serve the appetizer or snack version with an assortment of foods including the Flaked Salmon Salad, page 280. Serve the main-dish version over a bed of steamed white rice.

Appetizer or Snack Kushi Yaki

BROIL: *Makes 9 6-inch skewers*

1 sirloin steak, 1 inch thick (2 to 3 pounds), trimmed and cut into 1-inch cubes, about 24 to 28
1 can (8½ ounces) bamboo shoots, sliced

1 can (8 ounces) unsweetened pineapple chunks
1 large green pepper cut into 9 pieces

MARINADE–BASTE

½ cup soy sauce
¼ cup dry sherry
2 tablespoons brown sugar
3 tablespoons peanut oil

2 tablespoons grated onion
1 clove garlic, crushed
½ teaspoon ground ginger

TOPPING MIX

1 cup finely chopped cocktail peanuts
1 can (6 ounces) water chestnuts, shredded
1 tablespoon finely chopped candied ginger

1 tablespoon grated lemon peel
¼ cup chopped green onions (white and green part)

One hour in advance: Combine marinade-baste ingredients in a bowl. Add chunks of meat. Cover. Stir occasionally. In a small bowl, toss together topping ingredients. Set aside.

Before serving: Thread skewers as follows: BEEF . several bamboo shoots . BEEF . pineapple . BEEF . green pepper. Broil about 4 inches from source of heat for medium rare, 6 to 8 minutes; for medium, 9 or 10 minutes. For well done, broil about 4 to 5 inches from source of heat for 11 to 14 minutes. Turn once and baste often. Sprinkle topping mixture generously over each kebob and serve.

Main-Dish Kushi Yaki

BROIL: *Makes 4 10-inch skewers*

1 sirloin steak, 1½ inches thick (3 to 4 pounds), trimmed and cut into 1½-inch cubes, about 16 to 20
8 medium-size mushroom caps

Green onions cut into 1-inch pieces (about 32)
1 small green pepper cut into 4 pieces

MARINADE–BASTE–TOPPING

½ cup beef consommé
⅓ cup soy sauce
3 tablespoons sherry
2 tablespoons granulated sugar
2 teaspoons finely chopped crystallized (candied) ginger, sugar washed off

1 clove garlic, minced
1 tablespoon grated onion
1 teaspoon cornstarch dissolved in 2 teaspoons water

Two hours in advance: In saucepan, combine marinade-baste-topping ingredients except the cornstarch. Heat to boil. Cool. Pour over chunks of meat. Cover.

Before serving: Thread skewers as follows: mushroom . BEEF . 4 pieces of green onion . BEEF . green pepper . BEEF . 4 pieces of green onion . BEEF . mushroom. Broil about 4 inches from source of heat for medium rare, 7 to 9 minutes; for medium, 10 or 11 minutes. For well done, broil about 4 to 5 inches from source of heat for 12 to 15 minutes. Baste after turning. Add cornstarch dissolved in water to remaining marinade and heat and stir until thickened. Use as a topping sauce.

German Sauerbraten Kebobs

BROIL: *Makes 4 10-inch skewers*

Here you can capture the classic flavor of Sauerbraten without having to wait 3 to 5 days to márinate a 5- to 6-

pound hunk of whole meat and without having to wait three hours to cook it. Serve with potato dumplings.

1 sirloin steak, 1½ inches thick (3 to 4 pounds), trimmed and cut into 1½-inch cubes, about 16 to 20

1 jar (16 ounces) whole carrots
1 small green pepper cut into 4 pieces
4 whole boiled canned onions

MARINADE–TOPPING

1¼ cups (10½-ounce can) beef broth
1 tablespoon soy sauce
½ cup ruby Port
3 tablespoons red wine vinegar
2 tablespoons lemon juice
1 medium carrot, thinly sliced
⅓ cup sliced onion (about 1 medium)

¼ cup chopped celery
4 sprigs parsley
½ green pepper, sliced
8 peppercorns
4 whole allspice
4 whole cloves
1 clove garlic, minced
½ teaspoon sweet basil
1 slice lemon

TOPPING SAUCE

2 tablespoons butter
2 tablespoons flour
1 tablespoon granulated sugar

1 tablespoon tomato paste
3 gingersnaps, crushed (optional)

Two hours in advance: Add marinade ingredients in saucepan and heat to boiling. Let cool. Pour over meat chunks. Cover. Let stand at room temperature, turning meat occasionally.

Before serving: Remove meat from marinade and strain broth. In saucepan, melt butter and stir in flour to a paste consistency. Stir in sugar and heat until brown. Gradually add strained marinade and bring to a boil, stirring constantly until thickened and smooth. Stir in tomato paste and, if desired, crushed gingersnaps. If sauce becomes too thick, you might want to thin it with Port to taste. Thread cubes of meat on skewer alternately with carrots, allowing 1 piece of green pepper and 1 whole onion per skewer. Broil about 4 inches from source of heat for medium rare, 7 to 9 minutes; for medium, 10 or 11 minutes. For well done, broil about 4 to 5 inches from source of heat for 12 to 15 minutes. Turn several times during broiling. Top each kebob generously with sauce and serve.

Skewered Beef Duo

BROIL: *Makes 7 10-inch skewers*

Thread each skewer with four cubes of meat. Coat two cubes with a bread-crumb mixture and just before serving top the two plain cubes with a banana sauce. Perhaps the combination of ingredients may seem unusual, but you should find the result quite good.

1 sirloin steak, 1 inch thick (2½ to 3 pounds) trimmed and cut into 28 1-inch cubes	3 tablespoons French bread crumbs
Salt to taste	21 large whole canned mushrooms
2 tablespoons chili sauce	2 green peppers, cut into 14 pieces
3 tablespoons grated Parmesan cheese	

TOPPING SAUCE FOR PLAIN BEEF

1 cup mashed bananas	dry white wine
2 tablespoons orange juice	1 to 2 tablespoons prepared horseradish to taste
3 tablespoons brandy	
3 tablespoons Chablis or other	3 tablespoons melted butter

Season cubes of beef with salt to taste. Dip 14 cubes of beef in chili sauce and then dredge in Parmesan cheese combined with bread crumbs. In blender, combine topping sauce ingredients and blend until a smooth, creamy consistency. Pour into serving bowl. Thread skewers as follows: mushroom · COATED CUBE OF BEEF · green pepper · PLAIN CUBE OF BEEF · mushroom · COATED CUBE OF BEEF · green pepper · PLAIN CUBE OF BEEF · mushroom. Broil about 4 inches from source of heat for medium rare—6 to 8 minutes;

for medium—9 or 10 minutes; for well done—about 4 to 5 inches from source of heat for 11 to 14 minutes. Turn once about halfway through total broiling time. Just before serving, top only the plain cubes of beef with the banana sauce.

SKEWERED SIRLOIN STEAK WITH A SINGLE VEGETABLE

In this series, you might find that the vegetable on the skewer steals the spotlight from the sirloin.

Sirloin with Stuffed Artichoke Bottoms

BROIL: *Makes 4 10-inch skewers*

1 sirloin steak 1½ inches thick (3 to 4 pounds), trimmed and cut into 1½-inch cubes, about 16 to 20
1 clove garlic, split

1 tablespoon olive oil
¼ teaspoon freshly ground black pepper
2 cans (12 ounces) artichoke bottoms, drained (8 per can)

MARINADES

Tomato Butter for 8 artichoke bottoms

¼ cup melted butter
¼ cup tomato sauce

1 tablespoon lemon juice

Lemon Butter for 8 artichoke bottoms

¼ cup melted butter

¼ cup lemon juice

STUFFINGS

Rye Bread

16 thin slices cocktail rye bread, trimmed
2 tablespoons Madeira

2 tablespoons grated Parmesan cheese

Anchovy

3 slices (1 inch thick) Italian bread, trimmed

2 tablespoons dry Sauterne

1 teaspoon lemon juice

1 can (2 ounces) flat anchovy fillets, well drained

¼ teaspoon grated lemon rind

TOPPING SAUCE

3 tablespoons butter

¼ cup minced green onion

¼ cup minced onion

⅓ cup Madeira

1⅓ cup dry Sauterne

¼ teaspoon sweet basil

¼ teaspoon dried chervil

¼ teaspoon dried tarragon

2 tablespoons tomato paste

Salt and pepper to taste

One hour before serving: Rub each meat chunk with split garlic, then coat with olive oil and pepper, tossing well. In two small bowls, combine ingredients for the two versions of artichoke marinade. Add 8 artichoke bottoms to each, coating them well. Set aside. Sprinkle Madeira over rye bread to moisten. Add Parmesan cheese and use fingers to mix ingredients thoroughly. Roll into 4 balls. Sprinkle dry Sauterne over Italian bread to moisten. Add anchovy fillets, lemon juice, and lemon rind, using fingers to mix well. Roll into 4 balls.

Before serving: In saucepan, melt butter and add onions. Cook until translucent but not brown. Add Madeira and dry Sauterne and simmer until liquid is reduced to half the original amount. Add remaining ingredients and simmer until reduced one-third. Season with salt and pepper to taste. Set aside. Press one rye-bread-stuffing ball into each of 4 artichoke bottoms marinated in lemon-butter sauce; top with remaining 4 artichoke bottoms. Press one anchovy-stuffing ball into each of 4 artichoke bottoms marinated with tomato-butter sauce; top with remaining 4 artichoke bottoms. You now have 8 stuffed artichoke bottoms. Thread sirloin on skewers alternately with artichoke bottoms, beginning and ending with sirloin, allowing one of each differently stuffed artichoke bottom per skewer. Baste each artichoke with respective marinade before and during cooking. Broil about 4 inches from source of heat for medium rare, 7 to 9 minutes; for medium, 10 or 11 minutes. For well done, broil about 4 to 5 inches from source of heat for 12 to 15 minutes. Just before turning once, salt meat to taste. After turning kebobs, brush topping sauce lightly on the meat. Before serving, spread meat generously with topping sauce.

Sirloin with Mushrooms

BROIL: *Makes 4 10-inch skewers*

1 sirloin steak, 1½ inches thick (3 to 4 pounds), trimmed and cut into 1½-inch cubes, about 16 to 20

24 medium-size mushrooms, about 1 pound

MARINADES

For Mushrooms

3 tablespoons olive oil
3 tablespoons lemon juice
1 teaspoon minced parsley

¼ teaspoon mint flakes, crushed
1 teaspoon garlic juice

For Sirloin

⅓ cup melted butter
⅓ cup dry white Port
3 tablespoons tomato juice
¼ teaspoon instant minced onion

¼ teaspoon celery flakes, crushed
1 bay leaf
4 peppercorns, crushed

Two hours in advance: Remove stems from mushrooms. (By all means, keep stems for other uses.) Whiten caps by wiping them with a cloth dampened with a mixture of vinegar and water. In a bowl, combine marinade for mushrooms; add mushrooms, tossing gently and coating each of them thoroughly. Refrigerate and stir often. In another bowl, combine marinade for sirloin. Add sirloin cubes, coating well. Let stand at room temperature, stirring occasionally. Since this marinade will adhere to the meat, don't expect a liquid consistency when ready for threading.

Before serving: Thread mushroom caps alternately on skewer with sirloin, beginning and ending with mushroom. Broil about 4 inches from source of heat for medium rare, 7 to 9 minutes; for medium, 10 or 11 minutes. For well done, broil about 4 or 5 inches from source of heat for 12 to 15 minutes. Turn several times during broiling. After turning once, season with salt to taste. These kebobs won't require basting. If desired, serve with Instant Potato Balls, page 286.

Sirloin with Cucumber

BROIL: *Makes 4 10-inch skewers*

1 sirloin steak 1 inch thick (2 to 3 pounds), trimmed and cut into 1-inch cubes, about 24 to 28

10 slices (1¼ inches) unpared cucumber (use one large cucumber)

⅔ cup Italian-seasoned bread crumbs

MARINADE

3 tablespoons brandy
3 tablespoons olive oil

3 tablespoons melted butter

Three hours in advance: Combine marinade ingredients in a bowl. Add cubes of beef, rubbing and coating each piece of meat with marinade, mixing and tossing well. Let stand at room temperature, turning meat often.

Before serving: Halve the cucumber slices. Thread sirloin cubes on skewer alternately with 5 pieces of cucumber per skewer. Spear the skewer through the white and not the seed part of cucumber. Turn kebob in bread crumbs, coating well. Broil about 4 inches from source of heat for medium rare, 6 to 8 minutes; for medium, 9 or 10 minutes. For well done, broil about 4 to 5 inches from source of heat for 11 to 14 minutes. Turn two to three times during broiling.

Sirloin with Eggplant

BROIL: *Makes 5 10-inch skewers*

1 sirloin steak 1½ inches thick (3 to 4 pounds), trimmed and cut into 15 1½-inch cubes

1 small eggplant (about 1 pound) unpared and cut into 15 chunks

MARINADES

For Sirloin

3 tablespoons dry Sauterne
3 tablespoons olive oil

1 medium onion, sliced and separated into rings

For Eggplant

⅓ cup tomato juice
⅓ cup salad oil
1 teaspoon salt
¼ teaspoon freshly ground black pepper

2 tablespoons wine vinegar
1 tablespoon lemon juice
½ teaspoon sweet basil
½ teaspoon leaf marjoram

One hour in advance: Combine marinade ingredients for sirloin, add cubes of sirloin, and toss well. Cover. In another bowl, combine marinade for eggplant, stir, and add eggplant chunks. Cover.

Before serving: Thread eggplant alternately with sirloin, beginning with eggplant, allowing 3 pieces each of vegetable and meat per skewer. Broil 4 to 5 inches from source of heat 12 to 15 minutes or until eggplant is tender.

Sirloin with Onions

BROIL: *Makes 4 10-inch skewers*

1 sirloin steak 1½ inches thick
(3 to 4 pounds), trimmed and
cut into 1½-inch cubes, about
16 to 20
4 squares white onion*
4 squares red onion

4 squares yellow onion*
4 whole boiled canned onions
Green onions, cut into 16 1-inch
pieces
4 cocktail onions

MARINADE

1 teaspoon peppercorns
2 drops Tabasco
2 teaspoons Worcestershire
sauce

2 tablespoons lemon juice
3 tablespoons olive oil

TOPPING SAUCE

⅔ cup Chablis or other dry
white wine
¼ bay leaf
2 tablespoons chopped onion
1 teaspoon tarragon vinegar
1 can (10½ ounces) onion soup
made with beef stock

2 tablespoons flour
2 tablespoons butter
2 teaspoons Dijon-style
mustard
1 teaspoon Worcestershire
sauce
2 tablespoons tomato puree

Two hours in advance: Crush peppercorns into coarse pieces, using mortar and pestle or rolling pin. Rub into meat. Combine remaining marinade ingredients and coat each cube of meat thoroughly.

Fifteen minutes before serving: In saucepan, combine wine, bay leaf, onions, and vinegar and boil until reduced by one-third the original amount. Add the can of onion soup. Cream butter and flour together with mustard, Worcestershire sauce, and tomato puree and stir into liquid. Cook until thickened.

* If desired, let white onion pieces stand in a combination of 2 tablespoons water, 1 tablespoon granulated sugar, and 1 teaspoon vinegar. For the yellow onion, let stand in a combination of 1½ tablespoons salad oil and 1 teaspoon tarragon vinegar.

Before serving: Remove pieces of meat from marinade, wiping away peppercorns. Thread skewers as follows: white onion . SIRLOIN . red onion . SIRLOIN . boiled onion . SIRLOIN . yellow onion . green onion . SIRLOIN . cocktail onion. Broil about 4 inches from source of heat for medium rare, 7 to 9 minutes; for medium, 10 or 11 minutes. For well done, broil about 4 or 5 inches from source of heat for 12 to 15 minutes. Turn once about halfway through broiling time. Spread kebobs with topping sauce and serve.

SKEWERED BEEF WITH FRUIT
Canned Fruit Kebobs

BROIL: *Makes 4 10-inch skewers*

1 pound top round steak cut into 12 to 14 1-inch cubes
8 pineapple chunks

8 apricot halves, drained well
Maraschino cherries (optional)

MARINADE

1 package (¾ ounce) brown-gravy mix
½ cup orange juice
½ cup pineapple juice

¼ cup water
2 tablespoons lemon juice
2 whole cloves

Night before: Combine marinade ingredients in a bowl. Add cubes of beef. Cover and refrigerate overnight or at least 12 hours. Turn meat occasionally.

Before serving: Thread meat on skewers alternately with pineapple and apricots. Broil about 4 inches from source of heat for medium rare, 6 to 8 minutes; for medium, 9 or 10 minutes. For well done, broil about 4 to 5 inches from source of heat for 11 to 14 minutes. Turn once about halfway through total broiling time. If desired, garnish tips of skewers with maraschino cherries. I should also add that if you're a fan of meat tenderizer, you might want to use the instant unseasoned tenderizer before threading meat. Follow directions on label.

Fresh Fruit Kebobs

BROIL: *Makes 4 to 5 10-inch skewers*

2 pounds top sirloin cut into
  12 to 14 1½-inch cubes
1 pineapple, pared, cored and
  cut into 12 wedges

8 cantaloupe balls
8 chunks of banana, dipped in
  lemon juice, rolled in finely
  ground nuts

MARINADE–BASTE–TOPPING SAUCE

½ cup pineapple juice
¼ cup melted butter
¼ cup lemon juice
2 tablespoons light rum
2 to 5 tablespoons granulated
  sugar to desired sweetness

½ teaspoon ground ginger
1 tablespoon soy sauce
½ clove garlic, minced

Two hours in advance: Combine marinade–baste–topping sauce ingredients in a bowl. Add cubes of beef. Cover. Let stand at room temperature, turning occasionally.

Before serving: Thread beef on skewer alternately with pineapple and cantaloupe, beginning and ending with banana chunks. Broil about 4 inches from source of heat for medium rare, 7 to 9 minutes; for medium, 10 or 11 minutes. For well done, broil about 4 to 5 inches from source of heat for 12 to 15 minutes. Turn once about halfway through broiling time. Baste frequently. Heat remaining marinade–baste, thicken with 1 teaspoon cornstarch dissolved in 2 teaspoons cold water, and serve as a topping.

KEBOBS FROM SEVERAL SPIRIT SOURCES

My grandfather was not a little old winemaker; he was a big old winemaker . . . portly, large-framed, with a heart the size of a canyon. How I remember my grandfolks' huge house near the lake, and particularly those steep steps which led to the dark, grape-smelling cellar. It seemed that anyone who visited that house invariably received a personally conducted tour to Papoo's cellar, where propped on two-by-fours about a foot off the floor were four 50-gallon barrels of wine —dry red, rosé, retsina, and a sweet variety. Yes, the highlight of the ritual was the sampling. When Papoo removed the plug from the barrel of the guest's choice, all that could be heard was the trickling sound of cold wine spouting from the barrel, bouncing and foaming into the small crystal glass decanter on the cement floor. But the silence was quickly broken, for Papoo really loved company, loved to talk. He'd go on to tell his guests (every guest to him was a friend) all about the good and bad barrels through the years, using his combination of native Greek tongue, broken English, and gestures of waving hands. The tours always ended with a friend taking with him at least one gallon of wine. No one ever left the house empty-handed. The tours ceased, however, when the old winemaker left his trade. No tours, nor as many friends. In our family, winemaking became a lost art; now it is a memory, a memory which inspired the idea for this series of recipes.

Beef and Madeira Kebobs

BROIL: *Makes 4 10-inch skewers*

Serve with Madeira-Topped Potato Mounds, page 286.

2 pounds top sirloin cut into 12 to 14 1½-inch cubes
8 jumbo black pitted olives
8 tidbit pieces of chive cheese spread

8 jumbo Spanish pimiento-stuffed olives
4 whole canned mushroom caps

MARINADE–BASTE

⅓ cup Madeira
¼ cup olive oil
¼ cup tomato sauce
2 bay leaves, crumbled
1 clove garlic, minced

1 tablespoon finely chopped parsley
⅛ teaspoon freshly ground black pepper

Three hours in advance: Combine marinade–baste ingredients in a bowl, stirring vigorously. Add cubes of beef and cover. Let stand at room temperature, turning meat occasionally.

Before serving: Stuff centers of pitted olives with cheese. Thread meat on skewer, alternating with olives, and garnish tip with a mushroom. Broil about 4 inches from source of heat for medium rare, 7 to 9 minutes; for medium, 10 or 11 minutes. For well done, broil about 4 to 5 inches from source of heat for 12 to 15 minutes. Turn once about halfway through broiling time, basting generously near end of cooking.

Beef and Burgundy Kebobs

BROIL: *Makes 4 10-inch skewers*

Serve with Sautéed Onions, Mushrooms, and Green Pepper, page 282.

2 pounds top sirloin cut into 12 to 14 1½-inch cubes	8 small whole canned new potatoes
8 cucumber slices, 1 inch thick	4 cherry tomatoes (optional)

MARINADE–BASTE

1 cup Burgundy	2 tablespoons chopped parsley
½ cup beef bouillon (1 bouillon cube dissolved in ½ cup hot water) or ½ cup canned	2 cloves garlic, minced
	2 bay leaves, crumbled
¼ cup finely chopped onion	¼ teaspoon leaf thyme
	¼ teaspoon rosemary
2 tablespoons olive oil	3 peppercorns, crushed

Three hours in advance: Combine marinade–baste ingredients in a bowl. Add cubes of beef. Cover and let stand at room temperature, turning meat occasionally.

Before serving: Thread beef on skewers alternately with cucumbers and potatoes, allowing 2 each of the vegetables per skewer. Broil about 4 inches from source of heat for medium rare, 7 to 9 minutes; for medium, 10 or 11 minutes. For well done, broil about 4 to 5 inches from source of heat for 12 to 15 minutes. Turn once about halfway through broiling time. Baste with marinade—baste once or twice before and after turning. If desired, garnish tips with cherry tomatoes near end of cooking.

Variation: Dip the potatoes in melted butter and then roll gently in ground bouquet garni seasoning or in seasoned breading mix.

Beef and Beer Kebobs

BROIL: *Makes 6 10-inch skewers*

Note what happens here. The foods next to the meat on the skewer influence the taste of the meat more than does the sauce. Arrange strips of round steak in a spiral, snakelike fashion, enclosing your choice of food companions in the curves.

2 pounds top round steak ½ inch thick, commercially scored and cut into 6 to 7 ½-inch strips

MARINADE–BASTE

¾ cup beer
⅓ cup chili sauce
¼ cup ketchup
3 tablespoons granulated sugar
2 tablespoons Worcestershire sauce

1 teaspoon salt
⅛ teaspoon freshly ground black pepper

Choice of companions to thread skewers, each skewer with a different theme or all of them alike:

PICKLED FOODS: dill tomato, sweet pickle, dill cucumber, cauliflower, pickled pepper, *senf gurken*, olive, pickled honeydew, etc.
FRESH VEGETABLES: onion, cucumber, celery, etc.
FRESH FRUITS: pineapple, pear, banana, apple, etc.
CANNED FRUITS: kumquat, papaya, maraschino cherry, etc.

Night before: Combine marinade–baste ingredients in a bowl. Add round-steak strips. Cover and refrigerate, turning meat several times.

Before serving: Thread meat on skewer in a twisting, curving manner, alternating your choice of the above companions in the curves. Broil about 4 inches from source of heat for medium rare, 5 to 7 minutes; for medium, 8 or 9 minutes. For well done, broil about 4 to 5 inches from source of heat for 10 to 13 minutes. Turn once about halfway through broiling time. Baste frequently.

Beef and Bourbon Kebobs

BROIL: *Makes 4 10-inch skewers*

Serve with Sautéed Pea Pods, Water Chestnuts, and Bamboo Shoots, page 283.

2 pounds top sirloin, cut into 12 to 14 1½-inch cubes	8 large mushroom caps
8 whole boiled canned onions	2 green peppers, cut into 8 pieces (optional)

MARINADE–BASTE

⅔ cup tomato sauce	1 tablespoon soy sauce
¼ cup bourbon	¼ teaspoon ground ginger
¼ cup salad oil	⅛ teaspoon turmeric
2 tablespoons chopped parsley	⅛ teaspoon garlic powder
1 tablespoon granulated sugar	

Three hours in advance: Combine marinade–baste ingredients in a bowl. Add beef cubes. Cover. Let stand at room temperature, stirring occasionally.

Before serving: Thread beef on skewers alternately with onions and mushrooms and, if desired, green pepper pieces, beginning and ending with onion. Broil about 4 inches from source of heat for medium rare, 7 to 9 minutes; for medium, 10 or 11 minutes. For well done, broil about 4 to 5 inches from source of heat for 12 to 15 minutes. Turn once about halfway through broiling time. Baste generously near end of cooking.

Flank Steak Kebobs Oriental

BRAISE: *Makes 4 8-inch skewers*

Whatever it takes to get a top-quality flank steak, I believe you'll agree it's really worth it for this recipe.

1 top-quality flank steak (about 1½ pounds) scored lightly crisscross on both sides
2 eggs, slightly beaten
1 cup French-bread crumbs
1 green pepper, cut into 8 pieces
8 chunks canned pineapple
Bamboo shoots, sliced (about ½ of an 8½-ounce can)

16 1-inch pieces of green onion
4 whole boiled canned onions
8 medium pimiento-stuffed olives
2 tablespoons peanut oil
1 tablespoon butter or margarine

MARINADE

3 tablespoons soy sauce
1 tablespoon Worcestershire sauce

CRUNCH TOPPING

¼ cup shredded water chestnuts
¼ cup finely chopped walnuts

2 tablespoons finely chopped celery
2 tablespoons minced parsley

TOPPING SAUCE

3 tablespoons melted butter
3 tablespoons dry sherry
2 tablespoons soy sauce

1½ tablespoons prepared horseradish
¼ teaspoon ground ginger

Three hours in advance: Cut flank steak across the grain at an angle into 12 strips about ¾ inch wide. Combine marinade ingredients in a bowl. Add strips of flank and toss well. Cover. Let stand at room temperature. In a small bowl, combine crunch-topping ingredients, mixing well. Set aside.
Before serving: Dip strips of flank steak in egg and then

dredge in bread crumbs. Thread skewers as follows: green pepper . FLANK STEAK strip wrapped around two pineapple chunks . several bamboo shoots . FLANK STEAK strip wrapped around onion . 4 pieces of green onion . FLANK STEAK strip wrapped around two olives . green pepper. Heat oil and butter in skillet and brown kebobs 6 to 8 minutes; turn, cover, cook additional 7 to 9 minutes over low heat. Combine topping-sauce ingredients in saucepan and heat. Spoon warmed sauce over each kebob and sprinkle with crunch topping.

SPUR-OF-THE-MOMENT STEAK KEBOBS

You have a few steaks on hand that you need to serve pronto, but you want to do something other than just slap them on a broiler or grill. For such moments, try these.

Pronto Broiler Kebobs

BROIL: *Makes 8 6-inch skewers*

2 rib eye steaks 1 inch thick,
  cut into 24 1-inch cubes

OR

2 strip loin steaks 1 inch thick,
  cut into 24 1-inch cubes

2 tablespoons melted butter	2 tablespoons melted butter
2 tablespoons grated Parmesan cheese	4 tablespoons Italian-bread crumbs
2 tablespoons French-bread crumbs	8 whole canned mushrooms
1 tablespoon soy sauce	8 anchovy-stuffed olives
1 tablespoon dry sherry	8 canned boiled onions (or 8 pieces red pepper)
3 to 4 tablespoons finely ground almonds	

Dip 8 cubes of steak in melted butter and then roll in grated Parmesan cheese combined with French-bread crumbs. Dip 8 cubes of steak in soy sauce combined with dry sherry and roll in finely ground almonds, coating well. Dip 8 cubes of steak in melted butter and roll in Italian-bread crumbs. Thread each skewer with one of the three types of coated meat cubes, alternating with mushroom, olive, and onion. Broil about 4 inches from source of heat for medium rare, 6 to 8 minutes; for medium, 9 or 10 minutes. For well done, broil about 4 to 5 inches from source of heat for 11 to 13 minutes. For best results here, season with salt before coating meat.

Pronto Skillet and Baking-Pan Kebobs

GRIDDLE-AND-BAKE: *Makes 4 8-inch skewers*

3 slices (1½ to 2 inches thick)
   beef tenderloin cut into 12
   cubes

OR

2 slices (1½ to 2 inches thick)
   rib eye steak cut into 12 cubes

1 clove garlic, split
1 green pepper, parboiled 3 to
   5 minutes, cut into 8 pieces

8 whole mushrooms
1 tablespoon olive oil
1 tablespoon butter

SAUCE

3 tablespoons Madeira
2 tablespoons dry vermouth
1 tablespoon tomato juice
¼ teaspoon dried chervil
¼ teaspoon Worcestershire
   sauce

¼ teaspoon dry mustard
Freshly ground black pepper
   and salt to taste

Preheat oven to 350°. Rub beef cubes with garlic and thread on skewers alternately with green pepper and mushrooms, allowing 3 pieces of meat per skewer. In skillet, heat oil and butter until very hot. Brown kebobs over high heat a few seconds on all sides. Transfer kebobs to baking pan and bake in 350° oven 4 to 10 minutes depending on desired degree of doneness. While kebobs are in oven, combine sauce ingredients and swirl into the skillet, stirring thoroughly and scraping up meat drippings. Season cooked kebobs with salt and pepper to taste and spoon skillet sauce over them. Serve immediately.

Skewered Steak à la Sauce and Sauces

BROIL: *Makes 4 10-inch skewers*

Here you have a choice of topping sauces—six of them, to be exact—and they all share one base, the Quick Brown Sauce, page 260.

2 pounds top sirloin or rib eye
    steak cut into 12 to 14
    1½-inch cubes
2 tablespoons olive oil

2 green peppers cut into 12
    pieces
Salt to taste

CHOICE OF TOPPING SAUCES

Brown Sauce I, page 260
Brown Sauce II (or Bordelaise), page 261

MUSHROOM-MADEIRA SAUCE

¼ cup finely chopped onion
½ pound fresh mushrooms,
    diced
4 tablespoons butter
2 tablespoons tomato sauce

1 cup Quick Brown Sauce
⅛ teaspoon freshly ground
    black pepper
1 tablespoon minced parsley
¼ cup Madeira

In a large heavy saucepan, sauté onions with mushrooms in butter until tender and brown. Add tomato sauce and brown sauce; stir well. Add black pepper, parsley and Madeira. Heat thoroughly but do not boil. Makes 1⅓ cups.

HERB SAUCE

⅔ cup Chablis
1 small bay leaf
½ teaspoon leaf thyme
½ teaspoon sweet basil

4 peppercorns, crushed
½ teaspoon parsley flakes
1 cup Quick Brown Sauce
1 tablespoon brandy

Add herbs to wine and cook until liquid is reduced to one-half. Stir in brown sauce and then brandy. Heat thoroughly but do not boil. Makes 1⅓ cups.

SAUCE CHASSEUR

1 clove garlic, chopped
2 tablespoons chopped green onion
3 tablespoons chopped onion
3 tablespoons butter
⅓ cup tomato sauce

1 cup Quick Brown Sauce
1 can (2½ ounces) sliced mushrooms, drained well
2 tablespoons dry sherry
2 tablespoons brandy
1 tablespoon minced parsley

Sauté garlic and onions in butter until tender. Add tomato sauce and brown sauce, stirring well. Add remaining ingredients, heating sauce thoroughly. Do not boil. Makes 1½ cups.

SLIGHTLY HOT SAUCE

2 cloves garlic
¼ cup chopped onion
2 tablespoons butter
2 tablespoons finely chopped canned green chilies

3 tablespoons tomato sauce
½ teaspoon ground coriander seed
1 cup Quick Brown Sauce
2 tablespoons tequila

Sauté garlic and onions in butter until tender. Add green chilies, tomato sauce, and coriander. Stir, mixing well. Add brown sauce and tequila, heating sauce thoroughly but do not boil. Makes 1¼ cups.

Prepare the topping sauce of your choice. Rub cubes of beef with olive oil, tossing well. Thread beef on skewers alternately with green pepper, allowing three green peppers per skewer. Broil about 4 inches from source of heat for medium rare, 7 to 9 minutes; for medium, 10 to 11 minutes. For well done, broil about 4 to 5 inches from source of heat for

12 to 15 minutes. Just before turning once, salt meat to taste. Before serving, spread meat generously with choice of topping sauce.

BEEF KEBOBING OUTDOORS

These two recipes for kebobing beef outdoors are definitely casual. In fact, their key attraction, I think, is fun eating. With the first recipe, you provide several baste sauces to choose from. Near the grill have three basting brushes along with three sauce bowls identified as Sweet and Sour, Herb, and Mild. The second recipe, however, is perhaps the most fun. Here the meat is slid off long skewers into various loaves of differently seasoned bread. Although I like to refer to these sandwiches as Rich Boys, they make for an informal and interesting way to stretch steak economically.

Beef Kebobs, Individual Style

GRILL

2 sirloin steaks, 1½ inches thick (each 3 to 4 pounds), trimmed and cut into 1½-inch cubes, about 36 to 40
2 cups Basic (Mild) Tomato Barbecue Sauce, page 266 (for use as a marinade)

2 cups Basic (Mild) Tomato Barbecue Sauce (for preparing the Sweet and Sour and the Herb sauces)

1 tablespoon brown sugar
2 tablespoons crushed pineapple, drained
1 tablespoon wine vinegar
1 tablespoon orange juice
⅛ teaspoon ground ginger

1 teaspoon each of parsley flakes, basil, and tarragon
¼ teaspoon ground thyme
1 bay leaf, crumbled
1 tablespoon dry white wine

Three hours in advance: In a bowl, pour 2 cups Basic Tomato Barbecue Sauce over cubes of beef. Stir well. Cover. To prepare 1 cup Sweet and Sour Barbecue Sauce, combine 1 cup Basic Tomato Barbecue Sauce with brown sugar, crushed pineapple, wine vinegar, orange juice, and ginger. To prepare 1 cup Herb Sauce, combine 1 cup Basic Tomato Barbecue Sauce with parsley flakes, basil, and tarragon, ground thyme, bay leaf, and dry white wine. Keep sauces in separate serving containers ready for use at grill.

Before serving: Thread meat on six long skewers. Wipe off excess sauce, since marinade has considerable tomato and may cause charring before meat is cooked. Grill 4 inches from hot coals about 15 to 18 minutes for medium rare or longer, about 22 to 28 minutes, for those who insist on well done. Turn often. Apply each of the baste sauces generously to two skewers near the end of cooking. Serve meat according to the one baste preference indicated, or for a fun sampling presentation, serve kebobs basted with the three different sauces. Serves about 6 to 8 persons.

Beef Kebobs, Loaf Style

GRILL

1 sirloin steak 1 inch thick (about 2 to 3 pounds), trimmed and cut into 1-inch cubes, about 24 to 28

MARINADE

⅓ cup Rhine wine
⅓ cup olive oil
1 tablespoon lemon juice

1 clove garlic, minced
½ teaspoon coarsely ground black pepper

A SELECTION OF LOAVES

German Bread, Reuben Style

1 loaf unsliced pumpernickel bread (about 3 x 10 inches)
8 ounces shredded Swiss cheese
¼ cup melted butter

2 tablespoons brandy
1 can (16 ounces) sauerkraut, very well drained
1 piece heavy-duty foil, 17 x 16 inches

Italian Eggplant Bread

1 loaf (1 pound) unsliced
   Italian bread
4 tablespoons olive oil
½ cup chopped onion
½ cup chopped green onion
1 medium eggplant (about 1
   pound), unpared, cut into
   1-inch cubes
1½ teaspoons salt
½ teaspoon freshly ground
   black pepper

2 tablespoons minced parsley
2 tablespoons tomato paste
3 tablespoons Burgundy
¼ teaspoon each ground
   cinnamon and ground
   nutmeg
¼ cup grated Parmesan cheese
1 piece heavy-duty foil,
   17 x 17 inches

French Blue Cheese Bread

French bread cut into 4 5-inch
   lengths
¼ cup melted butter
2 tablespoons dry sherry
1 tablespoon lemon juice
1 cup crumbled blue cheese

½ teaspoon paprika
1 tablespoon finely chopped
   onion
4 pieces heavy-duty foil, each
   8½ x 12 inches

Three hours in advance: Combine marinade ingredients in a bowl and add meat cubes. Cover. Prepare the loaves of bread—two or all three, depending on preference. *To prepare German loaf,* cut bread lengthwise above halfway mark. Scoop out soft bread from bottom crust, leaving one-inch border. Combine soft crumbs with cheese, butter, brandy and sauerkraut, using fingers to mix well. Fill cavity of bread with mixture. Cover. Wrap with foil. Refrigerate. *To prepare Italian loaf,* cut bread lengthwise above halfway mark. Scoop out soft bread from bottom crust. Set aside. Heat 2 tablespoons oil in skillet. Sauté onions about 5 minutes. Season eggplant with salt and pepper and add to skillet with the remaining oil. Cover. Simmer for about 12 to 15 minutes until eggplant is tender. Let cool. Combine skillet ingredients with bread crumbs and remaining ingredients, mixing thoroughly. Fill cavity of bread. Cover. Wrap in foil. *To prepare French loaf,* cut bread lengthwise at halfway mark. Scoop out soft bread from top and bottom crusts. Mix crumbs with melted butter. Add remaining ingredients, mixing thoroughly. Fill cavity of bread, spreading one-fourth of mixture to each 5-inch roll. Cover. Wrap each roll in foil.

Before serving: Place foil-wrapped loaves on grill to heat about 15 to 20 minutes before starting kebobs. Thread beef cubes on long skewers. Grill 3 to 4 inches from hot coals 10 to 15 minutes for medium rare and about 22 minutes for well done. Slide meat off skewer into selected loaves. Cut each loaf in not less than 2-inch serving pieces. Note: The meat from one sirloin steak, 1 inch thick, will fill two of the three loaves suggested here. You could, if it appealed to you, substitute sirloin tip and use a commercial tenderizer, following directions on package.

Cold or Warmed Roast Beef Slices on a Skewer

Makes 4 10-inch skewers

When you're looking for something different to do with sliced cooked beef from the delicatessen, try this. Serve cold or hot.

8 thin slices (about 4 x 6 inches) roast beef
4 thin slices brick, Münster or other mild, semisoft cheese (about 4 x 6 inches)
4 tablespoons whipped cream cheese with bacon and horseradish

2 teaspoons anchovy paste
1 jar (4 ounces) pimiento
4 tablespoons processed sharp cheese spread
2 tablespoons finely ground almonds
Chunks of pickles, olives, fruits or vegetables

On a counter, spread 8 slices of beef. Place two slices of cheese over two slices of beef. Combine cream cheese with anchovy paste and spread two tablespoons of this mixture over two more slices of beef. Halve the pimiento and spread over two beef slices. Combine cheese with nuts and spread two tablespoons on each of the remaining slices. Roll each slice tightly and cut each rolled slice in half for 16 rolls. Thread four differently seasoned rolls on each of four skewers. Alternate the rolls on skewer with chunks of pickles, olives, mushroom caps, cucumbers, green peppers, kumquats—whatever strikes your fancy. To serve cold, place skewers on dark rye bread or serve as a food centerpiece with skewers speared into fruit, such as half a melon placed cut side down. To serve warm, place skewers on foil-lined bake pan and heat in oven until cheese begins to melt. If extra moistness is desired, top with a tomato sauce.

Variation: Instead of the sharp cheese spread, substitute 2 tablespoons garlic spread concentrate combined with 2 tablespoons soft butter.

LEFTOVER ROAST BEEF

There's no need for leftovers to be dull. Kebob them! As in the preceding recipe, to serve cold, thread beef roast or even leftover steak on 6- or 10-inch skewers, alternating with pickles, candied fruits, fresh vegetables, or chunks of cheese. For dunking foods, provide a variety of dip sauces (see pages 267–74). If, on the other hand you'd like to serve the kebobs hot, consider some of the following suggestions. Note that 2 cups of cooked roast beef yield approximately 18 to 22 1½-inch cubes.

Cheese-Coated Kebobs

BAKE: *Makes assorted amounts*

½ cup melted butter
1 teaspoon freeze-dried shallots
Cold roast beef, cut into cubes
½ cup grated cheese, Parmesan
  or Romano

Cherry tomatoes
Fresh mushroom caps

Thirty minutes to one hour in advance: Combine melted butter and shallots and add roast beef cubes.

Before serving: Roll meat in grated cheese. Thread on skewer, alternating with tomatoes and mushrooms. Place skewers on foil-lined baking pan and bake in preheated 350° oven for 8 to 10 minutes. Serve with dip sauces—Spicy Cocktail Dip Sauce, Version I: Mild and Different, page 267, or the Horseradish Dip Sauces, pages 268–69.

Sweet-Tangy Kebobs

BAKE: *Makes assorted amounts*

½ cup pineapple syrup (liquid from canned pineapple chunks)
¼ cup lemon juice

¼ teaspoon ground nutmeg
Cold roast beef, cut into cubes
Canned pineapple chunks
Mandarin oranges

Thirty minutes in advance: Combine pineapple syrup, lemon juice, and nutmeg in a bowl. Add roast beef chunks.

Before serving: Thread meat on skewer alternately with pineapple chunks and mandarin oranges. Place skewers on foil-lined bake pan and bake in preheated 350° oven for 8 to 10 minutes. Baste frequently. If desired, add cornstarch to thicken remaining baste and serve as topping.

Enchilada Kebobs

BAKE: *Makes assorted amounts*

1 cup canned enchilada sauce
¼ cup Chablis or other dry white wine
Cold roast beef cut into cubes
Green pepper wedges

Black pitted olives
Bacon strips, cut into 1½-inch pieces
Cheddar cheese chunks

One hour in advance: Combine enchilada sauce with wine and add cubes of roast beef.

Before serving: Thread meat on skewer with green pepper, olives, and bacon wrapped around cheese. Place skewers on foil-lined bake pan. Bake in preheated 350° oven until cheese begins to melt and bacon is semicrisp. If you wish, place kebobs in broiler the last few minutes of cooking. Baste generously near the end of cooking. Serve remaining sauce as topping.

Variations: If preferred, parboil bacon 3 to 5 minutes before threading on skewer. Or, instead of bacon, use sliced ham to wrap around cheese.

5 · GROUND BEEF

WHAT TO CONSIDER BEFORE
SKEWER-COOKING GROUND BEEF

In preparing ground-beef patties, you would use any of the standard varieties of ground beef available, such as hamburger, ground chuck, or ground sirloin, and you would handle it gently and mix very lightly. But in making burger kebobs you'll have different requirements.

With these, you must make sure that the meat stays on the skewer. First of all, use very lean meat such as ground round steak (hamburger can have up to 30 percent fat, whereas ground round contains an average of 11 to 12 percent). Secondly, add something such as bread crumbs to act as a cohesive element. Third, by all means get your fingers into the bowl, and work and mix meat with seasonings thoroughly. Finally, once you have shaped the burger kebobs in balls of appetizer or dinner size, always, always chill at least 45 minutes before threading onto skewer to cook. And, especially when broiling, allow at least one-half of the cooking time to elapse before gently turning skewers. If turned too soon, kebobs will slip off the skewer. The same applies to baking, although here in most cases they don't require turning. Avoid placing burger kebobs directly on flat bottom of pan. Turn to page 23 for ideas on how to arrange skewers on pan to broil or bake. If the meat should stick and you're tempted to tug at the skewer, don't. Loosen with a spatula or fork. In baking, you may wish to line the pan with foil.

TIMETABLE FOR BROILING

For the broiled burger kebob recipes in this section (except if indicated otherwise), cook 4 to 5 inches from source of heat.

Dinner Size: Broil 6 to 8 minutes, turn, and broil an additional 5 to 7 minutes.

Appetizer Size: Broil 4 to 6 minutes, turn, and broil an additional 4 to 5 minutes.

Ideas for threading on skewer and ways to serve depend strictly on preference and imagination. Here are a few suggestions to get started. Mix and shape the burger balls in the morning or several hours in advance, wrap with wax paper, and refrigerate until ready to cook. For dinner, cook and serve on 10-inch skewers—and note that one pound of seasoned burger yields 12 2-inch balls, serving three to four. For appetizers or snacks, cook and serve on 6-inch skewers and shape one pound of seasoned burger into 30 1-inch balls; this serves five or six. Thread only the meat or arrange alternately with fruits and vegetables. If you wish, thread two to three differently seasoned burger kebobs on one skewer or combine them with other meats such as sausages (see page 153). You can thicken remaining bastes to serve as a topping or place several cups of various dip sauces on each plate.

When you want something to break up ground-beef monotony, consider the attractive alternative of cooking and serving it on a skewer.

Plain Burger Kebobs

BROIL: *Makes 12 dinner-size or 30 appetizer balls*

Place burger kebobs on a French roll smothered with fried onions. Serve with spiced peaches.

THE BURGER

1 pound ground round steak	1 teaspoon salt
1 egg, slightly beaten	¼ teaspoon garlic salt
½ cup French-bread crumbs	(optional)
2 tablespoons milk	⅛ teaspoon freshly ground
2 tablespoons finely chopped parsley	black pepper

Mix together burger ingredients and shape into balls. Chill. Thread burgers on skewers. Broil.

Variations: To burger mixture, add one tablespoon of Angostura bitters, ground curry, caraway seed, or parsley flakes; thread burger balls on skewer with mushrooms, canned potatoes, or cherry peppers; baste with a Tomato Barbecue Sauce, pages 265–66; or serve the appetizer size with Sour Cream Dip Sauces, page 272, or Spicy Cocktail Dip Sauce, Version I: Mild and Different, page 267.

Spiced Burger Kebobs

BROIL: *Makes 12 dinner-size or 30 appetizer balls*

Here's a Greek combination of spices. Place burger kebobs on a bed of egg noodles and serve with Vegetable Verve, page 283. If serving the appetizer size, accompany with Sour Cream Dip Sauce, Mild and Different Version, page 273.

THE BURGER

1 pound ground round steak	1 teaspoon ground allspice
1 egg, slightly beaten	1 teaspoon freshly grated
½ cup dry bread crumbs	nutmeg
2 tablespoons finely chopped onion	½ teaspoon salt
	¼ teaspoon cinnamon
2 tablespoons milk	⅛ teaspoon ground cloves

Mix burger ingredients thoroughly. Shape meat into balls. Chill. Thread onto skewers, alternating burger with cherry tomatoes and slices of raw onion if desired. Broil. Squeeze fresh lemon over kebobs before serving.

Kefte Burger Kebobs

BAKE: *Makes 24 dinner-size or 60 appetizer balls*

This is one of my favorite burger kebobs, an adaptation of the Greek Yourvarlakia—dinner-size ground meat and rice balls with the Avgolemono Sauce. If you wish, serve the appetizer size with Greek Fondue Dip, page 273.

THE BURGER

2 pounds ground round steak
1 cup cooked rice
2 tablespoons each finely chopped onion and parsley
1 tablespoon hot water
1 teaspoon dried mint, crushed

1 medium egg, slightly beaten
1½ teaspoons salt
¼ teaspoon each allspice and cinnamon

Flour for dredging
Cherry tomatoes

Lemon wedges or slices
Avgolemono Sauce, page 262

Mix burger ingredients together thoroughly. Shape meat into 24 2-inch balls. Dredge lightly in flour. Chill. Thread 8 10-inch skewers, alternating kefte burger with cherry tomatoes. Garnish tips with lemon slices or wedges. If you don't like well-cooked tomatoes, alternate with lemon slices and garnish tip of skewer with tomato near end of cooking. Bake in preheated 350° oven for 30 to 35 minutes. Do not turn. While burger kebobs are baking, prepare sauce. Top the kebobs with sauce just before serving. Garnish with sprigs of fresh parsley, if desired.

Mexicali Burger Kebobs

BROIL: *Makes 12 dinner-size or 30 appetizer balls*

For dinner, accompany these with corn soufflé, Mexican fried beans, and a crisp green salad. For appetizer, serve with Guacamole, Version II: Golden, page 271; and corn chips.

THE BURGER

1 pound ground round steak
1 tablespoon chili powder
2 tablespoons chopped pimiento, canned

¼ teaspoon dried ground chili peppers
¼ teaspoon garlic powder

Green pepper, cut into pieces

Pimiento-stuffed olives

BASTE

1 cup tomato sauce (8-ounce can)
½ cup vegetable oil
½ cup red wine vinegar
1 Mexican red pepper, finely chopped

⅓ cup finely chopped onion
1 teaspoon chili powder
1 teaspoon salt

Mix burger ingredients together thoroughly. Shape into balls. Chill. Thread burgers on skewers alternately with green pepper pieces and pimiento olives (and for the daring, add a few hot peppers, too). Broil. Combine baste ingredients and brush burger kebobs often.

Parmesan Burger Kebobs

BROIL: *Makes 12 dinner-size or 30 appetizer balls*

Place burger kebobs on a bed of buttered green noodles. Serve with glazed carrots and a romaine salad.

THE BURGER

1 pound ground round steak
½ cup grated Parmesan cheese
1 tablespoon finely chopped
   onion

2 teaspoons ketchup
1 teaspoon salt
½ teaspoon freshly ground
   black pepper

Grated Parmesan cheese to coat
   burger balls

Mushroom caps
Cherry tomatoes (optional)

BASTE

½ cup Burgundy

Mix together burger ingredients and shape into balls. Roll in Parmesan cheese, coating well. Chill. Thread burgers on skewers alternately with mushroom caps. Garnish tips of skewers with cherry tomatoes, if desired. Broil. Baste frequently with Burgundy.

Pineapple Burger Kebobs

BAKE: *Makes 12 dinner-size or 30 appetizer balls*

This is only for those fond of the sweet. Serve with rice, buttered peas, and chopped pimiento.

THE BURGER

1 pound ground round steak
½ cup French-bread crumbs
1 egg, slightly beaten

2 tablespoons pineapple syrup
1 teaspoon salt
⅛ teaspoon ground cloves

Canned pineapple chunks, well
   drained

Maraschino cherries
Whole cloves

BASTE–TOPPING

½ cup light brown sugar
½ cup pineapple syrup
2 tablespoons cider vinegar

1 teaspoon dry mustard
¼ cup crushed pineapple

Mix together burger ingredients and shape into balls. Chill. Thread the burgers on skewers alternately with pineapple chunks. Garnish tips of skewers with maraschino cherries. Insert two whole cloves in each burger. Bake in preheated 350° oven for 25 to 30 minutes. In a saucepan, combine baste-topping ingredients except crushed pineapple. After 10 minutes of cooking, baste burger kebobs generously. Add crushed pineapple plus cornstarch dissolved in water to thicken remaining sauce to serve as a topping. Remove cloves before serving.

Dill Burger Kebobs

BROIL: *Makes 12 dinner-size or 30 appetizer balls*

Serve with crisp fried onion rings, sliced tomatoes, and a gelatin salad.

THE BURGER

1 pound ground round steak
1 egg, slightly beaten
1 tablespoon prepared dill mix,
   or 2 teaspoons dill weed

1 teaspoon salt

Dill pickles (slices or whole
   pickles cut into chunks)

TOPPING SAUCE

8 ounces dairy sour cream

2 teaspoons dill weed

Mix together the burger ingredients. Shape into balls. Chill. Thread burger on skewers alternately with dill pickle pieces. Broil. Combine topping-sauce ingredients. Scoop sauce over kebobs just before serving.

Pizza Burger Kebobs

BROIL AND BAKE: *Makes 12 dinner-size balls*

THE BURGER

1 pound ground round steak
1 egg, slightly beaten
½ cup Italian-seasoned bread crumbs
⅓ cup grated Parmesan cheese
1 tablespoon instant minced onion

½ teaspoon salt
½ teaspoon oregano
¼ teaspoon freshly ground black pepper

Italian-seasoned bread crumbs (to coat burger balls)
Mushroom caps

6 Italian hard rolls (about 3 x 5-inch size)

TOPPING SAUCE

1 cup prepared pizza sauce, without meat (8-ounce can)
1 8-ounce package shredded cheese (Cheddar or mozzarella)

Oregano to taste

Mix burger ingredients together thoroughly. Shape into 12 balls. Roll in Italian-seasoned bread crumbs, coating well. Chill. On 6-inch skewers, thread two burgers alternately with mushroom caps. Broil 4 to 5 inches from source of heat for 7 to 8 minutes; turn; broil another 3 to 4 minutes. Reduce oven temperature to 375°. Arrange hard rolls open-face on cookie sheet. Place filled skewer on each roll. Top generously with pizza sauce and then shredded cheese. Bake 5 to 6 minutes until cheese melts. Sprinkle oregano to taste. Serve immediately.

Variations: Instead of hard rolls you may wish to use English muffins. Or you can form meat mixture into six sausage shapes and serve in frankfurter rolls, substituting a quick spaghetti-sauce mix for the pizza sauce.

Pecan Burger Kebobs

BROIL: *Makes 12 dinner-size or 30 appetizer balls*

Serve with a cottage cheese vegetable salad. For appetizer size, serve with Sour Cream Dip Sauces, Cheddar or Sweet Accents, page 272.

THE BURGER

1 pound ground round steak	2 tablespoons soy sauce
½ cup finely chopped pecans	¼ teaspoon cinnamon
1 egg, slightly beaten	

Green-tipped bananas, cut into
1-inch chunks (covered with
orange juice)

Mix burger ingredients together thoroughly. Shape into balls. Chill. Thread on skewers, alternating burger with banana chunks. Broil. After turning, baste with orange juice if desired.

Variations: Thread bacon in a twisting, curving manner, alternating burger with banana and pineapple chunks in curves. Garnish tip of skewer with maraschino cherry. Note: For crisper bacon you may wish to parboil it 3 to 5 minutes before threading on skewer.

Coated Burger Kebobs

BAKE: *Makes 12 dinner-size or 30 appetizer balls*

Here you have a choice of coatings, chip or flake. Serve over a bed of sautéed Chinese vegetables or with a spinach soufflé.

THE BURGER

1 pound ground round steak	1 teaspoon garlic salt
1 tablespoon soy sauce	2 teaspoons minced parsley
¼ cup melted butter or margarine	Cherry tomatoes, or fruit, if preferred
Green pepper	

COATINGS

Chip Coating

⅔ cup finely crushed potato
   chips

Flake Coating

⅔ cup finely crushed cornflakes

Mix burger ingredients together thoroughly. Shape into balls. Roll in melted butter and then roll in flake or chip crumbs, coating well. Chill. Thread coated burgers on skewers alternately with green pepper pieces, cherry tomatoes, or fruit. Bake in preheated 350° oven for 30 to 35 minutes.

Variations: Serve each person a double treat—one burger kebob chip-coated and the other flake-coated. However, when using both varieties for one pound of meat, remember to crush only half of each coating.

Anchovy-Stuffed Burger Kebobs

BROIL: *Makes 12 dinner-size or 30 appetizer balls*

Serve with Wild Rice and Mushrooms, page 290.

THE BURGER

1 pound ground round steak	1 teaspoon garlic salt
1 tablespoon soy sauce	

Anchovy-stuffed olives

BASTE

½ cup sweet vermouth

Mix burger ingredients together. Roll into balls, then flatten. Embed anchovy-stuffed olive in center and shape meat around it to form perfect balls. Chill. Thread on skewer, making certain to spear center of olive. If desired, thread burger alternately with more anchovy-stuffed olives or black pitted olives stuffed with cheese. Broil. Baste frequently with sweet vermouth.

Variations: Serve with saffron rice and substitute a Roquefort baste: 1 cup vegetable oil, ½ cup crumbled Roquefort cheese, ⅓ cup freshly squeezed lemon juice, 1 teaspoon salt, ½ teaspoon ground black pepper and ½ teaspoon paprika.

Texas Burger Kebobs

BROIL: *Makes 4 elongated shapes (long stars)*

Serve on a toasted frankfurter roll, or accompany with sorghum wheat cakes.

THE BURGER

1 pound ground round steak
1 egg, slightly beaten
⅓ cup dry bread crumbs
2 tablespoons finely chopped
  onion

2 teaspoons chili powder
½ teaspoon freshly ground
  black pepper
¼ teaspoon dry mustard
⅛ teaspoon Tabasco sauce

Small boiled onions

BASTE

Tomato Barbecue Sauce,
  Version II: Uncooked,
  page 266

Mix burger ingredients together thoroughly. Divide meat into 4 equal portions. Shape into 4 balls. Roll each ball into a 5- or 6-inch length. Chill. Thread one long-star burger on 10-inch skewer. Garnish both ends of skewer with small cooked onions, or cherry tomatoes if preferred. Broil 4 to 5 inches from source of heat 7 to 8 minutes; turn; broil another 7 to 8 minutes. Baste generously with sauce.

Variation: See Wiener and Burger Kebobs, page 252.

Beer Burger Kebobs

BROIL: *Makes 12 dinner-size or 30 appetizer balls*

This might interest the chef who likes to nip. The baste requires only 8 ounces of beer—so if you open a 12-ounce can or bottle, by all means chugalug. Serve with German potato salad, caraway sauerkraut, and corn on the cob.

THE BURGER

1 pound ground round steak	2 teaspoons ketchup
½ cup cracker meal	1 teaspoon salt
1 tablespoon instant minced onion	⅛ teaspoon freshly ground black pepper

Small boiled onions   Green pepper pieces

BASTE

1 cup beer	1 teaspoon salt
⅔ cup ketchup	⅛ teaspoon freshly ground black pepper
3 tablespoons granulated sugar	
2 tablespoons Worcestershire sauce	

Mix together burger ingredients. Shape into balls. Chill. Thread burgers on skewers alternately with onions and green pepper. Broil. Combine baste ingredients and baste burger kebobs generously.

Burgundy Burger Kebobs

BROIL: *Makes 12 dinner-size or 30 appetizer balls*

Here you have a choice of burger—Burgundy or Roquefort. Place burger kebobs on French bread spread with parsley butter.

THE BURGUNDY BURGER

1 pound ground round steak
½ cup French-bread crumbs
¼ cup Burgundy
1 teaspoon salt

1 teaspoon chopped parsley
Freshly ground black pepper to taste

OR, IF YOU CHOOSE, THE ROQUEFORT BURGER

1 pound ground round steak
½ cup Roquefort cheese, crumbled

2 tablespoons chopped parsley
1 teaspoon garlic salt

Fresh mushroom caps (or 1 4-ounce jar, drained)

BASTE

2 tablespoons minced onion
2 tablespoons butter

½ cup Burgundy
Salt to taste

Mix ingredients of your burger choice thoroughly. Shape into balls. Chill. Thread burgers on skewers alternately with mushrooms. Sauté onions in butter until tender. Add wine and salt. Broil burgers. Baste with warmed sauce frequently.

Citrus Burger Kebobs

BROIL: *Makes 12 dinner-size or 30 appetizer balls*

Place on a bed of white or brown rice and serve with crab apples.

THE BURGER

1 pound ground round steak
⅓ cup graham cracker crumbs
2 tablespoons freshly squeezed
   orange juice

1 teaspoon salt

MARINADE–BASTE

1 cup freshly squeezed orange
   juice
¼ cup Cointreau
¼ cup freshly squeezed lemon
   juice

2 bay leaves
3 whole cloves
Salt and pepper to taste

Pieces of thick orange peel
Pieces of lemon peel

Whole bay leaves (optional)

Forty-five minutes in advance: Mix burger ingredients together. Shape into balls. Combine marinade–baste ingredients in a bowl. Add burger balls. Cover. Refrigerate.

Before serving: Thread burgers on skewers alternately with orange and lemon peels and bay leaves. Broil. Baste generously with the marinade–baste.

More Surprise Burger Kebobs

BROIL: *Makes 12 dinner-size or 30 appetizer balls*

Here we have surprise centers: soft . . . crunchy . . . crisp . . . mild . . . sharp.

THE BURGER

1 pound ground round steak
1 tablespoon soy sauce
1 tablespoon milk

2 teaspoons horseradish
1 teaspoon onion powder

TIDBIT VARIATIONS FOR SURPRISE CENTERS

Pimiento slices

Blue cheese or Cheddar tidbits

Bacon-flavored chips

Cocktail onions

Cocktail olives

Pickled fruits

BASTE

It's up to you! Thin Sweet-Sour Sauce, page 264, or for a choice of barbecue sauces, pages 265–67. For the appetizer sizes, serve with dip sauces, pages 267–74.

Mix burger ingredients together thoroughly. Shape meat into balls. Flatten and embed surprise tidbits in center and roll into balls. Chill. Thread burgers on skewers alternately with olives, pickles, fruits, and vegetables. Broil. Baste with your favorite sauce.

Variations: Alternate a variety of burgers on one skewer, one surprise after another. If you wish, roll some of the burgers in grated cheese or dry bread crumbs.

6 · VEAL

WHAT TO CONSIDER BEFORE
SKEWER-COOKING VEAL

Essentially veal is a dependent. Lacking the fullness of flavor found in meats such as beef and pork, veal needs seasoning to give it some vitality. For this reason, it adapts especially well to the braised method of skewer cooking. That, of course, is because veal has little marbleization of fat and abundant connective tissue. But if you prefer all meats broiled or baked, then cook veal kebobs that way too. If you broil, extra attention will be required to achieve acceptable tenderness; by the time the veal is sufficiently cooked, it tends to become quite dry. To help overcome this, use cuts only from the leg or loin, always marinate at room temperature for three hours, and baste often. I've obtained good results with portable appliances that have an infrared element.

For all methods of skewer-cooking veal, I use meat from the loin or leg; but for braising you could use that from the shoulder, which is about one half the price (remember, veal steak labeled "arm" or "blade" comes from the shoulder, whereas veal steak labeled "sirloin" and "round" comes from the loin and leg, respectively).

Although I'm certain veal kebobs make appealing appetizers or snacks, to me they seem most appropriate as a main dish. Allow one-third to one-half pound of boneless meat per person. Please also turn to pages 239, 240, 241. There you'll find recipes for veal braised on a skewer together with several other meats—perfect for times when you want kebobs of considerable contrast.

Tangy Skewered Veal

BROIL OR BAKE: *Makes 4 10-inch skewers*

Serve with corn soufflé and a bacon-lettuce salad.

1 pound veal steak cut into 20 to 22 1-inch cubes	8 mild cherry peppers
1 green pepper cut into 8 pieces	8 canned whole onions
	4 cherry tomatoes (optional)

MARINADE–BASTE–TOPPING SAUCE

½ cup tomato sauce	1 tablespoon prepared mustard
¼ cup ketchup	2 teaspoons Worcestershire sauce
¼ cup vegetable oil	
2 tablespoons brown sugar	

Three hours in advance: Combine sauce ingredients in a bowl. Add cubes of veal, cover, and marinate at room temperature.

Before serving: Thread each skewer as follows: onion . VEAL . cherry pepper . VEAL . green pepper . VEAL . onion . VEAL . cherry pepper . VEAL . green pepper. *If you choose to broil:* Broil 4 to 5 inches from source of heat 12 to 15 minutes on each side. Baste frequently near end of cooking. *If you choose to bake:* Bake in preheated 375° oven for 30 to 35 minutes. Baste often. If desired, serve remaining baste as a topping sauce.

Variations: Garnish tips of skewers with cherry tomatoes near end of cooking. Or substitute 1 cup Tomato Barbecue Sauce, Sweet-Sour Variation, page 266, for marinade–baste–topping sauce.

City Chicken

BRAISE: *Makes 6 6-inch skewers*

"City Chicken" is perhaps the most familiar braised skewered dish. It is cubes of veal cooked on short skewers in a skillet. The term "Mock Chicken Legs" refers to ground veal (sometimes combined with ground pork) shaped on skewers to resemble poultry legs. Both are usually found with wooden skewers at fresh-meat counters.

1 pound veal shoulder (boned), cut into 20 to 22 1-inch cubes	2 tablespoons milk
	⅓ to ½ cup fine cracker crumbs
Salt to taste	2 tablespoons margarine or
1 egg, slightly beaten	butter

SKILLET SAUCE

1 cup chicken broth (bouillon cube dissolved in 1 cup hot water)	¼ teaspoon thyme
	¼ teaspoon nutmeg
	⅛ teaspoon freshly ground
1 teaspoon paprika	black pepper

One-half hour in advance: Season cubed veal with salt to taste. Mix slightly beaten egg with milk. Dip meat into milk-egg mixture. Roll in cracker crumbs, coating well. Refrigerate.

Before serving: Thread three or four veal cubes on each skewer. Melt margarine in skillet and brown veal on all sides. Combine sauce ingredients and pour over kebobs. Cover. Simmer 35 to 40 minutes, turning at least once.

Skewered Veal Vermouth

BROIL: *Makes 6 10-inch skewers*

Dry (or French) vermouth is a fortified wine blended with many different herbs and spices. Its use here enhances this

rather mild and dry kebob. Serve with a sweet potato casserole and a spinach-and-lettuce salad.

2 pounds veal steak, cut into
38 to 40 1-inch cubes
18 whole canned onions

2 green peppers, each cut into
9 pieces

MARINADE–BASTE

⅓ cup dry vermouth
⅓ cup vegetable oil
¼ cup finely chopped onion

¼ cup chopped parsley
2 tablespoons lemon juice
¼ teaspoon celery salt

Three hours in advance: Combine marinade–baste ingredients in a bowl and add veal cubes. Cover. Let stand at
room temperature.

Before serving: Thread veal on skewers alternately with
onions and peppers, beginning and ending with onion. Broil 4
to 5 inches from source of heat 12 to 15 minutes on each
side. Baste frequently. Before serving, brush kebobs generously with remaining sauce.

Skewered Veal with Apricots

BRAISE: *Makes 4 8-inch skewers*

1 pound veal steak, cut into
20 to 22 1-inch cubes
Salt to taste
24 dried apricots
2 tablespoons margarine or
butter

4 round pieces thick orange
peel
4 maraschino cherries

SKILLET SAUCE

½ cup apricot brandy
½ cup orange juice
1 tablespoon grated orange
rind

½ teaspoon soy sauce
¼ teaspoon rosemary leaves
⅛ teaspoon ground ginger

Season cubes of veal with salt to taste. Thread meat on skewers alternately with apricots, beginning and ending with apricots. Combine sauce ingredients. Melt margarine in a skillet and brown kebobs on all sides. Pour sauce over kebobs. Cover. Simmer for 15 minutes. Spoon sauce over kebobs. Add orange peel on end of each skewer. Cover. Simmer an additional 20 minutes. Sauce will thicken. Before serving, garnish tips of skewers with maraschino cherries.

Cointreau Veal Kebobs

BRAISE: *Makes 4 8-inch skewers*

The white-colored Cointreau and Triple Sec and the orange-colored Curaçao are similar liqueurs—that is, they are principally flavored with orange. In this recipe, use whichever you have handy.

1 pound veal shoulder (boned), cut into 20 to 22 1-inch cubes
Salt to taste
12 canned pineapple chunks

1 thick-skinned orange, unpeeled, cut into 12 sections
2 tablespoons butter or margarine

SKILLET SAUCE

¼ cup pineapple juice
¼ cup Cointreau
¼ cup water
1 tablespoon wine vinegar

1 teaspoon soy sauce
¼ teaspoon garlic powder
½ teaspoon ground ginger

Season cubes of veal with salt to taste. Thread on skewer alternately with pineapple chunks and orange sections, beginning with pineapple and ending with orange. Combine sauce ingredients. Melt butter in skillet and brown kebobs on all sides. Pour sauce over kebobs. Cover. Simmer 30 to 35 minutes. Sauce will thicken.

Veal Kebobs Parmesan

BAKE: *Makes 4 10-inch skewers*

Serve with asparagus tips and sautéed mushrooms.

1 pound veal steak cut into 20 to 22 1-inch cubes	8 cherry tomatoes
Salt to taste	1 green pepper, cut into 8 pieces
¼ cup melted butter	2 strips bacon, halved crosswise
½ to ¾ cup grated Parmesan cheese	

Season cubes of veal with salt to taste. Dip meat in melted butter. Roll in Parmesan cheese. Thread meat on skewer alternately with tomatoes and green pepper, beginning and ending with veal. Wrap a piece of bacon tightly around last piece of meat on each skewer. Bake in preheated 350° oven 45 to 50 minutes.

Variations: Use only 4 cherry tomatoes and garnish tips of skewers near end of cooking. Substitute ½-inch-thick slices of cucumber, halved, for tomatoes.

A Skewer of Veal and Salty Accents

BROIL: *Makes 6 10-inch skewers*

Depending on one's affinity for salt, the onions wrapped with anchovy fillets may or may not be desired. At least— give friends a warning.

1 can (2 ounces) anchovy fillets, drained	2 pounds veal steak, cut into 38 to 40 1-inch cubes
Green onions, cut into 12 3-inch pieces	1-pound jar boiled onions, about 18

MARINADE–BASTE

½ cup Chablis
¼ cup olive oil
¼ cup chopped parsley
2 tablespoons lemon juice

1 clove garlic, minced
1 tablespoon anchovy paste
1 large onion, sliced

Three hours in advance: Combine marinade–baste ingredients in a bowl. Add veal cubes. Cover and let stand at room temperature.

Before serving: Lay anchovy fillets over slices of green onions and roll tightly. Thread veal on skewers alternately with whole onion and rolled green onion. Broil 4 to 5 inches from source of heat 12 to 15 minutes on each side. Baste frequently. Before serving, brush each kebob generously.

Veal Kebobs Italiano

BRAISE: *Makes 4 8-inch skewers*

Serve these moist and well-seasoned kebobs over a bed of green noodles or spaghetti.

1 pound veal shoulder (boned), cut into 20 to 22 1-inch cubes
Salt to taste
8 thin strips of boiled ham (optional)
8 jumbo pimiento-stuffed olives

8 large whole mushrooms, canned
1 onion, cut into 8 pieces
2 tablespoons butter or margarine

SKILLET SAUCE

½ cup dry sherry
¼ cup chopped parsley
¼ cup tomato sauce
2 tablespoons olive oil
½ teaspoon paprika

½ teaspoon dry mustard
¼ teaspoon rosemary
⅛ teaspoon nutmeg
1 clove garlic, minced

Season cubes of veal with salt to taste. Thread skewers as follows: folded ham strip . olive . VEAL . mushroom .

VEAL . onion . VEAL . mushroom . VEAL . onion . VEAL . olive . folded ham strip. Combine sauce ingredients. Melt butter or margarine in skillet. Brown kebobs on all sides. Pour sauce over kebobs. Cover. Simmer about 30 to 35 minutes. Occasionally scoop sauce over kebobs. After removing kebobs from skillet, stir two more tablespoons of wine into remaining sauce and spoon over kebobs.

Variation: To make 6 6-inch skewers. Instead of using meat from the shoulder, you might prefer veal cutlet. If so, make the following substitutions in the recipe above: Use 1 pound veal cutlet, cut into 18 strips; 12 medium-size pimiento-stuffed olives; 6 medium-size canned mushrooms; 1 small onion cut into 6 pieces. To thread veal strips on skewer, fold them over once. Thread 6-inch skewers as follows: olive . VEAL . mushroom . VEAL . onion . VEAL . olive. Cook as above.

Dilled Veal Kebobs

BRAISE: *Makes 4 8-inch skewers*

1 pound veal shoulder (boned) cut into 20 to 22 1-inch cubes
Salt to taste

24 pickled green tomato wedges, 15-ounce jar (found in refrigerator sections of supermarkets)
2 tablespoons butter or margarine

SKILLET SAUCE

1 cup Rhine wine
1 cup dairy sour cream

2 teaspoons dill weed

Season cubes of veal with salt to taste. Thread veal on skewers alternately with pickled tomato wedges, beginning and ending with tomato wedges. Melt butter or margarine in skillet. Brown kebobs on all sides. Add wine. Cover. Simmer 30 to 35 minutes, adding more wine if needed. Remove kebobs to platter. Combine dill with sour cream and add to skillet, stirring well. Turn off heat. Return kebobs to skillet. Spoon sauce over them. Serve immediately. (If you wish, don't return kebobs to skillet and pour sauce in a bowl for self-servings.)

7 · LAMB

WHAT TO CONSIDER
BEFORE SKEWER-COOKING LAMB

In spring, lamb is most abundant—and at its best. At that time, you'll find genuine spring lamb that's been slaughtered at 3 to 5 months, with a leg weighing around 4 or 5 pounds. If the lambs are allowed to grow, by winter the leg ranges anywhere from 8 to 10 pounds. Generally, the older the sheep when slaughtered, the tougher and more pronounced in flavor.

The image that flashes in my mind of the most tender, delicately flavored, succulent lamb is *arni too yalatos*—Greek for milk-fed young things carefully sheltered until slaughtered between the ages of 2 and 3 months. Perhaps you identify these as suckling lambs, which are marketed under the name Hothouse. This may surprise you, but if I'm serving a meal to guests who thoroughly relish lamb, I don't kebob it. With sections of very young lamb, to do anything other than roast, broil, or grill and season with garlic, freshly ground black pepper, and a combination of freshly squeezed lemon juice and a little olive oil—to me, it just doesn't seem right. And to serve it with mint jelly . . . that's unthinkable.

For those who like lamb, certainly kebobs make for an interesting treat. And for those indifferent to lamb, kebobs could be instrumental in stimulating greater interest in this meat. To achieve superb kebobs, note three things. First, the meat should come from young lamb. Secondly, it should have some marbleization of fat (and the surface fat should be very white). Even a small lamb, with a leg of 4½ to 5½ pounds, can be tough if it's too lean. Finally, when you're broiling or grilling, cook the kebobs until pink or slightly pink. To my chagrin, even many people with Middle Eastern heritages, who are perhaps the largest group of consumers of this meat, abuse it by overcooking. But as always, keep in mind the preferences of those you're cooking for—if necessary, serve it well done.

The cut of lamb to use for kebobs is the leg—particularly the sirloin part (sometimes called butt), which is generally more tender than the bottom shank end. A boned loin section is also fine. Ideally, the leg should weigh from 4 to 6 pounds. However, depending on where you shop, you may have a difficult time securing that size leg, especially in late fall and winter. In that case, the sirloin part from a leg of 8 to 10 pounds would equal the weight of a full leg from a smaller lamb. You can find small legs throughout the year in specialty and imported-food markets with meat departments that cater to customers who generally purchase baby lamb, not by small cuts, but by sections such as a quarter or a half or the entire carcass. Depending on the demand for lamb in an area, meat markets might sell the sirloin and shank parts separately or the full leg only. Some butchers will cut the sirloin part of the leg and sell lamb steak, but others won't. In a few markets you can find PRIME lamb, which of course is excellent.

There are many resourceful ways to use a leg of lamb. If, for instance, you had a 6- to 8-pound leg, you could take pieces from it for a kebob recipe and freeze the remainder for kebobs another time. Or you could use the entire leg for kebobs at one time to serve 6 to 8. Another way is to use the sirloin part of the leg for kebobs to serve 3 or 4 and use the shank end for a stew to serve 4 or 5. Still another way is to roast the leg for a meal and then prepare the leftovers as kebobs for another meal or snack. Do also consider using the bone as stock for soup or a stew; and for a specific idea, use it for stock to prepare Dolmathes (stuffed grape leaves), page 277.

Some like to prepare kebobs with the meat from the

shoulder. If you want meat for only a few kebobs, consider lamb steaks from the leg (if it's available) or even the meat trimmed from loin chops. And for lamburger kebobs, use lamb that comes packaged and already ground (usually meat from the neck, breast or flank) or, as I prefer to do, have the butcher grind it from the leg. In the following recipes, although I prefer to use 4½- to 5½-pound legs of lamb, you'll find that I've indicated boned leg by the pound and by the kebob-chunk count. After you've boned the leg (and I always have this done by the butcher), remove any fell (the thin, paperlike membrane covering the leg) as well as any gristle or unwanted fat and then cut into pieces for kebobs. Remember to count for a weight loss from the bone. A 5½-pound leg, for example, will yield about 3 pounds of meat.

Minted Lamb Kebobs Avgolemono

BROIL: *Makes 4 10-inch skewers*

Serve these when the occasion demands something elegant.

1¼ to 1½ pounds boned leg of lamb cut into 12 1½-inch pieces

1 can (14 ounces) artichoke bottoms (8 per can)
8 pieces hearts of palm (1 14-ounce can)

MARINADE FOR LAMB

⅓ cup melted butter
2 tablespoons dry Marsala
2 tablespoons orange juice
⅛ teaspoon ground nutmeg

¼ teaspoon ground cinnamon
1 clove garlic, crushed
2 bay leaves, crushed

MARINADE FOR ARTICHOKES

¼ cup melted butter

¼ cup tomato sauce

Stuffing for Artichokes

4 slices white bread, trimmed
2 tablespoons dry Marsala

1 tablespoon minced onion
½ teaspoon crushed dried mint

BASTE

2 to 3 tablespoons white crème
de menthe

TOPPING SAUCE

Avgolemono Sauce (1½ cups),
page 262

Two hours in advance: Combine marinade ingredients for
lamb. Add lamb, coating well. Let stand at room temperature. In small bowl, combine marinade for artichokes. Add
artichokes, coating well. Set aside. Sprinkle Marsala over
bread to moisten. Add minced onion and dried mint, using
fingers to mix thoroughly. Roll into 4 balls and set aside.
Before serving: Prepare Avgolemono Sauce. Embed one
of the bread-stuffing balls into each of 4 artichoke bottoms
and top with remaining 4 artichoke bottoms, thereby creating
4 stuffed artichokes. Thread skewers as follows: LAMB .
heart of palm . LAMB . stuffed artichoke . LAMB . heart of
palm. Broil 4 inches from source of heat for 14 to 16 minutes for medium, 18 to 20 minutes for well done. Turn often
and baste the hearts of palm with crème de menthe near end
of cooking. Top kebobs with Avgolemono Sauce and serve.

Lamb Kebobs Latholemono

BROIL: *Makes 6 10-inch skewers*

Among Greeks, perhaps the favorite sauce next to Avgolemono (egg-lemon) is Latholemono (oil-lemon). And to flavor
lamb kebobs (*arni souvlakia*), that seasoning is used almost
exclusively. The proportions of oil to lemon might be 4 or
3 to 1, or a little tangier yet, 2 to 1. Rarely are the *souvlakia*
removed from the grill or broiler and not bathed with freshly
squeezed lemon juice.

3 pounds boned leg of lamb,
cut into 30 to 32 1½-inch
pieces

12 lemon wedges or slices
12 bay leaves (optional)

MARINADE–BASTE (Latholemono)

½ cup olive oil
Juice of 1 lemon (¼ cup)
¼ cup chopped parsley
1 clove garlic, minced

1 teaspoon salt
½ teaspoon freshly ground
black pepper

Three hours in advance: Combine marinade–baste ingredients in a large bowl. Beat to blend well. Add lamb. Cover. Let stand at room temperature, turning meat occasionally.

Before serving: Thread lamb on skewers, with two lemon wedges or slices and two bay leaves per skewer. Broil 4 inches from source of heat 14 to 16 minutes for medium, 18 to 20 minutes for well done. Turn several times and baste generously. Sprinkle with leaf thyme or oregano, if desired.

Variation: If you wish to serve these as a *meze* (an appetizer or snack), cut three pounds of boned leg of lamb into 1-inch pieces and thread on 6-inch skewers. Omit bay leaves. Makes 10 to 12 6-inch skewers. Broil 3 inches from source of heat 10 to 12 minutes for medium, 14 to 16 minutes for well done.

Skewered Lamb with Orange Overtones

BRAISE: *Makes 4 8-inch skewers*

1¾ to 2 pounds boned leg of
lamb cut into 16 1½-inch
pieces
8 whole canned mushrooms

Green onions (the green part)
cut into 36 1-inch pieces
2 tablespoons butter or
margarine

ORANGE TOPPING MIXTURE

½ cup candied orange peel
½ cup coarsely chopped
walnuts

½ teaspoon crushed dried mint

SKILLET SAUCE

⅓ cup orange juice
2 tablespoons Curaçao or other
    orange-flavored liqueur

2 tablespoons lemon juice
2 tablespoons dry vermouth
¼ teaspoon leaf thyme

In blender, add topping-mixture ingredients and chop. Set aside. Thread skewers as follows: mushroom . LAMB . 3 pieces of onion . LAMB . 3 pieces of onion . LAMB . 3 pieces of onion . LAMB . mushroom. Melt butter or margarine in skillet. Add kebobs and brown 6 to 8 minutes, turning often. Combine sauce ingredients and pour over kebobs. Cover. Simmer 10 minutes; turn kebobs, scooping sauce over them. Cover and cook an additional 8 to 10 minutes. Garnish each kebob with a generous sprinkling of the orange topping mixture.

Skewered Lamb with Zucchini Surprises

BROIL: *Makes 5 10-inch skewers*

1¾ to 2 pounds boned leg of
    lamb, cut into 15 1½-inch
    pieces
4 small to medium unpared
    zucchini (about 5 inches
    long)
10 whole canned mushrooms
½ to 1 tablespoon grated
    Parmesan cheese

5 canned boiled onions
1 to 2 teaspoons melted butter
¼ teaspoon dill weed
5 canned pineapple chunks,
    well drained
2 teaspoons white crème de
    menthe
5 cherry tomatoes

MARINADE

⅓ cup melted butter
⅓ cup tomato sauce
2 tablespoons dry Marsala
¼ teaspoon leaf marjoram

¼ teaspoon rosemary
¼ teaspoon sweet basil
⅛ teaspoon freshly ground
    black pepper

Two hours in advance: Combine marinade ingredients and add lamb. Cover. Let stand at room temperature. Proceed then to prepare the zucchini surprises. Place zucchini in boiling water and boil 5 to 8 minutes. Rinse in cold water. Cut crosswise into 20 1-inch pieces. Hollow pieces by scraping out seed pulp (which can be kept for other uses). Coat mushrooms with grated cheese, tossing well. Place two mushrooms, side by side, in the center of each of 5 hollowed zucchini. Dip onions in melted butter combined with dill weed and insert in center of 5 zucchini. Toss pineapple chunks with crème de menthe and place in center of 5 zucchini. Insert a cherry tomato in each of the remaining 5 zucchini. Set zucchini surprises aside.

Before serving: For each skewer, thread four different zucchini surprises alternately with lamb, beginning and ending with zucchini and allowing three pieces of meat per skewer. As a suggestion, you might consider this order: zucchini with mushroom . LAMB . zucchini with dilled onion . LAMB . zucchini with pineapple . LAMB . zucchini with tomato. Broil 4 inches from source of heat 14 to 16 minutes for medium, 18 to 20 minutes for well done. Turn twice.

Skewered Lamb with Eggplant

BROIL: *Makes 4 10-inch skewers*

1¼ to 1½ pounds boned leg
of lamb cut into 12 1½-inch
pieces

1 small unpared eggplant
(about ¾ pound) cut into
16 chunks

MARINADE FOR LAMB

¼ cup olive oil
¼ teaspoon sweet basil
¼ teaspoon marjoram
1 medium onion, sliced and
separated into rings

2 cloves garlic, minced
¼ teaspoon freshly ground
black pepper

MARINADE FOR EGGPLANT

⅓ cup vegetable oil	¼ teaspoon dill weed
⅓ cup tomato juice	½ teaspoon crushed dried mint
2 tablespoons lemon juice	⅛ teaspoon ground cinnamon

Two hours in advance: Combine marinade ingredients for lamb. Add lamb and toss well. Cover. Let stand at room temperature. In another bowl, combine marinade ingredients for eggplant; add the eggplant chunks and toss very well.

Before serving: Thread skewers, beginning and ending with eggplant, allowing 4 chunks of eggplant and 3 pieces of lamb per skewer. Broil 4 inches from source of heat 15 to 18 minutes or until eggplant is tender. Turn often.

Lamb Kebobs Cosmopolitan

BRAISE: *Makes 4 8-inch skewers*

8 large whole canned mushroom caps	4 thin slices lemon
8 square pieces onion	4 slices (¼ inch thick) unpared cucumber
1¾ to 2 pounds boned leg of lamb cut into 16 1½-inch pieces	2 tablespoons butter or margarine

TOPPING MIXTURE

½ cup salted cashews	1½ tablespoons finely chopped green onion
¼ cup candied citron	½ teaspoon crushed dried mint
1 teaspoon grated lemon rind	
1 teaspoon grated cucumber	

SKILLET SAUCE

¼ cup tomato sauce	⅛ teaspoon freshly ground black pepper
½ cup dry vermouth	⅛ teaspoon garlic powder
¼ teaspoon leaf marjoram	1 cup dairy sour cream
¼ teaspoon leaf thyme	
¼ teaspoon rosemary	

In a blender, chop cashews and citron. Stir in cucumber, green onion, mint, and lemon rind until thoroughly mixed. Set aside. Thread skewers as follows: mushroom . onion . LAMB . onion . LAMB . lemon . LAMB . cucumber . LAMB . mushroom. Combine sauce ingredients except sour cream and 1½ tablespoons vermouth. Melt margarine or butter in skillet and brown kebobs 6 to 8 minutes, turning often. Pour skillet sauce over kebobs. Cover and simmer 10 minutes. Turn kebobs and scoop sauce over them. Cover. Cook an additional 10 minutes. Remove kebobs to a warm platter. Combine 1½ tablespoons vermouth with sour cream and gradually stir into sauce. Heat but do not boil. Spoon sauce over kebobs and sprinkle topping mixture over each.

Lamb Kebobs with Onion

BROIL: *Makes 4 10-inch skewers*

The potency of this recipe makes it strictly for onion lovers.

2 pounds boned leg of lamb cut into about 20 1½-inch pieces	8 canned whole onions
8 3-inch pieces of green onion, folded once	1 green pepper, cut into 8 pieces

MARINADE

1 package onion-soup mix	⅓ cup vegetable oil
⅔ cup Chablis or other dry white wine	2 tablespoons lemon juice

Three hours in advance: Combine marinade ingredients in a bowl. Add lamb. Cover. Let stand at room temperature, turning meat occasionally.
Before serving: Thread lamb on skewers as follows: green onion . LAMB . whole onion . LAMB . green pepper . LAMB . green onion . LAMB . whole onion . LAMB . green pepper. Broil 4 inches from source of heat 14 to 16 minutes for medium, 18 to 20 minutes for well done. Turn once.

Lamb Kebobs, Turkish Accent

BRAISE: *Makes 4 8-inch skewers*

Here the bay leaves threaded on skewers and the yogurt give a Turkish twist to the kebobs.

1¼ to 1½ pounds boned leg of lamb, cut into 12 1½-inch pieces
1 small unpared eggplant, ¾ to 1 pound, cut into 16 chunks

12 bay leaves
2 tablespoons olive oil

SKILLET SAUCE

⅓ cup tomato sauce
⅓ cup Burgundy
¼ teaspoon dillweed
1 clove garlic, crushed

¼ teaspoon freshly ground black pepper
½ cup plain yogurt

Thread lamb on skewer, beginning and ending with eggplant, allowing 4 chunks of eggplant, 3 pieces of lamb and 3 bay leaves per skewer. Combine sauce ingredients except yogurt. Heat oil in skillet, add kebobs and brown 6 to 8 minutes, turning several times. Pour skillet sauce over kebobs. Cover. Simmer 10 minutes, turn kebobs, and cook additional 8 to 10 minutes. Transfer kebobs to warm platter. Remove skillet from heat. Stir in yogurt. Spoon skillet sauce generously over kebobs and serve.

Shashlik, Russian Accent

BROIL: *Makes 5 10-inch skewers*

Shashlik, the Russian version of skewered meat, is flavored mildly with pomegranate. The key ingredient here, then, is grenadine, a syrup made from the juice of that fruit. Note the cast of green and red hues which make these kebobs especially appropriate for serving around the holidays.

1½ to 1¾ pounds boned leg of lamb cut into 15 1½-inch pieces	20 slices (1 inch thick) unpared cucumber

MARINADE

½ cup vegetable oil	1 tablespoon tarragon leaves
2 tablespoons red wine vinegar	¼ teaspoon freshly ground
1 medium onion, sliced and separated into rings	black pepper

BASTE–TOPPING SAUCE

1 tablespoon grenadine	¼ cup melted butter
2 tablespoons lemon juice	1 teaspoon ground coriander

One and a half hours in advance: Combine marinade ingredients, add lamb, toss well. Cover. Turn and toss meat occasionally. Let stand at room temperature.

Before serving: Thread lamb on skewers alternately with cucumbers, beginning and ending with cucumbers. In saucepan, combine baste–topping sauce ingredients, stirring with brush to blend well. Broil 4 inches from source of heat 14 to 16 minutes for medium, 18 to 20 minutes for well done. Turn kebobs often. Baste frequently with sauce, especially near end of cooking, and spread generously with remaining sauce before serving.

South African Sosaties

BROIL: *Makes 4 10-inch skewers*

It appears that the dish Sosaties (skewered meats) was originally introduced to South Africa by Malaysians during the early 19th century. Since the dish was then characterized by liberal amounts of strong spices which didn't agree with the South African taste, eventually wine and dried fruits such as peaches and apricots replaced the spices. This highly favored adaptation has a slightly peppery, sweet-and-sour tang.

1¼ to 1½ pounds boned leg of lamb cut into 12 1½-inch pieces	1 can (13¼ ounces) pineapple chunks
16 large dried apricots	¼ cup chopped salted peanuts

MARINADE–BASTE–TOPPING SAUCE

¾ cup apricot nectar	1 teaspoon mild curry powder
3 tablespoons apricot preserves	¼ teaspoon freshly ground black pepper
2 tablespoons orange juice	
2 tablespoons soy sauce	⅛ teaspoon cayenne pepper
3 tablespoons cider vinegar	½ teaspoon cornstarch
1 clove garlic, crushed	1 tablespoon dry vermouth
1 medium onion, sliced, rings separated	

Three hours in advance: In a saucepan combine marinade ingredients except cornstarch and vermouth and bring to a boil. Cool. Pour over meat. Let stand at room temperature. Cook dried apricots in boiling water 4 to 5 minutes. Set aside.

Before serving: Strain marinade. Dissolve cornstarch in dry vermouth and add to marinade. Stir over low heat until smooth and thickened. Thread skewers as follows: 3 chunks pineapple . apricot . LAMB . apricot . pineapple chunk . LAMB . apricot . pineapple chunk . LAMB . pineapple chunk . apricot . 3 chunks pineapple. Broil 4 inches from source of heat 14 to 16 minutes for medium, 18 to 20 minutes for well done. Turn several times. Baste near end of cooking and spread generously with sauce just before serving. Garnish top of each kebob with one tablespoon of chopped nuts.

Spanish Pinchos

BROIL: *Makes 5 6-inch skewers*

Pincho refers to food cooked on small skewers, usually served as an appetizer. This adaptation of Spanish-style skewered meats is certainly colorful. Note, too, the use of ingredients characteristic of Spanish cooking—olive oil, of course, plus garlic, pimiento, and hard-cooked eggs.

1 to 1¼ pounds boned leg of lamb cut into 15 1-inch pieces

20 whole canned mushrooms
10 square pieces of onion

MARINADE

⅓ cup olive oil
1 tablespoon lemon juice
2 tablespoons dry sherry
½ teaspoon paprika

2 cloves garlic, crushed
⅛ teaspoon freshly ground black pepper

TOPPING MIXTURE

2 hard-cooked eggs, diced fine
2 tablespoons finely chopped parsley
2 tablespoons chopped pimiento, well drained

½ cup slivered almonds, crushed
¼ teaspoon salt
⅛ teaspoon freshly ground black pepper

Two hours in advance: Combine marinade ingredients and add lamb, tossing vigorously and coating well. Let stand at room temperature.

Before serving: In small bowl, combine topping mixture and toss lightly. Thread skewers as follows: mushroom . LAMB . onion . mushroom . onion . LAMB . mushroom . LAMB . mushroom. Broil 3 inches from source of heat 10 to 12 minutes for medium, 14 to 16 minutes for well done, turning several times during cooking. Garnish each kebob liberally with topping mixture and serve.

MOROCCAN-INSPIRED LAMB KEBOBS

Savored as sandwiches—that's one of the ways Moroccans enjoy kebobs. The following snack-style presentation of lamb kebobs is sure to appeal to those who like lamb. The second, more highly seasoned, version could obscure the identity of the meat.

Mildly Seasoned Lamb Kebob Sandwich

BROIL: *Makes 1 sandwich (1 6-inch skewer)*

French bread, cut to 6-inch
length
1 tablespoon finely chopped
parsley
½ teaspoon leaf thyme

1 teaspoon chopped lemon pulp
1 tablespoon melted butter
½ tablespoon chopped onion
5 1-inch cubes of lamb steak*
4 square pieces of onion

Halve French bread lengthwise at center. Scoop out bread, using fingers. In a bowl, combine bread, parsley, thyme, lemon, butter, and chopped onion, mixing thoroughly. Spread this filling on one side of bread. Thread lamb chunks on 6-inch skewer alternately with onion. Broil 3 inches from source of heat 10 to 12 minutes for medium, 14 to 16 minutes for well done. Turn often. Place bread on small baking sheet and heat in preheated 350° oven until thoroughly warmed—about 8 minutes. Season cooked kebobs with salt to taste and place on unseasoned side of bread. Serve immediately. Note: These are especially good when grilled over coals.

Nippy Seasoned Lamb Kebob Sandwich

BROIL: *Makes 1 sandwich (1 6-inch skewer)*

French bread, cut into 6-inch
length
¼ cup finely crushed corn chips
½ teaspoon chili powder
2 tablespoons melted butter

1 whole canned pimiento
2 thin slices sharp Cheddar
cheese
4 1-inch cubes of lamb steak*
4 anchovy-stuffed olives

Halve French bread lengthwise at center. Scoop out bread with fingers. In a bowl, combine bread, corn chips, chili

* A 1-inch-thick slice of lamb steak can stretch to make 4 sandwiches. Cut steak into 1-inch cubes. One pound yields approximately 18 to 20 cubes.

powder, and melted butter. Stuff pimiento with corn-chip mixture. With sharp knife, cut stuffed pimiento in half and press halves next to each other, filling one side of bread. Top with sharp cheese. Thread lamb chunks on skewer alternately with olives. Broil 3 inches from source of heat 10 to 12 minutes for medium, 14 to 16 minutes for well done, turning often. While meat is cooking, place bread on small baking sheet and heat in preheated 350° oven until thoroughly warmed—about 8 minutes, or until cheese begins to melt. Season cooked meat with salt to taste and place immediately on unseasoned side of bread.

Lamb Kebobs Caribbean

BROIL: *Makes 5 6-inch skewers*

Serve on appetizer or platter plates with dip-sauce cups. This makes for a very interesting snack or a substantial appetizer.

1 to 1¼ pounds boned leg of
  lamb cut into 15 1-inch pieces
1 large green pepper, cut into
  10 pieces

1 small pineapple, pared, cored
  and cut into 10 chunks

MARINADE

⅓ cup melted butter
2 tablespoons lemon juice
¼ teaspoon turmeric
⅛ teaspoon ground ginger

¼ teaspoon mild curry powder
⅛ teaspoon freshly ground
  black pepper

DIP SAUCE

⅓ cup peanut butter
½ cup mashed bananas
1 tablespoon soy sauce
1 tablespoon light rum
1 tablespoon lemon juice
1 teaspoon Worcestershire
  sauce

¼ teaspoon dry mustard
⅛ teaspoon ground ginger
½ teaspoon grated lemon rind
2 drops Tabasco

Two hours in advance: Combine marinade ingredients in a bowl. Add meat. Cover and let stand at room temperature. The marinade will adhere to the meat. Turn meat occasionally. In a blender, combine dip-sauce ingredients and blend until smooth. Pour into container. Seal tightly with a cover. Refrigerate.

Before serving: Stir dip sauce and pour into dip-sauce cups for serving with kebobs. Thread skewers as follows: LAMB . green pepper . pineapple . LAMB . green pepper . pineapple . LAMB. Broil 3 inches from source of heat 10 to 12 minutes for medium, 14 to 16 minutes for well done. Turn often.

Variation: Instead of pineapple, substitute preserved kumquats. If desired, too, remove pulp from kumquats and stuff with seedless grapes that have marinated in a combination of rum and fresh or dried mint.

Lamb Kebobs Mediterranean

BRAISE: *Makes 4 8-inch skewers*

Serve Roditys (Greek rosé wine) with these kebobs.

1¾ to 2 pounds boned leg of lamb, cut into 16 1½-inch pieces
8 whole canned mushrooms

1 green pepper, cut into 8 pieces
½ medium onion, cut into 12 1½-inch pieces

SKILLET SAUCE

½ cup chicken bouillon (1 cube dissolved in ½ cup hot water)
⅓ cup Roditys
3 tablespoons Metaxa brandy

¼ teaspoon leaf thyme
¼ teaspoon leaf marjoram
¼ teaspoon sweet basil
⅛ teaspoon garlic powder

2 tablespoons olive oil
4 tablespoons grated Parmesan cheese

Thread skewers as follows: mushroom . green pepper . LAMB . onion . LAMB . onion . LAMB . onion . LAMB . green pepper . mushroom. Combine skillet-sauce ingredients. Heat oil in skillet. Brown kebobs 5 to 8 minutes, turning often. Pour sauce over kebobs. Cover. Simmer 10 minutes. Turn kebobs. Cover and cook 5 minutes. Uncover and cook an additional 6 to 8 minutes, spooning sauce over kebobs frequently. Sprinkle one tablespoon cheese over each kebob and serve.

Lamb Kebobs Scandinavian

BROIL: *Makes 4 10-inch skewers*

The Scandinavians, I think, have such interesting ingredients to work with—particularly, the lingonberries.

1¾ to 2 pounds boned leg of lamb cut into 16 1½-inch pieces

12 whole cooked white potatoes (1-pound can)

12 whole cooked carrots (1 1-pound jar)

8 slices (¼ inch thick) unpared cucumber

MARINADE

⅓ cup melted butter or margarine

2 tablespoons lemon juice

⅛ teaspoon each ground cardamom, cinnamon, and allspice

¼ teaspoon dill weed

⅛ teaspoon freshly ground black pepper

TOPPING SAUCE

½ cup lingonberry preserves

1 tablespoon lemon juice

2 tablespoons dry vermouth

½ teaspoon grated lemon rind

Two hours in advance: Combine marinade ingredients. Add meat and toss well. Marinade will adhere to meat. Cover and let stand at room temperature, turning and rubbing meat occasionally. In a bowl, combine topping-sauce ingredients and set aside.

Before serving: Thread skewers as follows: potato . LAMB . carrot . cucumber . LAMB . potato . carrot . LAMB . potato . carrot . LAMB . cucumber. Broil 3 inches from source of heat 13 to 16 minutes for medium, 17 to 19 minutes for well done. Turn often. Spread each kebob with topping sauce and serve.

Spur-of-the-Moment Lamb Kebobs

BROIL: *Makes 2 10-inch skewers*

Serve this when you have loin chops available and you want to do something other than just broil them plain.

4 loin lamb chops, 1 inch thick
2 tablespoons Dijon-style mustard
3 to 4 tablespoons French-bread crumbs
4 slices (½ inch) unpared cucumber

3 dashes of pure mint and peppermint extract (a combination of spearmint and peppermint)
4 preserved kumquats
4 slices dilled cucumber pickle

Trim meat from bone. (Each loin chop yields one large piece and a small tenderloin piece.) Toss meat from 2 of the chops in mustard. Roll in bread crumbs, coating well. Sprinkle cucumber slices with mint and peppermint extract, tossing well. Remove pulp from kumquats and stuff with pickle. Thread skewer as follows: coated LAMB . stuffed kumquat . coated LAMB . cucumber . stuffed kumquat . plain LAMB . cucumber . plain LAMB. Broil 3 inches from source of heat 10 to 12 minutes for medium, 14 to 16 minutes for well done, turning several times.

LAMBURGER KEBOBS

In this series of recipes—ground lamb on a skewer—select the one with your favorite seasonings or alternate the dill and mint versions on one skewer and serve the curry-flavored on separate skewers. To chill lamburgers adequately before cooking, allow a minimum of 45 minutes.

Dilled Lamburger Kebobs

BROIL: *Makes 3 or 4 10-inch skewers*

THE LAMBURGER

1 pound lean ground lamb	1 teaspoon dill weed
¼ cup cracker crumbs	1 egg, slightly beaten
1 tablespoon finely chopped onion	1 teaspoon salt
8 wedges pickled green tomatoes	4 large black pitted olives
8 pieces (3 inches) green onion, folded once	

BASTE

½ cup melted butter
½ to 1 teaspoon dill weed to taste

Mix together the lamburger ingredients. Shape into 12 balls. Chill. Thread lamburger kebobs on skewers alternately with tomato wedges and green onions and end with black olive. Combine baste ingredients. Broil kebobs 4 inches from source of heat for 6 to 7 minutes, turn and broil another 7 minutes, basting generously.

Minted Lamburger Kebobs

BROIL: *Makes 3 or 4 10-inch skewers*

THE LAMBURGER

1 pound lean ground lamb
¼ cup dry bread crumbs
2 tablespoons freshly squeezed
   lemon juice

1 teaspoon grated lemon rind
   (optional)
1 teaspoon salt
1 tablespoon chopped parsley

1 lemon, cut into 8 wedges or
   slices

BASTES

I

⅓ cup melted butter
½ to 1 teaspoon crushed dried
   mint, to taste

1 tablespoon freshly squeezed
   lemon juice

OR

II

⅓ cup melted butter
2 tablespoons white crème de
   menthe

Mix together lamburger ingredients. Shape into 12 balls. Chill. Thread balls on skewers, alternating with lemon wedges or slices, beginning and ending with lamburger. Combine baste ingredients of your choice. Broil kebobs 4 inches from source of heat 6 to 7 minutes, turn, baste, and broil another 5 to 6 minutes. Baste generously throughout cooking.

Curried Lamburger Kebobs

BROIL: *Makes 3 or 4 10-inch skewers*

THE LAMBURGER

1 pound lean ground lamb
¼ cup cracker crumbs
2 tablespoons chopped parsley
1 tablespoon grated onion

1 teaspoon salt
1 small egg, slightly beaten
¼ teaspoon freshly ground
   black pepper

16 1-inch chunks of green-tipped
    bananas dipped in orange
    juice and rolled in finely
    chopped peanuts

BASTE

½ cup melted butter
¼ cup lemon juice
2 tablespoons granulated sugar
1 tablespoon finely chopped
   onion

1 teaspoon Indian-style curry
   powder
½ teaspoon freshly ground
   black pepper

OR

TOPPING SAUCE

1 cup (8 ounces) plain yogurt
2 tablespoons onion juice
1 teaspoon prepared mustard

½ teaspoon mild Indian-style
   curry powder

Mix together the lamburger ingredients. Shape into 12 balls. Chill. Thread lamburger kebobs on skewer alternately with nut-coated bananas. Broil 4 inches from source of heat 5 to 7 minutes. Turn and broil another 6 to 7 minutes. If you prefer a thin covering of curry flavor, combine baste ingredients and baste lamburger kebobs generously during cooking. If, however, you prefer a thick curry-flavored covering, then combine topping sauce ingredients, mixing well; put in a bowl with a ladle and serve with cooked lamburger kebobs.

Variation: Thread lamburger kebobs alternately with pieces of bacon.

Lamb Kebobing Outdoors for a Family of 8 to 10

Weather permitting, the Tatosians of a Chicago suburb serve lamb kebobs to their family once a week in the back yard of their home. The kebobs are cooked on a *skara* (grill) which was designed by Mariam Tatosian's father when he arrived in this country from Armenia over sixty years ago. The *skara,* which is placed over a bed of coals, consists of 9 skewers, each 24 inches long. The skewers are connected to one another by gears. Thus, when the handle attached to the center skewer is turned manually, the other skewers rotate simultaneously. This portable *skara* fits in the back-yard barbecue pit or packs conveniently in the trunk of a car for when the family vacations. The following recipe is the way Mariam prepares kebobs for her family. For the menu, see page 309.

GRILL

1 leg of lamb (about 7 pounds)	Salt to taste
4 medium onions, finely sliced	Whole tomatoes
Freshly ground black pepper to taste	Whole green peppers

Natural wood charcoal

Two hours in advance: Mariam bones the lamb and cuts it into 1½-inch pieces, leaving a little fat on meat to prevent dryness. She places the pieces of meat in a roasting pan, mixing and tossing with onions and pepper.

Twenty to thirty minutes in advance: Mariam's husband starts the fire. The Tatosians never use commercially processed charcoal. They insist on natural wood charcoal, which they feel gives the kebobs a distinctive flavor. (In fact, they have this charcoal delivered to their home from the coal yards in 20-pound bags.)

Before serving: Mariam seasons the pieces of meat lightly with salt and threads them on the long skewers that belong to the *skara*. The whole tomatoes and green peppers are threaded on separate skewers. The vegetables take about 10 minutes to cook and the meat 12 to 15 minutes until pink. With a fork, Mariam pushes the cooked meat from the skewers into a large roasting pan, which is lined with Syrian or other hard-crust bread to absorb the juices from the meat. She places the meat on a platter, slices the bread and serves that on another dish. It's good!

LEFTOVER LAMB ROAST

Lamb should be served either hot or cold, never lukewarm. Unadorned slices of leftover cold roast lamb appeal to those who like this meat. If, however, you'd like it enhanced with skewers and served hot, then the following recipes might interest you. Note that 18 to 20 1½-inch pieces of leftover roast lamb fill approximately 2 cups.

Kebobs, Sweet Version

BAKE: *Makes assorted amounts*

1 jar (1 pound 13 ounces) canned fruit (large fruits for salad)
Leftover roast lamb, cut into 18 to 20 1½-inch pieces

2 teaspoons rum flavoring (imitation rum extract)

Forty-five minutes in advance: Place fruit and its syrup in a bowl. Add meat to soak thoroughly.

Before serving: Drain fruit and meat and combine rum flavoring with syrup to use as a baste. Thread lamb on skewers alternately with fruit. Bake in preheated 350° oven 8 to 10 minutes until heated through, basting generously.

Variation: Rather than use the assortment of large fruits for salad, you might instead prefer to use only one canned fruit such as pineapple, spiced peaches, or apricots. For a less sweet version, select diet-pack canned fruits.

Kebobs, Tart Version

BAKE: *Makes assorted amounts*

1 cup Tomato Barbecue Sauce, Version II, page 266, or prepared barbecue sauce from the bottle
Orange juice for thinning to taste

Leftover roast lamb cut into 18 to 20 1½-inch pieces
Canned whole potatoes
Canned whole mushrooms
Pitted black olives
Green pepper pieces (optional)

Thirty minutes in advance: In a saucepan, heat barbecue sauce with orange juice. Add pieces of lamb and let steep.

Before serving: Thread lamb on skewer alternately with potatoes, mushrooms, black olives and green peppers. Bake in preheated 350° oven 8 to 10 minutes until heated through, basting generously with sauce. Serve with remaining sauce as a topping if desired.

8 · FRESH PORK AND HAM

WHAT TO CONSIDER BEFORE
SKEWER-COOKING FRESH PORK AND HAM

No other animal offers such a variety of fresh and processed parts for skewer cooking as does the pig. These parts include fresh pork; cured and smoked ham and picnic ham; and bacon, a side of pork cured and smoked with the ribs removed. On a skewer these cuts can be broiled, baked, or braised. Fresh pork and fresh ham must always be cooked until well done. When serving pork as a main dish, allow one-third to one-half pound of boneless meat per person; for appetizers or snacks, one-fourth pound.

Since all pork is tender, no one cut is better than another for skewer cooking. "Better" is determined by personal taste and pocketbook. Select cuts from the tenderloin, loin, or if you wish, the shoulder, which is less expensive per pound. Since meat from the shoulder has more fat, you can count on its being juicier, but since it also has more bone, allow for more waste too. To prepare one or two kebobs you could use even the meat from chops.

In many cookbooks and meat-cookery publications, you'll find the admonition "Never Broil Pork." The reasons are, one, a safety precaution to have you cook the meat thoroughly, and two, palatability. To comment briefly on safety, it is necessary to cook this meat long enough to destroy the parasite, *Trichinella spiralis,* known to infect pork. There was, years ago, considerably more concern with the incidence of trichinosis transmitted from pork to man than there is today with controlled inspection and processing of meats. Reports indicate it occurs rarely. Nevertheless, it is important to take the precaution of cooking the meat completely. Palatability is another reason broiling has not been recommended. Pork often becomes dry by the time it reaches the well-done stage during broiling. Knowing these objections, if you still prefer your meats cooked this way, go ahead and use this method for pork kebobs too. Select meat from the loin, and broil slowly and long. You might want to consider threading some fruits and vegetables on separate skewers to avoid overcooking them.

A few suggestions. For kebobing pork outdoors over a grill, serve it Latholemono style; see page 256. Substitute pork loin for lamb, omit the bay leaves, and add one large onion sliced and separated to the marinade-baste. This, by the way, goes well with tomato and cucumber wedges, feta cheese, crusty bread, and chilled Soave. And here's an idea for those of you who make use of canned sauces (about 14 or 16 ounces). Use them also as skillet sauces for braising pork kebobs. For example, you could thread green pepper and onions alternately with cubes of pork, brown the kebobs, add one cup of canned barbecue sauce, cover, cook over low heat, and add remaining sauce from can before serving. For an idea on timing, review the recipes in this section that indicate "Braised."

Now for ham. Cook fresh ham well done—which means longer cooking than for those hams labeled "Fully Cooked" or "Cook Before Eating." (These two can be used interchangeably whenever a recipe in this section calls for one or the other.) Most canned hams sold in retail stores today are fully cooked. This means they have been cured, smoked, and brought to a suitable internal temperature for serving without further cooking if desired. Not processed as long, the cook-before-eating hams improve in texture and palatability when cooked, although they can be safely eaten without further cooking. The center slices of ham found at meat counters are usually from cook-before-eating hams. Resembling the shape of beef round steak, they come in various thicknesses from 1 to 2 inches. Ask the butcher to cut the size you want for kebobs. For quick kebobs that require no cooking, packaged ham slices can take on interesting shapes when speared on a skewer. Try, too, cooked pork roast threaded alternately with slices and chunks of ham. Now, that's a resourceful and appealing way to dress up leftovers.

One thing to remember about ham is that skewer cooking influences the taste of cured and smoked meat only slightly, if at all. As with sausage, the smoked flavor of ham may range in strength from mild to very pronounced, depending on the meat packer's recipe. And of course, the milder the smoked flavor, the more the sauces will influence the taste of the meat.

As for bacon, it can be sliced thin or thick. Cut pieces crosswise or thread the entire strip in a snakelike curving manner as suggested for Pecan Burger Kebobs, page 81. Thread Canadian bacon, too, in slices or cubes. Since bacon combines well with almost any meat broiled or baked on a skewer, keep it in mind whenever there's a need for extra flavor and moisture. Also—if you want bacon to be done at the same time as the other items, you may prefer to parboil it 3 to 5 minutes or partially cook it in a skillet before threading on skewers.

On-the-Range Pork Kebobs

BRAISE: *Makes 4 8-inch skewers*

Here the kebobs and the accompanying vegetables are cooked on top of the range at one time in a skillet and a saucepan. Serve with a gelatin salad.

8 jumbo black pitted olives
1½ pounds boned pork loin, cut into 15 to 16 1-inch cubes
1 jar (4 ounces) whole pimiento, contents divided into 8 pieces

8 canned whole mushrooms
Green onions, cut into 8 3-inch pieces, folded once (optional)

SKILLET SAUCE

⅓ cup Chablis
½ cup beef bouillon (bouillon
cube dissolved in ½ cup hot
water)

2 tablespoons finely chopped
onions
¼ teaspoon ground marjoram
⅛ teaspoon tarragon leaves

2 tablespoons margarine or
butter
2 packages (10 ounces) frozen
unseasoned green vegetables
(such as asparagus, green
beans, or broccoli)

1 cup dairy sour cream

Thread each skewer as follows: olive . PORK . pimiento
. PORK . mushroom . green onion . olive . PORK . pimiento
. PORK . green onion . mushroom. Combine sauce ingredients. Melt margarine or butter in skillet and brown kebobs
4 to 5 minutes on each side. Remove kebobs from skillet.
Stir sauce into skillet. Return kebobs. Cover. Cook over low
heat until liquid is reduced by about half—about 15 to 20
minutes. Place kebobs on individual serving plates. Stir sour
cream into skillet. Heat but do not boil. In saucepan, cook
frozen vegetables according to directions on package. Place
the cooked vegetables next to the kebobs for each serving.
Use the sauce from the skillet to spread over the vegetables—
not the kebobs.

Sweet-and-Sour Skewered Pork

BAKE: *Makes 5 10-inch skewers*

Serve with sautéed Chinese vegetables and crisp fried
noodles.

1½ to 2 pounds pork shoulder
(boned and trimmed), cut
into 25 1-inch cubes

Salt to taste
10 pineapple chunks
10 whole water chestnuts

MARINADE–BASTE

¼ cup brown sugar	1 tablespoon soy sauce
¼ cup ketchup	⅛ teaspoon ginger
¼ cup pineapple juice	⅛ teaspoon dry mustard
3 tablespoons vinegar	

Night before: In saucepan, heat marinade-baste ingredients. In a bowl, place cubes of meat and pour warmed sauce over them. Stir. Pierce each cube several times with fork. Cover. Refrigerate overnight.

Before serving: Salt meat to taste, remembering salt in soy sauce used in marinade. Thread meat alternately with pineapple and water chestnuts, beginning and ending with pork. Bake in preheated 350° oven 40 to 45 minutes until well cooked. Baste generously near end of cooking.

Variation: For snack kebobs grilled over a small hibachi, thread cubes of pork loin on 6-inch skewers, alternating with green pepper and onions. Serve with Sweet-Sour Dip Sauce, page 269.

Peppery Pork Kebobs

BROIL: *Makes 4 10-inch skewers*

With pepper in particular, the amount considered pleasant by one person is unpleasant to another. Here you determine how much you want to use—a heap or a hint of it.

1 pork tenderloin, about 1½ pounds, cut into 14 to 16 1-inch cubes	1 green pepper, cut into 8 pieces
1 to 2 tablespoons prepared lemon-pepper marinade from the jar (add to taste)	1 jar (4 ounces) whole red pimiento, contents divided into 8 pieces
	1 small onion cut into 4 wedges

BASTE

½ cup dry vermouth

Thirty minutes in advance: Rub cubes of pork with lemon-pepper marinade. Cover. Let stand at room temperature.

Before serving: Thread on skewer as follows: green pepper . PORK . pimiento . PORK . onion wedge . PORK . pimiento . PORK . green pepper. Broil 4 to 5 inches from source of heat for 10 minutes, turn, and baste with vermouth. Broil an additional 12 to 15 minutes until well cooked, basting generously with vermouth.

Variation: Make the dry marinade a liquid marinade as suggested in directions on jar.

Kümmel Pork Kebobs

BAKE: *Makes 5 10-inch skewers*

Unlike the well-known liqueurs that are made from fruits, Kümmel takes its flavor from the seeds of a plant—caraway.

2 pounds pork shoulder (boned and trimmed), cut into 20 1½ x 1-inch pieces	2 green peppers, cut into 10 pieces
	1 small onion, cut into 5 wedges

MARINADE–BASTE

¾ cup tomato sauce	½ small onion, finely chopped
¼ cup Kümmel	2 cloves garlic, minced
2 bay leaves, crumbled	⅛ teaspoon oregano

One hour in advance: Combine marinade–baste ingredients in a bowl. Add pork pieces. Cover. Let stand at room temperature.

Before serving: Thread pork on skewer alternately with green pepper and onion, beginning and ending with pork. Bake in preheated 350° oven 40 to 45 minutes until well cooked, basting generously.

Sage Skewered Pork

BROIL: *Makes 3 10-inch skewers*

In this recipe, you can use either ground or leaf sage, depending on how moist you want your kebobs.

1 pound pork tenderloin, cut   6 lemon wedges
  into 9 to 12 1½-inch pieces

MARINADES

For drier pork kebobs:

Ground sage   Salt to taste

For more moist kebobs:

¼ cup olive oil   ½ teaspoon *leaf* sage
¼ cup lemon juice   1 teaspoon salt

To prepare the drier version: Rub meat with sage and salt. Thread on skewers alternately with lemon wedges, beginning and ending with pork. Broil 4 to 5 inches from source of heat for 20 to 25 minutes until cooked well. Squeeze fresh lemon juice over each kebob.

To prepare the more moist version: One hour in advance mix oil, lemon juice, sage, and salt in a bowl. Add pork. Cover. Let stand at room temperature. *Before serving* thread meat alternately with lemon wedges, beginning and ending with pork. Broil 4 to 5 inches from source of heat for 20 to 25 minutes until well cooked. Baste generously and often.

Pork Kebobs Portokali

BRAISE: *Makes 4 8-inch skewers*

This is the highly accepted version of pork with orange. Serve with green peppers stuffed with sweet potatoes, and Feta and Cream Cheese Balls, page 275.

1½ pounds boned pork loin cut
  into 15 to 16 1-inch cubes
20 square pieces of thick
  orange peel (from two
  oranges)

SKILLET SAUCE

½ cup beef bouillon (bouillon
  cube dissolved in ½ cup hot
  water)
¼ cup orange juice
¼ cup Chablis
2 tablespoons lemon juice

2 tablespoons olive oil

1 tablespoon finely chopped
  parsley
⅛ teaspoon freshly ground
  black pepper
⅛ teaspoon oregano
⅛ teaspoon garlic powder

¼ cup grated orange rind

Thread cubes of pork on skewer alternately with pieces of orange peel, beginning and ending with orange peel, allowing 5 pieces of peel per skewer. Combine sauce ingredients. In skillet, heat oil and brown kebobs 4 to 5 minutes on each side. Pour skillet sauce over kebobs. Cover. Cook over low heat 20 to 25 minutes, occasionally spooning sauce over kebobs. Before serving, top each kebob with one tablespoon of grated orange rind.

Pork and Apple Kebobs

BAKE: *Makes 4 10-inch skewers*

1½ pounds boned pork loin, cut
  into 15 to 16 1-inch cubes
1-pound jar whole crab apples,
  about 8 to 10 apples

12 chunks of canned pineapple

MARINADE–BASTE

½ cup apple juice
⅓ cup applesauce
¼ cup pineapple syrup
2 tablespoons soy sauce

2 tablespoons chopped onion
⅛ teaspoon ginger
⅛ teaspoon nutmeg

One hour in advance: Combine marinade–baste ingredients in a bowl. Add cubes of pork. Cover. Let stand at room temperature. To drain apples well, place on paper towel until ready to use.

Before serving: Thread pork on skewer alternately with pineapple and apples, allowing two apples per skewer. Bake in preheated 350° oven 35 to 40 minutes until done, turning once. Baste often near end of cooking.

Mixed Pork Kebobs

BRAISE: *Makes 3 8-inch skewers*

½ pound pork tenderloin, cut into 6 1½ x 1-inch pieces
½ pound Canadian bacon, cut into 6 1½ x 1-inch pieces
½ pound fresh ham, cut into 6 1½ x 1-inch pieces

2 strips of thick-sliced bacon cut in pieces (optional)
1 tablespoon margarine or butter

SKILLET SAUCE

½ cup chicken bouillon (bouillon cube dissolved in ½ cup hot water)
⅓ cup Chablis or other dry white wine
¼ cup red currant jelly

1 teaspoon instant minced onion
⅛ teaspoon freshly ground black pepper
⅛ teaspoon each ground nutmeg and cinnamon

Thread the meats alternately on skewers. Add bacon if desired, but note it will add to saltiness. Melt butter or margarine in skillet. Brown kebobs 4 to 5 minutes on each side. In a saucepan, combine sauce ingredients and heat until jelly dissolves. Pour over kebobs. Cover. Simmer 20 to 25 minutes, occasionally spooning sauce over kebobs.

Variations: Thread skewer with other pork products such as smoked butt and cuts of pork from the shoulder and loin.

Rather than braise, broil or grill and serve with a choice of dip sauces, pages 267–74, or marinate pork meats for two hours in 1 cup of the Herb Variation of Tomato Barbecue Sauce, page 266, and use sauce as a baste also.

Porkburger Kebobs

BROIL: *Makes 12 dinner-size or 30 appetizer balls*

THE BURGER

1 pound ground pork	1 teaspoon salt
1 egg, slightly beaten	1 teaspoon instant minced
1/3 cup cracker crumbs	onion
2 teaspoons soy sauce	

Fresh pineapple chunks
Banana chunks, dipped in orange
   juice and rolled in finely
   ground nuts

BASTE

1/4 cup light rum	1/8 teaspoon garlic powder
1/4 cup soy sauce	1/4 teaspoon ground ginger
2 tablespoons brown sugar	1/4 teaspoon dry mustard

Mix together burger ingredients. Chill. Thread burgers on skewers alternately with pineapple and banana chunks. Broil 4 to 5 inches from source of heat. Dinner size (2-inch balls): 7 to 9 minutes, turn, and broil an additional 5 to 7 minutes or until well done. Appetizer size (1-inch balls): 5 to 7 minutes, turn, and broil an additional 4 to 5 minutes. Combine baste ingredients. Baste burger kebobs generously during last 5 minutes of broiling.

Variation: Thread pieces of bacon on every other skewer.

Sparerib Kebobs

BROIL: *Makes 4 to 5 10-inch skewers*

These are so good I doubt seriously you'll have any left-overs.

2 cups beer
½ cup tomato juice
¼ cup lemon juice
4 peppercorns
4 whole cloves

1 large onion, quartered
5 pounds baby spareribs, cut into 2-rib pieces
1 fresh pineapple, pared, cored and cut into 20 chunks

BASTE–TOPPING SAUCE

½ cup honey
¼ cup soy sauce
¼ cup chili sauce
¼ cup red wine vinegar
1 cup orange juice

1 teaspoon grated orange rind
¼ teaspoon Worcestershire sauce
1 clove garlic, mashed
1 teaspoon salt

Forty minutes in advance: In a sauce pot, combine beer, tomato and lemon juices, peppercorns, cloves, and onion. Add ribs. Cover. Bring to a boil. Reduce heat and simmer for 35 minutes. (Do this far ahead of time, if desired.)

Before serving: Combine sauce ingredients in a bowl. Remove the ribs from kettle with long fork and place on platter. Dip ribs in sauce, coating well. Thread skewers alternately with chunks of fresh pineapple, beginning and ending with pineapple. Broil 4 to 5 inches from source of heat 6 to 8 minutes, turn, and brush generously with sauce. Broil an additional 6 to 8 minutes until brown. If grilling outdoors, thread meat on long skewers and brown over low glowing coals that are covered with gray ash and show no signs of flames, about 10 to 12 minutes.

Ham Kebobs Madeira

BRAISE: *Makes 4 8-inch skewers*

An elegant way to present ham.

12 whole canned mushrooms
 1 pound cook-before-eating
   ham, cut into 14 to 16 1-inch
   cubes
 1 green pepper, cut into 8
   pieces

 4 bay leaves
 4 king-size pitted Spanish
   olives
 2 tablespoons butter or
   margarine

SKILLET SAUCE

⅓ cup Madeira
¼ cup tomato sauce
¼ teaspoon dry mustard

¼ teaspoon cinnamon
 2 tablespoons brown sugar

Thread each skewer as follows: mushroom . HAM . green pepper . mushroom . HAM . bay leaf . olive . green pepper . HAM . mushroom. Combine sauce ingredients. Melt butter or margarine in skillet. Brown kebobs 3 to 4 minutes on each side and remove to platter. Stir skillet sauce into skillet. Return kebobs. Cover. Simmer until liquid is reduced to half, about 10 to 12 minutes. Occasionally spoon sauce over kebobs.

Skewered Ham with Eggplant

BRAISE: *Makes 4 8-inch skewers*

 1 small eggplant (about ¾
   pound), unpared and cut into
   12 chunks
½ cup sweet vermouth
⅛ teaspoon allspice
 1 pound fully cooked ham, cut
   into 14 to 16 1-inch cubes

16 square pieces onion
 1 green pepper, cut into 8
   pieces
 2 tablespoons olive oil

MARINADE FOR EGGPLANT

¼ cup orange juice	¼ teaspoon leaf thyme
1 tablespoon lemon juice	2 tablespoons finely chopped
1 tablespoon tomato paste	onion
3 tablespoons vegetable oil	¾ to 1 teaspoon salt
¼ teaspoon sweet basil	

3 to 4 tablespoons grated
Parmesan cheese

One hour in advance: Combine marinade ingredients for eggplant in a bowl. Add eggplant chunks. Set aside 3 tablespoons sweet vermouth. In another bowl, season remaining sweet vermouth with allspice and add ham cubes. Occasionally toss contents of each bowl.

Before serving: Thread each skewer as follows: HAM . onion . eggplant . HAM . green pepper . eggplant . HAM . onion . eggplant . HAM. In skillet heat oil and brown kebobs 3 to 4 minutes on each side. Combine the 3 tablespoons sweet vermouth with the marinade from eggplant and pour over kebobs. Cover. Cook over low heat an additional 8 to 10 minutes or until eggplant is tender. Occasionally spoon sauce over kebobs. Sprinkle kebobs with Parmesan cheese and serve.

Variations:

To serve as appetizers, thread eggplant and ham on 6 6-inch skewers.

If you wish to double this recipe and use two skillets simultaneously, note that a center slice of ham, 1 inch thick (about 2 pounds), will very nicely yield 30 to 32 1-inch cubes.

Instead of braising, thread the marinated eggplant and ham on skewers and grill. Or broil on 10-inch skewers 4 to 5 inches from source of heat 12 to 15 minutes until eggplant is tender. Baste with melted butter or sweet vermouth. If desired, substitute for the Parmesan cheese a cheese topping mixture consisting of 1 cup shredded Provolone cheese, 1 tablespoon canned chopped chilies and ⅓ cup finely chopped celery.

HAM SLICES ON SKEWERS

Use slices of boiled ham rolled and speared on a skewer to serve two ways. The first—actually, a centerpiece arrangement—consists of slices of boiled ham cut in strips, rolled around cheese balls and threaded on skewers alternately with finger-size bread rolls and speared into half a grapefruit. In the second, the slices of boiled ham are first spread with soft cheese, then rolled, and each end of the roll is speared with a 6-inch skewer; this is heated in broiler and basted with a barbecue sauce.

Ham Slices 1: Served Cold

Makes 5 8-inch skewers

2 3-ounce packages of cream cheese
1 tablespoon sweet pickle relish
¼ cup chopped nuts
½ teaspoon paprika
2 tablespoons milk
2 frankfurter rolls, split and cut into thirds crosswise
Salad fillings such as chicken, fish, egg—or cheese spreads

5 slices boiled ham cut lengthwise into 1½ x 6-inch strips
10 stuffed olives
1 banana cut into 5 chunks, dipped in orange juice
1 grapefruit, halved

DIP SAUCES

Horseradish Dip Sauces, page 268; Mustard Dip Sauces, page 269; or Sour Cream Dip Sauces, page 272.

Combine one package of cream cheese with relish. Shape into 5 balls. Combine the other package of cheese with nuts, paprika and milk. Mix well. Shape into 5 balls. Chill the 10 balls. Spread choice of filling on frankfurter rolls. Wrap ham strips around cheese balls to make ham rolls. Thread skewer as follows: olive . HAM roll . banana . frankfurter roll .

olive . HAM roll. Spear into half grapefruit placed on platter cut side down. Serve with choice of dip sauces. Note: You'll have one extra frank roll—so munch on it or start a sixth skewer of your own fancy.

Ham Slices 2: Served Hot

BROIL: *Makes 4 Ham Roll Twins (2 6-inch skewers per twin)*

8 slices boiled ham
2 teaspoons prepared mustard
Sharp cheese spread (soft for spreading)
Crisp-cooked bacon, drained and finely crumbled, or imitation bacon bits

16 pineapple chunks
16 mandarin oranges
16 pimiento-stuffed olives
16 black pitted olives

BASTE–TOPPING

Basic Tomato Barbecue Sauce with your favorite additions, see page 266.

Spread mustard and softened cheese on each slice of ham. Sprinkle center with bacon bits. Roll ham slices to make 8 ham rolls. Spear one 6-inch skewer on each side of two ham rolls, alternating olives on each end and fruit in center between the rolls. In the broiler, heat about 5 to 8 minutes until cheese begins to melt. Brush with barbecue sauce. Do not overheat since cheese will seep from sides. If desired, serve with a gelatin salad and blueberry muffins.

HAM CHUNKS ON SKEWERS, SANDWICH STYLE

Here are two ways to serve the well-liked combination of ham and Swiss cheese. Select the cold version, in which skewered chunks of ham and slices of Swiss cheese are wrapped in rye bread, or serve the hot version of a ham kebob placed on a roll with melted Swiss cheese.

Ham Chunks 1: Served Cold

Makes 6 6-inch skewers

¾ pound cook-before-eating ham cut into 12 1-inch cubes
6 large pimiento-stuffed olives
6 pitted black olives
Swiss cheese slices cut in 1-inch squares (4 squares stacked together)

6 dill pickle slices, about ¾ inch thick
6 large slices rye bread, lightly buttered

TOPPING SAUCE

Equal parts of prepared mustard and creamed horseradish sauce.

Thread ham chunks alternately on skewer with olives, cheese stack, and pickle. Place kebobs on rye bread, wrapping bread halfway around. Secure with toothpicks. Combine sauce ingredients and serve as a topping. If desired, accompany with a hot spiced fruit.

Ham Chunks 2: Served Hot

BAKE: *Makes 4 6-inch skewers*

4 frankfurter rolls
Butter to spread on rolls
2 slices Swiss cheese, each cut into 2 strips
½ to ¾ pound cooked smoked ham cut into 8 to 12 1-inch cubes

4 1-inch pieces candied sweet or dill pickles
4 cherry tomatoes
1 green pepper, cut into 8 pieces

TOPPING SAUCE

¼ cup unsweetened pineapple
   juice
¼ cup orange juice
⅛ teaspoon nutmeg

⅛ teaspoon ground cloves
1 teaspoon cornstarch dissolved
   in 2 teaspoons water

Arrange buttered rolls on cookie sheet. Place cheese strip on one side of each roll. Thread ham, pickle, tomato, and pepper on 6-inch skewers. Combine sauce ingredients in saucepan, thickening with cornstarch dissolved in water. Bring to a slow boil, stirring constantly. Place kebobs on remaining halves of rolls. Brush with sauce. Heat in preheated 350° oven 5 to 8 minutes or until cheese melts. If desired, serve with coleslaw and potato chips.

A MEDLEY OF HAM
AND FRUIT KEBOBS

"Music is the only language in which you cannot say a mean or sarcastic thing." That quote by John Erskine inspired the idea for this series. But then, of course, I've always advocated the placement of music on each and every guest list. After all, a medley of tunes played in good taste garnishes any menu sweetly. And that thought on music triggered the one on meat. Of all meats, ham takes to sweetness the best . . . and the rest, the recipes on ham and fruit, follow; some taste sweet and others slightly sweet.

Orange Ham Kebobs

BROIL: *Makes 4 10-inch skewers*

1 pound cook-before-eating
   ham, cut into 10 to 12
   1½ x 1-inch cubes
1 orange (navel or other eating
   orange), unpeeled, sliced
   into 8 sections

4 bay leaves (optional)

MARINADE

⅓ cup orange juice
¼ cup melted butter
2 tablespoons brown sugar
1 tablespoon grated orange rind

1 teaspoon minced parsley
¼ teaspoon each of ground clove and nutmeg
1 bay leaf

Three hours in advance: Combine marinade ingredients in a bowl. Add ham squares. Cover. Let stand at room temperature.

Before serving: Thread ham alternately with orange slices and bay leaves on skewer. Broil 4 to 5 inches from source of heat at 425° for 10 to 15 minutes, turning once (if desired, heat marinade and baste. Goes well with steamed rice, chive cottage cheese and corn relish.

Pineapple Ham Kebobs

BAKE: *Makes 4 10-inch skewers*

1 pound cook-before-eating ham, cut into 10 to 12 1½ x 1-inch cubes
1 egg, slightly beaten
1 can (3½ ounces) sweetened coconut

8 maraschino cherries
1 fresh pineapple, pared, cored and cut into 16 wedges

Dip ham squares in beaten egg and then roll in coconut. Thread skewer as follows: cherry . pineapple . HAM . pineapple . HAM . pineapple . HAM . pineapple . cherry. Bake in preheated 350° oven for 15 to 20 minutes, turning once. If desired, serve with cranberry-orange gelatin salad and assorted cold cooked vegetables.

Apricot Ham Kebobs

BRAISE: *Makes 4 8-inch skewers*

8 canned whole mushrooms
16 dried apricots
1 pound cook-before-eating
ham cut into 14 to 16 1-inch
cubes

Green onions cut into 8 3-inch
pieces, folded once
2 tablespoons butter or
margarine

SKILLET SAUCE

½ cup apricot nectar
⅓ cup apricot brandy
3 tablespoons lemon juice

¼ teaspoon cinnamon
⅛ teaspoon ginger

Thread skewers as follows: mushroom . apricot . HAM . onion . apricot . HAM . onion . apricot . HAM . apricot . mushroom. Combine skillet-sauce ingredients. Melt margarine in skillet. Brown kebobs 3 to 4 minutes on each side and remove to platter. Stir sauce into skillet. Return kebobs. Cover. Simmer for 10 to 12 minutes, spooning skillet sauce over kebobs, turning once. If desired, serve with a romaine salad.

Variations: For a more subtle apricot flavor, substitute Chablis for apricot brandy. If desired, green onion can be removed before serving.

Hawaiian Ham Kebobs

BROIL: *Makes 4 10-inch skewers*

1 pound fully cooked ham, cut
into 10 to 12 1½-inch cubes
2 green-tipped bananas cut
into 8 1½-inch chunks
⅓ cup chopped macadamia nuts
(or chopped almonds), about
2½-ounce can

4 canned papaya chunks
(reserve syrup)
4 canned pineapple chunks

MARINADE–BASTE

½ cup Chablis
¼ cup melted butter or
   margarine
2 tablespoons pineapple syrup

1 tablespoon soy sauce
¼ teaspoon ginger
¼ teaspoon dry mustard
⅛ teaspoon leaf thyme

Two hours in advance: Combine marinade–baste ingredients. Add ham cubes. Cover. Let stand at room temperature.
   Before serving: Dip bananas in papaya syrup and roll in chopped nuts. Thread ham on skewers alternately with papaya, pineapple, and banana. Broil 4 to 5 inches from source of heat at 425° for 10 to 15 minutes, turning once, and basting occasionally. If desired, serve with buttered asparagus tips and baked stuffed sweet potatoes.

LEFTOVER PORK AND HAM ROAST

Regardless of how you now use leftover ham—perhaps in a casserole or just sandwiches—on occasion you might want to serve kebobs for a change. Do take a good look at the snack platter suggestion—it's exceptionally attractive and adaptable to various needs.

Skewered Pork and Pineapple

BROIL (*griddle-broil*) : *Makes assorted amounts*

Cooked cold pork roast, cut into
   10 to 12 1-inch cubes (about
   1 cup)
Green pepper, cut into 1-inch
   pieces

Pineapple chunks, fresh or
   canned

MARINADE–BASTE

½ cup unsweetened pineapple
   juice

¼ cup soy sauce

Thirty minutes in advance: Combine marinade–baste ingredients in a bowl. Add cubes of pork. Cover.

Before serving: Thread on skewers alternately with pineapple and green pepper. Broil 4 to 5 inches from source of heat at 425° for about 8 to 10 minutes, basting occasionally, until lightly browned.

Variation: Substitute Thin Sweet-Sour Sauce, page 264, for marinade–baste.

Griddled Ham Kebob Snacks

BROIL *(griddle-broil)* : *Makes assorted amounts*

Leftover ham cut into 1-inch cubes
Choice of foods threaded on skewer (pickled cauliflower, dill peppers, pickled dill tomatoes, bananas, pimiento slices, olives, whatever is available)

2 tablespoons margarine

DIP SAUCES

Mustard, page 269; Sweet-Sour Dip Sauce, page 269; Sour Cream Dip Sauces, page 272; Spicy Cocktail Dip Sauce, Version I: Mild and Different, page 267; or Guacamole, Version I, Traditional, page 270.

Thread ham on skewers with accompaniments. Melt margarine in griddle and brown kebobs, about 5 to 8 minutes. Serve with dip sauces in individual cups.

Broiled Ham Kebob Snacks

BROIL: *Makes assorted amounts*

Leftover ham, cut into 1-inch cubes
Medium-size apple, unpared, cored, cut into quarters

2 to 3 green-tipped bananas cut into 1-inch cubes

BASTE

½ cup brown sugar
¼ cup honey
¼ cup orange juice

1 tablespoon cider vinegar
(if sweet-sour flavor is
desired)

Thirty minutes in advance: In a saucepan, combine marinade–baste ingredients. Heat until sugar dissolves (note: if
sweet-sour flavor is desired, add vinegar or make half sweet
and the other sweet-sour).

Before serving: Thread ham on skewers alternately with
apple and banana. Broil 4 to 5 inches from source of heat at
425° until thoroughly heated, about 8 minutes. Baste only
near end of broiling time.

Platter of Chilled Ham Kebobs

6 1-inch cubes of leftover ham
6 chunks canned pineapple
(use spears from 8¾-
ounce can and cut into
1-inch chunks)
6 1-inch cubes Italian bread,
crust removed
1 package (8 ounces) cream
cheese, room temperature
1½ tablespoons mayonnaise

Yellow food coloring
Almond extract
⅓ to ½ cup finely chopped
pecans or walnuts
3 red maraschino cherries,
well drained
3 green maraschino cherries
(mint-flavored), well
drained

Beginning one inch from tip of skewer, thread 6 6-inch
skewers as follows: HAM . pineapple chunk . bread. Beat
cream cheese and mayonnaise with electric mixer until
smooth. Divide mixture in half, adding one drop of yellow
food coloring to one portion and one drop of almond extract
to the other. Mix each portion well. With a spatula, spread
three kebobs with the white mixture and the remaining three
kebobs with the yellow mixture, coating thoroughly. Sprinkle
each kebob with about one tablespoon chopped nuts. Alternate red and green cherries on tips of each skewer. Arrange

kebobs on large platter, handle-side near rim and skewer points radiating from center. Chill.

Variations: Breadless version—omit bread and place two cubes of ham on each skewer with the pineapple. Or, instead of two cubes of ham, use four ½-inch-thick chunks of ham.

Children's version: Instead of metal skewers, use wooden sticks. The length of the handle provides an easy hand grasp for eating kebob right from the stick, Indonesian style.

Holiday version: Divide cream cheese mixture and add a drop of red food coloring to one portion, mixing thoroughly, and add a drop of green food coloring to the other, mixing well.

Island version: Substitute papaya chunks for pineapple; rather than the almond extract, use rum extract; and instead of walnuts or pecans, use macadamia nuts.

Calorie counter's version: Substitute Neufchâtel cheese for cream cheese and also omit mayonnaise. As for the pineapple, use the diet pack.

9 · VARIETY MEATS

WHAT TO CONSIDER BEFORE
SKEWER-COOKING VARIETY MEATS

Variety meats come from all animals and consist specifically of viscera—the edible parts such as heart, liver, kidney, sweetbreads, lung, tripe and brains. Some refer to variety meats as entrails, offal, innards, intestines, or internal organs, and a few call them guts.

These meats are quite well liked abroad. Peruvian "anticuchos" are cubes of beef heart marinated for two days in a mixture of wine vinegar and oil, seasoned with garlic and cumin, and served as an appetizer or snack accompanied with corn on the cob or sweet potatoes. "Kokoretsi souvlakia" are popular in Greece around Easter—the time when these souvlakia appear as appetizers to the feast of Pascal Lamb. The kokoretsi include pieces of lamb heart threaded alternately on a wooden skewer (*souvla*) with kidney, spleen, sweetbreads and lung. Generally, they're marinated for several hours before threading, basted with olive oil and lemon juice and sprinkled with thyme or oregano. French cuisine features a variety of brochettes—*foie de veau* (calf's liver) . . . *ris de veau* (sweetbreads) . . . *rognons de mouton* (lamb kidneys)—which may be threaded with pieces of bacon or dipped in a butter sauce, rolled in fine bread crumbs and basted with melted butter. Among the many Spanish skewered appetizers called "pinchos" are *riñones* (kidneys). And then there is the Moroccan "boulfaf"—skewer of sheep's or calf's liver with sheep's caul (the fold of fatty tissue around the abdomen), seasoned as a Moroccan might say "with a pinch of cumin and a suspicion of pimiento."

To many, I'm certain some of the above preparations seem a bit bizarre. Understandably, however, if these were part of one's diet from a very young age, they would be much-sought-after delicacies.

In the United States, the most favored variety meat is liver. The kind found most readily in supermarkets is beef liver; and where veal is available, you'll often find calf's liver, too. As for serving these livers kebobed, I do that only as something different for an everyday meal. Use the beef liver or calf's liver interchangeably in the recipes here, depending on taste preference. (And this might interest those who eat liver because it's good for you: Although calf's liver costs almost three times the price of beef liver, it's basically comparable to the beef liver in nutrient value.)

Another equally nutritious liver, and one that I think adapts the best to party or company meals, is chicken liver. Note the following for skewer-cooking them successfully. Thread livers whole and fold over once, or, as I prefer, cut them in half. When spearing the skewer through them, secure well to avoid their slipping off during cooking. For exceptionally moist and flavorful livers, I suggest braising. If you do broil or bake, be sure to allow space between the liver and other foods on skewer to facilitate even cooking. Also baste frequently, since livers have little fat for self-basting. A suggestion: Try chicken and turkey livers threaded alternately on a skewer with those of beef, pork and lamb . . . rather interesting textures, if you like liver.

As an entree for lunch or brunch, allow one-half pound of chicken livers per serving; for appetizers or snacks, one-quarter pound. Remember, they are substantially filling, and might be (depending on the entree) too heavy as an appetizer. For an impressive snack at your fingertips, keep handy at least two eight-ounce frozen packages. In my freezer, they're a staple item.

Skewered Chicken Livers, Georgia's Style

BRAISE: *Makes 4 8-inch skewers or 6 6-inch skewers*

Here's something simple, and based on the unsolicited comments I receive it's special, too. If served as a snack, accompany with Feta and Cream Cheese Balls, page 275.

1 pound chicken livers, cut in half (about 24 pieces)
Salt to taste
16 large whole mushrooms, canned
1 jar (4 ounces) whole pimiento divided into 12 pieces

8 whole water chestnuts
1 green pepper, cut into 8 pieces
2 tablespoons butter or margarine

SKILLET SAUCE

⅓ cup sweet vermouth
⅓ cup tomato sauce

2 tablespoons soy sauce

Season livers with salt to taste, keeping in mind the salt in soy sauce and tomato sauce. Thread livers on 8-inch skewers as follows: mushroom . LIVER . pimiento . LIVER . water chestnut . mushroom . green pepper . LIVER . pimiento . LIVER . water chestnut . mushroom . green pepper . LIVER . pimiento . LIVER . mushroom. Combine sauce ingredients. Melt margarine or butter in skillet and brown kebobs about 10 minutes, turning several times. Pour skillet sauce over kebobs. Cover and simmer an additional 10 to 15 minutes, occasionally turning kebobs and scooping sauce over them. Serve with a favorite pasta as a light meal. For appetizer or snacks, thread on 6-inch skewers and serve on small trays.

Skewered Chicken Livers with Sesame Bananas

BROIL: *Makes 4 10-inch skewers*

Here you'll find a crisp surface texture complemented with a soft center of sweet fruit.

1 pound chicken livers, cut in half (about 24 pieces)
3 green-tipped bananas cut into 16 1-inch pieces
¼ cup orange juice

⅓ cup sesame seeds
Salt to taste
Canned pineapple chunks (optional)

MARINADE–BASTE

2 tablespoons dark molasses
2 tablespoons peanut oil

3 tablespoons each of orange juice and lemon juice

Thirty minutes in advance: In a bowl, combine marinade–baste ingredients, mixing well. Add chicken livers. Cover and let stand in refrigerator.

Before serving: Dip banana chunks in orange juice and roll in sesame seeds, coating well. Remove livers from marinade–baste and season with salt to taste. Thread two liver pieces alternately with sesame-covered banana, beginning and ending with banana. Broil 4 to 5 inches from source of heat for 7 to 9 minutes; turn; then broil another 8 to 10 minutes. Baste generously near end of broiling. If desired, garnish tips of skewer with canned pineapple chunks before serving.

Coated Chicken Liver Kebobs

BAKE: *Makes 6 10-inch skewers*

1 package (2½ ounces)
  seasoned coating mix for
  chicken
1½ pounds chicken livers, cut
  in half (about 36 pieces)
⅓ cup melted butter
1 teaspoon paprika
¼ teaspoon dill weed

⅛ teaspoon cardamom
12 whole boiled onions (1
  16-ounce jar)
9 slices cucumber (about ½
  inch thick), halved
3 strips bacon, each cut into
  4 pieces

Empty package of seasoned coating mix into a bowl. Add chicken livers, coating thoroughly. In another bowl, combine melted butter, paprika, dill weed and cardamom. Add onions and toss well. Thread skewers as follows: cucumber . onion . two LIVERS . bacon . two LIVERS . cucumber . two LIVERS . bacon . onion . cucumber. Brush some of remaining butter mixture from onions onto foil-lined baking pan. Bake in preheated 350° oven 10 to 15 minutes; turn; then bake an additional 15 minutes.

Variation: Use cherry tomatoes instead of cucumber.

Children's Favorite Cold Beef Liver Kebobs

Makes 8 8-inch skewers

Make this dish attractive to children by spearing apple halves with liver and fruit threaded on wooden skewers with cartoon-designed handles. Of all meats, liver is the richest source of vitamin A and iron. And liver eaten cold tastes a good deal like sausage. This recipe just might help establish a liking for a nutritious food that children might otherwise avoid.

1 pound sliced beef liver
Salt to taste
¼ cup flour for dredging
2 tablespoons melted butter
(for liver)
Bananas, cut into 1-inch chunks
¼ cup melted butter (for bananas)
Sugar and cinnamon mixture
(5 or 6 parts sugar to 1 part cinnamon)

Fruits for spearing on skewer: pineapple, orange sections, pears, or whatever your child likes
3 or 4 apples, unpared, halved crosswise

One day in advance: Trim membrane from liver. Season with salt to taste. Dredge with flour. Brush 2 tablespoons melted butter on foil-lined bake pan and bake liver slices in preheated 350° oven for 15 minutes. Turn. Bake an additional 10 minutes. Refrigerate.

Before serving: Cut liver into 32 bite-size pieces. Dip banana chunks in ¼ cup melted butter and roll in cinnamon-sugar mixture. Thread liver on 8-inch wooden skewers, alternating with bananas and other fruits, allowing 4 pieces of liver per skewer. In center of individual plates, place apple cut side down. Spear two kebobs into each half. Surround with rice, potato chips, vegetables, or whatever your children are particularly fond of. For older children (or for adults), accompany with Horseradish Dip Sauces, page 268.

Beef Liver and Onion Kebobs

BROIL: *Makes 4 10-inch skewers*

For a change of pace, serve the popular liver and onion combination with a new twist. Accompany with baked squash and corn muffins.

1 pound beef liver, cut into
16 pieces
2 tablespoons melted butter
1 teaspoon dried mint, crushed
2 teaspoons grated orange rind
1 jar (16 ounces) whole boiled
onions, drained

Salt to taste
Green onions (the green part),
cut into 16 3-inch pieces,
each folded once

MARINADE–BASTE

½ cup Madeira
¼ cup salad oil
¼ cup finely chopped onion

2 tablespoons chopped parsley
½ teaspoon salt
1 bay leaf

Twenty minutes before serving: In a bowl, combine marinade–baste ingredients, mixing well. Remove membrane from liver, then add liver pieces to marinade, cover, and refrigerate. In a small bowl, combine melted butter with mint and orange rind. Toss with boiled onions and let stand at room temperature.

Before serving: Season liver with salt to taste. Thread liver alternately with green onion strips and boiled onions. Broil 4 to 5 inches from source of heat for 6 to 7 minutes. Turn, baste, and broil an additional 7 to 8 minutes.

Skewered Calf's Liver

BAKE: *Makes 4 10-inch skewers*

3 medium zucchini, unpared
12 small whole boiled onions,
canned
1 tablespoon melted butter
2 tablespoons grated Parmesan
cheese

1 pound calf's liver, cut into
16 pieces
½ cup Italian-flavored bread
crumbs

BASTE

1 cup Tomato Barbecue Sauce,
Version II, page 266

Cook zucchini in boiling salted water 6 minutes. Drain and rinse with cold water. Cut crosswise into 12 1-inch slices. Scoop out center and discard (or reserve for other use). Roll onions in melted butter and then in grated cheese, coating well. Insert onions in center of zucchini slices. Remove any skin covering from liver and roll in bread crumbs. On each skewer thread 4 pieces of liver alternately with 3 onion-stuffed zucchini slices. (Note: Spear skewer through skin of zucchini and the onion as well.) Place on foil-lined baking pan and bake in 350° oven for 15 minutes. Turn, baste with sauce, and bake an additional 15 to 18 minutes. Before serving, brush each skewer generously with remaining sauce.

Skewered Lamb Kidneys

BROIL: *Makes 4 10-inch skewers*

Here you have a choice between two bastes. Serve with saffron rice and a gelatin salad mold.

8 lamb kidneys
Salt to taste
16 whole canned mushrooms

8 whole boiled onions, canned
1 green pepper, cut into 8
  pieces

BASTES

I

½ cup Claret
¼ cup salad oil
1 clove garlic, minced

2 teaspoons minced parsley
1 teaspoon salt

OR

II

½ cup melted butter

2 teaspoons minced parsley

Wash kidneys and remove outer skin covering. Split in half lengthwise, removing fat and tubes. Rinse with cold water. Season with salt to taste. Allow 2 kidneys (each

cut into 4 pieces) per skewer. Thread as follows: mushroom
. KIDNEYS . onion . green pepper . KIDNEYS . mushroom .
onion . green pepper . KIDNEYS . mushroom . KIDNEYS .
mushroom. Broil 4 to 5 inches from source of heat for 10 to
12 minutes. Turn and baste. Broil an additional 6 to 8 minutes. Just before serving, brush each skewer generously with
remaining baste.

Variation: Use two strips of bacon cut in half crosswise
and wrap one piece of kidney on each skewer.

10 · SAUSAGE

WHAT TO CONSIDER BEFORE
SKEWER-COOKING SAUSAGES

Of all meats, this category is the most versatile for serving kebobs in countless ways. And it's no wonder with over 200 types of seasoned chopped meats in casings. From hot and spicy to quite mild and even sweet, sausages fall into at least one of six categories. The first two—fresh and smoked —require cooking and the remaining four do not. These latter ready-to-eat sausages include: cooked . . . cooked/smoked . . . dry and semidry . . . plus the cooked meat specialties, perhaps better known to you as luncheon meats, loaves and spreads.

With the wide assortment of shapes and textures in the ready-to-eat sausages, it's easy to see the endless possibilities for creating kebob conversation pieces. One way is to spear these meats on skewers and serve cold as centerpieces for buffet tables. Another way is to heat kebobs by whatever method you prefer and serve them as hearty snacks or as attractive main dishes. In the cooked/smoked category, the one sausage which still ranks as America's favorite is the wiener—or perhaps you refer to it as frankfurter, frank, or simply, hot dog. Although it doesn't require cooking, heating enhances its flavor considerably.

One fact to remember about skewer-cooking sausage is that the foods next to it on the skewer and the sauces won't influence its flavor as they would fresh unseasoned meat;

and, of course, the more strongly spiced varieties are influenced the least.

Tropicana Frank Kebobs

BROIL: *Makes 4 10-inch skewers*

Here, reserve the syrup and remaining chunks from a can of pineapple to prepare and serve with A Tropical Drink, page 293.

1 green pepper, parboiled, cut into 8 pieces
1 package (12 ounces) knackwurst or jumbo-size franks, cut into 1-inch pieces

4 canned yams, cut in half (8-ounce can)
8 pineapple chunks from a 13¼-ounce can
¼ cup ground macadamia nuts

BASTE

¼ cup melted butter
3 tablespoons orange juice
1 tablespoon soy sauce
2 tablespoons lemon juice

1 teaspoon dry mustard
⅛ teaspoon ground cloves
⅛ teaspoon ground cinnamon

Thread skewers as follows: green pepper . FRANK . yam . FRANK . pineapple . FRANK . green pepper . FRANK . yam . FRANK . pineapple. Combine baste ingredients in saucepan and heat. Baste kebobs generously before, during and after cooking. Broil 4 to 5 inches from source of heat for 10 to 12 minutes, turning once. Before serving, sprinkle one tablespoon nuts over each kebob.

Variation I: As a baste substitute, use 1 cup of the Sweet-Sour Variation, Tomato Barbecue Sauce, page 266.
Variation II: Omit the yams and green pepper and instead thread franks and pineapple with stuffed prunes and apple slices. Soak 12 dried pitted prunes in 1 tablespoon water combined with 1½ teaspoon rum flavoring. Before threading,

stuff centers of prunes with 12 canned or fresh seedless grapes. Combine 1½ cups water with ½ teaspoon cinnamon and 2 tablespoons granulated sugar. Add 12 dried apple slices and cook until partially tender, 10 to 15 minutes. Set aside to cool. When threading, fold each apple slice once.

FRANK KEBOBS IN SEASONED BUNS

In the first version below, the bun is seasoned, moist, and soft; and in the second, it is crisp and crunchy.

Franks in a Bun, Banana Version

BROIL AND BAKE: *Makes 5 10-inch skewers*

5 frankfurters, each cut into 3 pieces, about 1½ inches each	2 medium-size bananas
	½ teaspoon cinnamon
	1 tablespoon orange juice
10 pineapple chunks	5 frankfurter buns, split

Thread frankfurter pieces on skewer alternately with pineapple chunks, beginning and ending with frankfurter. Broil 4 to 5 inches from source of heat for 8 to 10 minutes or until delicately brown, basting with pineapple syrup from can if desired. In a bowl, mash bananas together with cinnamon and orange juice. Place buns open-face on foil-lined baking sheet. Butter one side of bun and spread banana mixture on the other side. Place kebobs on the banana mixture and then heat buns in 400° oven for several minutes until buttered side of bun becomes slightly toasted. Serve with a side dish of cucumber slices in sour cream.

Franks in a Bun, Almond Version

BROIL AND BAKE: *Makes 5 10-inch skewers*

5 frankfurters, each cut into 3 pieces, about 1½ inches each
10 mixed stuffed olives
5 frankfurter buns, split

¼ cup melted butter
1 teaspoon lemon juice
1 teaspoon almond extract
⅔ cup chopped almonds

Thread frankfurters on skewer alternately with olives, allowing 2 olives per skewer. Broil 4 to 5 inches from source of heat about 8 to 10 minutes, turning once. Place buns open-face on foil-lined baking sheet and brush both sides of each bun generously with a mixture of melted butter, lemon juice and almond extract. On one side of each bun add chopped nuts and then kebobs. Place in 400° oven just a few minutes to heat thoroughly.

Variation without the bun: Rather than use the mixture of butter, lemon juice and almond extract to season the bun, instead, use it to baste the kebobs and to coat an accompaniment of cooked green vegetables. Sprinkle the almonds generously over vegetables or kebobs.

Biscuit-Ringed Knackwurst Kebobs

BAKE: *Makes 5 10-inch skewers*

Here, use both sauces and baste only *after* the kebobs are cooked. These must be served immediately.

5 knackwurst (12-ounce package)
1 package (8 ounces) refrigerator buttermilk biscuits
15 medium pimiento-stuffed olives

1 small onion cut into 5 thin wedges
1 red pepper cut into 10 pieces
5 tablespoons grated Parmesan cheese
5 tablespoons ground pecans

BASTES

Anchovy Butter

⅓ cup melted butter
1 can (2 ounces) flat anchovy
   fillets, well drained

Soy Sauce

¼ cup melted butter   2 tablespoons soy sauce

Halve the knackwurst crosswise and separate the 10 biscuits. Push each piece of knackwurst through center of a biscuit. (To assist here, slit each biscuit in the center with pointed knife.) Squeeze biscuit dough firmly around knackwurst. Thread on skewers as follows: olive . biscuit-ringed KNACKWURST . onion . red pepper . olive . biscuit-ringed KNACKWURST . red pepper . olive. Place on greased baking pan and bake in preheated 475° oven (or temperature indicated on biscuit package) for 8 to 10 minutes, or until biscuits are golden. Heat butter and anchovies, mixing well. Also combine soy sauce baste ingredients. In the baking pan, baste one of the biscuit-ringed knackwurst on each skewer with the anchovy butter sauce and baste the other biscuit-ringed knackwurst with the soy sauce mixture. Place kebobs on serving plates and top each of the anchovy basted knackwursts with 1 tablespoon grated cheese and the soy-sauce basted ones with 1 tablespoon of ground nuts.

Variation: For the traditional hot dog taste, baste the biscuit-ringed knackwurst with equal parts of melted butter and prepared mustard and top with sweet relish.

Pepperoni-Accented Kebobs

BROIL: *Makes 4 10-inch skewers*

Serve with spaghetti topped with tomato sauce, and a mixed green salad.

4 thin, square-shaped slices of bologna or other luncheon meat, halved
6 ounces aged Cheddar cheese, cut into 8 1-inch cubes
½ pound pepperoni, skinned and cut into ½-inch slices
1 green pepper, cut into 8 pieces
4 frankfurters, cut into 2-inch pieces

Wrap bologna or other luncheon meat around cheese cubes. Thread skewer as follows: bologna wrapped around cheese . PEPPERONI . green pepper . frankfurter (lengthwise) . PEPPERONI . bologna wrapped around cheese . green pepper . frankfurter (lengthwise) . PEPPERONI. Broil 4 to 5 inches from source of heat for 8 to 10 minutes, or until cheese begins to melt.

KEBOBS OF CHEESE AND SAUSAGE TIDBITS

The first of these snack foods makes a colorful food centerpiece, ideal for St. Patrick's Day. Spear an array of kebobs into a cucumber half and accompany with a dip sauce. Serve the second version hot right from the griddle, anytime.

Cold Version: Cheese and Sausage Balls

Makes 8 6-inch skewers

SAUSAGE BALLS

½ pound Braunschweiger liver sausage
¼ cup finely ground cracker crumbs
8 small stuffed olives
8 tidbit pieces of dill pickle
¼ cup chopped parsley

CHEESE BALLS

2 3-ounce packages of chive cream cheese
¼ cup chopped pecans

1 long cucumber, halved lengthwise, unpared (plus ⅓ cup chopped cucumber)

Tiny sweet gherkins

Black pitted olives (small size)

½ cup mayonnaise

½ teaspoon celery salt

Dash of green food coloring (optional)

In advance: In a bowl, mix liver sausage and cracker crumbs. Shape mixture into a large ball, roll lengthwise and then divide into 16 pieces. Roll these between the palms of your hands to shape into small balls and then flatten. Place an olive in the center of 8 flattened balls and a pickle tidbit in the other 8. Shape into balls again and coat only the pickle-stuffed balls by rolling in chopped parsley. Chill. Shape soft-ened cream cheese into 8 balls and coat by rolling in chopped pecans. Chill.

Before serving: Place halved cucumber flat-side-down on a platter. Thread liver sausage balls and cream cheese balls on skewers alternately with pickles, cucumber chunks, and black olives, allowing two liver sausage balls and one cream cheese ball per skewer. Spear kebobs into the cucumber half. Combine ⅓ cup finely chopped cucumber (from remaining cucumber half) with the mayonnaise, mixed with food color-ing, if you are using it, and celery salt. Place in serving cup on platter.

Hot Version: Cheese and Sausage Chunks

BROIL (*griddle-broil*): *Makes 4 10-inch skewers*

12 jumbo-size black pitted olives

1 to 2 ounces aged sharp cheese, cut into tidbit pieces

16 dill pickle slices

8 cocktail wieners, canned or packaged

12 ¾-inch chunks of salami, summer sausage, or bologna

1 tablespoon butter

Stuff centers of black olives with tidbit pieces of cheese. Thread each skewer as follows: pickle . olive stuffed with CHEESE . wiener (lengthwise) . olive stuffed with CHEESE . SAUSAGE chunk . pickle . olive stuffed with CHEESE .

SAUSAGE chunk . pickle . wiener (lengthwise) . SAUSAGE chunk . pickle. Melt butter on griddle. Brown kebobs, turning often, and heat until cheese begins to melt. Serve immediately in one of the following ways: over a bed of vegetables and then topped with a cheese sauce; or in a frankfurter bun or in Italian bread; or placed on top of a thick slice of pumpernickel bread and accompanied with choice of dip sauces—Horseradish, Mustard, Sweet-Sour Dip Sauce and Guacamole, pages 268–71.

SKEWERED LUNCHEON MEATS

When the time seems appropriate for luncheon meats—as an appetizer, snack, or lunch—thread them on skewers to serve hot or cold. To serve cold, here are a few ideas. Use several varieties of square-shaped slices of luncheon meat to make different shapes—rolls, folds, stacks. Spread soft cheese on some slices and then roll and wrap around an olive, banana chunk or other fruit. Halve other slices, spread a favorite condiment on them, and then either roll tightly or simply fold over several times to make a triangle shape. Use other slices to make large or small stacks; divide one slice into a stack of 4 pieces or divide one slice into 12 pieces to make 2 stacks of 6 pieces. Alternate the various luncheon meat shapes with cherry tomatoes or cucumber chunks or favorite fruit (an idea: cut raw pear slices ½ inch thick and remove core center and replace with dark sweet cherry; spear skewer through cherry only). Spear kebobs into large candles, a head of cabbage, an eggplant, a pineapple, Styrofoam, or simply place on a platter over lettuce leaves.

A Sandwich on a Stick Idea . . . for youngsters who like peanut butter: Spread a mixture of equal parts peanut butter and mashed banana on one side of a split frankfurter bun. Cover and cut crosswise into 3 pieces. Thread these on 10-inch skewers alternately with small stacks or rolled pieces of luncheon meat. Thread with a choice of pineapple chunks and candied cherries for something colorful, or thread with liver sausage balls rolled in crushed potato chips, shredded coconut, or perhaps wheat germ.

For serving luncheon meat hot, try the following recipes, especially the second one.

Chopped Luncheon Meat Kebobs

BROIL: *Makes 5 10-inch skewers*

4 packages (3 ounces each) of wafer-sliced, ready-to-eat luncheon meat (turkey, ham, corned beef, and roast beef)
10 strips bacon, halved crosswise

10 chunks cucumber
1 large green or red pepper cut into 10 pieces

BASTE–TOPPING SAUCE

½ cup Thin Sweet-Sour Sauce,* page 264

Divide each package of luncheon meat into 5 equal portions. Wrap each portion tightly with a piece of bacon. Thread skewers as follows: MEAT . cucumber . MEAT . pepper . MEAT . cucumber . MEAT . pepper. Broil 4 to 5 inches from source of heat for 10 to 12 minutes or until bacon is cooked, basting kebobs frequently. Serve remaining sauce as topping.

Variations: For sweet version, substitute pineapple chunks and maraschino cherries for cucumber and red or green pepper. For crisper bacon and for kebobs broiled in half the cooking time above, cook bacon in a skillet for 2 to 3 minutes before wrapping luncheon meat.

* If more convenient, use a 2-ounce package of sweet-sour mix and follow directions on package.

Cubed Luncheon Meat Kebobs

BRAISE: *Makes 6 6-inch skewers*

1 can (12 ounces) luncheon
meat cut into 12 cubes
6 pieces (1-inch square)
pickled sweet banana peppers
1 package (4 ounces)
Braunschweiger liver
sausage cut into 6 ½-inch
slices and shaped into cubes

6 slices sweet pickled
cucumbers
6 pimiento-stuffed olives
1 egg, well beaten
½ cup flour
2 tablespoons butter

TOPPING SAUCE

6 tablespoons butter
2 tablespoons lemon juice
2 tablespoons Dijon-style
mustard

1 tablespoon Worcestershire
sauce

Thread skewers as follows: luncheon MEAT cube . sweet banana pepper . liver sausage . pickled cucumber . luncheon MEAT cube . olive. Dip skewers in beaten egg and then roll in flour, coating well. Heat butter in skillet and add kebobs. Brown on all sides in covered skillet 6 to 8 minutes, turning often. In saucepan, combine topping-sauce ingredients, stirring well. Spread over kebobs and serve.

TRIANGLE KEBOBS

The main feature here is triangular-shaped sausage. You might consider the first recipe below eccentric (and it is).

Sweet and Cordial Triangles

BROIL: *Makes 6 10-inch skewers*

1 pound chub mild bologna, cut
into 6 1-inch slices

36 dark pitted sweet cherries

MARINADE–BASTE

⅓ cup cherry syrup from
canned sweet cherries
¼ cup cherry-flavored brandy

¼ cup firmly packed brown
sugar
1 teaspoon dry mustard

One hour in advance: Cut each bologna slice into three triangular shapes. Combine marinade-baste ingredients. Add bologna and let stand at room temperature.

Before serving: Thread each skewer as follows: BOLOGNA triangle . two cherries . BOLOGNA triangle . two cherries . BOLOGNA triangle . two cherries. Broil 4 to 5 inches from source of heat for 8 to 10 minutes. Baste near end of broiling.

Variation: If you wish, use a 12-ounce can of luncheon meat to cut into 12 cubes and a small can (8 ounces) of cherries to thread four 10-inch skewers. Since canned luncheon meat isn't generally as highly seasoned as bologna, it will better absorb the marinade-baste flavoring.

Nonsweet Triangles

BRAISE: *Makes 6 6-inch skewers*

¾ pound chub (about 2½-inch
diameter) soft cooked salami,
cut into 4 1-inch slices
12 medium black pitted olives

1 jar (4 ounces) whole
pimiento, cut into 12 pieces
12 tiny whole onions (about 1
8-ounce can)

SKILLET SAUCE

⅓ cup Rhine wine
¼ cup apple juice
⅓ cup tomato sauce

¼ teaspoon nutmeg
¼ teaspoon freeze-dried chives

Cut each salami slice into three triangular shapes. Thread skewers as follows: olive . SALAMI triangle . pimiento . onion . SALAMI triangle . pimiento . onion . olive. Heat kebobs in lightly greased skillet and brown 3 to 5 minutes. Combine skillet-sauce ingredients and add to skillet. Cover and simmer 10 to 12 minutes.

Skewered Greek Sausages

BROIL: *Makes 6 10-inch skewers*

If you're not familiar with Greek sausages, let me introduce you to loukanika. What you might find unique about them is their peppery seasoning and the orange rind. In my opinion, loukanika are best used only as an accent. The distinctive flavor in the sauce can be attributed to the Greek Mavrodaphne wine. Accompany with a side dish of Angouro Salata, page 292.

3 bratwurst (about 12 ounces) each cut into ten ½-inch pieces
3 loukanika (about 12 ounces) each cut into ten ½-inch pieces

2 green peppers cut into 12 pieces
4 pickled sweet banana peppers, cut into 12 pieces

MARINADE–TOPPING SAUCE

½ cup Mavrodaphne wine
½ cup orange juice

¼ cup tomato juice
1 tablespoon finely chopped parsley

BASTE

¼ cup lemon juice

One and one-half hours in advance: Combine marinade–topping sauce ingredients in a bowl and add bratwurst. Let stand at room temperature, turning occasionally.

Before serving: For each skewer: begin and end with green pepper, thread two pickled peppers, and arrange 5 bratwurst alternately with 5 loukanika. Broil 4 to 5 inches from source of heat for 10 to 12 minutes, turning often and basting generously with lemon juice. Heat the marinade in saucepan and thicken by stirring in 2 teaspoons flour mixed with 2 tablespoons water. Serve as a topping over each kebob.

Skewered Italian Sausages

BROIL: *Makes 4 10-inch skewers*

1 pound Italian sweet (mild) sausages, cut into 1½-inch slices, about 10 to 12 pieces
1 jar (4 ounces) whole pimiento
1 package (10 ounces) frozen Brussels sprouts, partially cooked

Long French bread cut into 4 10-inch pieces
Shredded mozzarella cheese (optional)

MARINADE–BASTE

1 cup (8-ounce can) prepared pizza sauce mix

½ cup Rhine wine*
1 tablespoon soy sauce

Thirty minutes in advance: Use a sharp knife to cut sausages, being careful not to tear casings. Divide pimiento into 12 pieces. Combine marinade–baste ingredients in a bowl and add sausage pieces.

Before serving: Thread sausage on skewer alternately with pimiento and Brussels sprouts, spearing skewer through the center of sausage and not the casing. Broil 4 to 5 inches from source of heat about 10 minutes; turn; then baste and broil another 15 to 20 minutes until cooked. Place kebobs on bread and brush with remaining sauce. If desired, sprinkle top with shredded mozzarella.

* If you're going to serve an Italian dry white wine for a beverage, use that instead of the Rhine wine.

Skewered Sausages, Viennese Accent

BROIL: *Makes 8 10-inch skewers*

16 pork sausage links (1-pound package)
½ cup Rhine wine
1 medium-size cooking apple, unpared, cut into 8 wedges
2 tablespoons melted margarine
3 to 4 tablespoons finely ground walnuts

4 beef knackwurst sausages (12-ounce package)
16 small chunks of unpared cucumber
1 small bunch green onions, the green part cut into 32 1-inch pieces

TOPPING MIXTURE

1 4-ounce package shredded sharp Cheddar cheese (1 cup)

⅓ cup finely chopped onion
½ cup finely chopped celery
¼ cup finely chopped parsley

Thirty minutes in advance: Place link sausages in a pan of boiling water and cook 5 minutes. Handle links carefully to avoid pricking the casing. Place links on paper towel to drain and then soak them in Rhine wine for about 15 minutes, tossing frequently. Combine topping-mixture ingredients in a bowl and set aside.

Before serving: Dip apple pieces in melted margarine and then roll in nuts to coat thoroughly. Halve the knackwurst crosswise.

Thread each skewer as follows: SAUSAGE LINK wrapped around cucumber . apple wedge . KNACKWURST (speared lengthwise) · 4 pieces green onion · SAUSAGE LINK wrapped around cucumber. Broil 4 to 5 inches from source of heat for about 10 to 12 minutes, turning frequently until sausages are evenly browned. Spread topping mixture over each kebob and serve.

Skewered Mixed Sausages

BRAISE: *Makes 6 6-inch skewers*

A meaty snack, this is certain to appeal to the savorer of sausage.

2 green peppers, cut into 18 pieces
2 knackwurst, cut into 6 1½-inch pieces
2 bratwurst, cut into 6 1½-inch pieces

6 little smoked links
2 Polish sausages, cut into 6 1½-inch pieces

SKILLET SAUCE

⅓ cup beer
⅓ cup tomato sauce

¼ teaspoon caraway seed

Thread each skewer as follows: green pepper . KNACK-WURST . BRATWURST . green pepper . SMOKED LINK . POLISH SAUSAGE . green pepper. Heat kebobs in skillet until brown, about 3 to 5 minutes. Combine skillet-sauce ingredients. Add to skillet. Cover. Simmer 15 to 18 minutes.

11 · POULTRY

WHAT TO CONSIDER BEFORE
SKEWER-COOKING POULTRY

Kebobed poultry—boned, skinned, cut into pieces, then cooked on a skewer—is a neat, convenient and attractive food to serve and eat. No unsightly bones remain on the plate. The meat is eaten simply by sliding it off the skewer with a fork. And certainly that's one good reason for skewer-cooking poultry more often.

Here is another reason. A three-ounce portion of chicken breasts (the part best suited for kebobs) with the skin removed comes to about 115 calories. Sauces do add calories, but during broiling or baking much of the sauce drips to the bottom of the pan. As for the number-one reason for kebobing chicken—it's, of course, flavor.

If you're a beginner at boning chicken, to acquire the knack often requires patience and practice. But if you follow these instructions, you should be quite satisfied with your results. First, you need a sharp-edged knife, preferably one with a 5- to 6-inch blade. On a cutting board, place the whole breast, which should be three-fourths to one pound, and remove wings, neck, and back, if they're attached. Next, remove the skin, using the knife to assist in cutting and pulling it away from the flesh. Then flatten the breast and with your knife slit the thin membrane covering the keel bone, the bulky one in the center. Remove this bone by loosening and tugging a bit, using your fingers and the knife if necessary. Cut the breast into two parts where the bone was removed. The objective now is to remove the flesh from each half in one piece. To do this, insert the point of the knife by the first (largest) rib bone, freeing the flesh. Continue to cut the flesh away from each rib until you've worked up to the last bone of the cage. You now should be in the wishbone area. Cut the tendons, loosen, and then detach the meat, thereby separating flesh from the ribcage in one piece. And there's your boned breast of chicken. (If breasts come already halved, as they do in some markets, insert and maneuver the tip of the knife in a way that slits the membrane between the flesh and the keel bone and then proceed as above to free the flesh from the ribcage.)

Cut each breast half into four or five 1½- to 2-inch pieces, which makes eight to ten for a medium-to-large-size breast. If the breast happens to be small, cut fewer pieces rather than smaller ones. Although in skewer-cooking other meats you might consider reducing the size of pieces for appetizers, here you don't because during cooking they'll become too dry. For a main dish serving, allow one whole breast per person, threading the chicken on 8- or 10-inch skewers. For appetizers, allow one-half breast per person and use 6-inch skewers.

Should you braise, broil, or bake? Really, all three methods are acceptable. Personally, I recommend braising because it keeps the chicken moist. But baking is also very satisfactory. Broiling must be done carefully. Broil until tender and brown, yet still juicy; baste frequently, cook at a lower temperature or farther from source of heat, and don't overcook.

Now for a few suggestions. Instead of chicken breasts, try turkey for a change. Use skin and bone remains to prepare a soup stock. For convenience, bone poultry the night before or in the morning and have ready to cut into pieces when needed. And one thing more—if you think you'll want to experiment with red wine as the predominant liquid in a marinade, let me save you a disappointment: don't, unless you like your chicken blue.

Chicken and Pimiento Kebobs

BROIL OR BRAISE: *Makes 4 10-inch or 5 8-inch skewers; or 5 to 6 6-inch skewers*

Here you have a choice of cooking methods—broiling or braising.

2 whole chicken breasts, skinned, boned, and cut into 16 to 20 1½-inch pieces
2 whole pimientos, each cut into 4 pieces (4-ounce jar)

1 green pepper, cut into 8 pieces
8 jumbo black pitted olives
2 tablespoons butter or margarine (for braising)

MARINADE–BASTE (if you choose to broil)

½ cup dry sherry
¼ cup melted butter

1 teaspoon paprika
1 teaspoon salt

SKILLET SAUCE (if you choose to braise)

½ cup chicken bouillon (one cube dissolved in ½ cup hot water)
½ cup dry sherry

1 teaspoon paprika
½ teaspoon salt
½ cup dairy sour cream

TO BROIL . . .
One hour in advance: Combine marinade–baste ingredients in a bowl. Add chicken pieces. Cover. Let stand at room temperature.

Before serving: Thread chicken on 10-inch skewers alternately with pimiento, green pepper, and black olives, allowing about 5 pieces of chicken per skewer. Heat the remaining marinade and stir. Broil at 400° 4 to 5 inches from source of heat for 10 to 12 minutes; turn; baste with sauce; and broil another 8 to 9 minutes. Baste generously during cooking and before serving.

TO BRAISE . . .
Season chicken with salt to taste. Thread on 8- or 6-inch skewers with the pimiento, green pepper, and olives. Melt butter or margarine in skillet and brown kebobs on all sides. Combine skillet-sauce ingredients except sour cream, and pour over kebobs. Cover. Simmer about 20 to 25 minutes, occasionally turning kebobs. Transfer kebobs to a warm platter. Stir sour cream into skillet. Heat but do not boil. Scoop sauce over kebobs as a topping. Garnish with chopped parsley if desired. Serve immediately.

Midwestern Chicken Kebobs

BRAISE: *Makes 4 8-inch skewers*

Serve over a bed of steaming rice for a main dish.

2 whole chicken breasts, skinned, boned, and cut into 16 to 20 1½-inch pieces
Salt to taste
8 1-inch pieces of celery

8 thin wedges of onion
1 green pepper cut into 8 pieces
2 tablespoons olive oil

SKILLET SAUCE

½ cup Rhine wine
¼ cup brandy
2 tablespoons tomato paste
1 tablespoon lemon juice
3 tablespoons orange juice
1 clove garlic, crushed

¼ teaspoon each of parsley flakes, dried tarragon, and freeze-dried chives
¼ teaspoon freshly ground black pepper

Season chicken with salt to taste. Thread each skewer as follows: celery . CHICKEN . onion . CHICKEN . green pepper . CHICKEN . onion . CHICKEN . green pepper . CHICKEN . celery. Combine skillet-sauce ingredients, mixing well. Heat oil in skillet and brown kebobs, turning several times. Pour sauce over kebobs. Cover. Simmer 20 to 25 minutes, occasionally turning kebobs and scooping sauce over them. Note: The celery will remain crisp.

Chicken Kebobs Confetti

BRAISE: *Makes 5 or 6 6-inch skewers*

These make perfect appetizers or snacks.

2 whole chicken breasts, skinned, boned, and cut into 16 to 20 1½-inch pieces
Salt to taste
16 small pimiento-stuffed olives (one 3-ounce jar)
½ medium onion cut into 5 thin wedges
1 large red pepper cut into 10 pieces
1 tablespoon butter or margarine
2 tablespoons olive oil

SKILLET SAUCE

½ cup beef bouillon (one cube dissolved in ½ cup hot water)
3 tablespoons Curaçao (or other orange-flavored liqueur)
3 tablespoons brandy
¼ teaspoon each of dried tarragon, basil and leaf marjoram

CONFETTI COATING

½ cup sliced blanched almonds, crushed
¼ cup imitation bacon bits or 5 strips crisp cooked bacon, finely crumbled
2 tablespoons grated Parmesan cheese
3 to 4 tablespoons finely chopped parsley or 2 tablespoons parsley flakes
2 tablespoons finely chopped candied orange peel

TOPPING SAUCE

¼ cup Sweet-Sour Sauce, page 269

Season chicken with salt to taste. Thread chicken on skewers alternately with olive, red pepper and onion, allowing 3 olives, 2 red peppers, 1 onion, and 3 to 4 pieces of chicken per skewer. Combine skillet-sauce ingredients. Heat oil and butter or margarine in skillet and brown kebobs 5 to 8 minutes, turning several times. Pour skillet sauce over kebobs. Cover. Simmer 20 minutes, occasionally turning kebobs and scooping sauce over them. In a platter, combine confetti-coating ingredients, using fingers to crumble well. Roll hot kebobs from skillet first in Sweet-Sour Sauce, and then in confetti until thoroughly coated. Place on individual serving plates and sprinkle kebobs with remaining confetti.

Polynesian Chicken Kebobs

BAKE: *Makes 8 10-inch skewers*

4 whole chicken breasts, skinned, boned, and cut into 32 1½-inch pieces
Salt to taste
16 maraschino cherries
1 unpeeled thick-skinned orange, cut into 8 pieces

16 pineapple chunks
1 unpeeled grapefruit, cut into 8 pieces
⅓ cup chopped macadamia nuts or sliced almonds or shredded coconut

MARINADE–BASTE–TOPPING SAUCE

½ cup unsweetened pineapple juice (or syrup from canned chunks)
½ cup brown sugar
6 tablespoons cider vinegar
2 tablespoons soy sauce

1½ teaspoons salt
¼ teaspoon ginger
2 teaspoons cornstarch dissolved in 2 tablespoons cold water
1 cup crushed pineapple

One hour in advance: Season chicken pieces with salt to taste. Thread skewers as follows: cherry . CHICKEN . orange . CHICKEN . pineapple . CHICKEN . grapefruit . CHICKEN . pineapple . cherry. Place kebobs in foil-lined baking pan. In saucepan, combine sauce ingredients omitting cornstarch mixture and crushed pineapple and heat until sugar dissolves.

Spoon half the sauce over kebobs. Let stand at room temperature.

Before serving: Drain kebobs and arrange on baking pan with skewer tips suspended from edges of pan. Bake in preheated 350° oven for 15 to 20 minutes. Turn and bake another 10 minutes. Add crushed pineapple and cornstarch mixture to thicken remaining sauce in saucepan. Spoon over kebobs about 5 minutes before done. Sprinkle with chopped nuts or coconut.

Variation: On skewer, substitute or add sliced papaya or kumquats.

HIGHLIGHTS OF ONE SPICE

A Selection of Single-Spiced Chicken Kebobs

BROIL: *Each of the recipes makes 6 10-inch skewers*

4 whole chicken breasts,
   skinned, boned, and cut into
   36 to 40 1½-inch pieces

Skewered GINGER Chicken . . . ginger, the rhizome (root) of a tuberous plant, imparts a fragrant, pungent spiciness. Available as whole and ground.

MARINADE–BASTE

½ cup dry sherry	1 to 1½ teaspoons ground
¼ cup melted butter	ginger, to taste
1 clove garlic, minced	1 teaspoon salt
Green onions, cut into 24 3-inch	18 cherry tomatoes
pieces, folded once	

ROSEMARY Chicken Kebobs . . . rosemary, a spiked-leaved herb that looks like curved pine needles, tastes sweet and fresh. Available as leaves and ground.

MARINADE–BASTE

½ cup Chablis
½ cup chopped onion
¼ cup vegetable oil

1½ teaspoons rosemary leaves
1 teaspoon salt

18 jumbo mushrooms

24 black pitted olives

CUMIN Chicken Kebobs . . . cumin, a small dried fruit oblong in shape, resembles caraway seeds. The flavor is sharp. Available as seeds and ground.

MARINADE–BASTE

⅓ cup melted butter
¼ cup tomato sauce
¼ cup sliced onion
1 teaspoon salt

½ teaspoon ground cumin
¼ teaspoon freshly ground
black pepper

2 green peppers cut into 18
pieces

24 tomato wedges

TARRAGON Chicken Kebobs . . . tarragon, a small perennial plant which forms tall stalks, is minty and mildly anise-like in flavor. Available as leaves.

MARINADE–BASTE

¼ cup safflower oil
¼ cup lemon juice
1 clove garlic, minced

1 teaspoon tarragon leaves
1 teaspoon salt
⅛ teaspoon ground marjoram

18 artichokes
2 4-ounce jars pimiento, cut
into 24 pieces

One hour in advance: Combine marinade–baste ingredients of your choice. Add pieces of chicken. Cover. Let stand at room temperature.

Before serving: Thread chicken on skewers, alternating with suggested accompaniments. Broil at 400° 4 to 5 inches from source of heat for 10 to 12 minutes; turn; baste and broil an additional 8 to 10 minutes, until chicken is tender and still juicy.

Note on side dishes: Avoid serving other foods that are highly seasoned. Let the spice in the kebobs predominate. You might consider carrot soufflé, baked or boiled potatoes, buttered vegetables.

Skewered Chicken, Soup-Inspired

BROIL: *Makes 6 10-inch skewers*

Here you have kebobs with your choice of flavor accents —oregano or paprika. Serve with potato croquettes, a crisp green salad, and, of course, the Chicken Soup Avgolemono, page 281.

1 whole breast of roaster chicken (reserved from chicken soup, page 281), skinned, boned, and cut into 8 to 10 1½-inch pieces

3 whole chicken breasts, skinned, boned, and cut into 28 to 30 1½-inch pieces
30 onion wedges or 30 cherry tomatoes

MARINADE–BASTES

Paprika

½ cup safflower oil
¼ cup freshly squeezed lemon juice (1 lemon)

1 tablespoon flour
1 teaspoon salt
1 teaspoon paprika

. . . OR . . .

Oregano

½ cup olive oil
¼ cup freshly squeezed lemon juice (1 lemon)
1 small onion, sliced and separated into rings

1 teaspoon salt
1 teaspoon oregano leaves

One hour in advance: Combine marinade–baste ingredients of your choice. Mix very well. Add chicken. Cover. Let stand at room temperature.

Before serving: Thread chicken on skewers alternately with the onions or tomatoes, beginning and ending with chicken. Broil at 400° 4 to 5 inches from source of heat for 10 to 12 minutes; turn; baste and broil an additional 8 to 10 minutes until done.

Skewered Chicken, Japanese Accent

BRAISE: *Makes 4 6-inch skewers*

Serve as a substantial appetizer . . . a very interesting, even exceptional snack.

2 whole chicken breasts, skinned, boned, and cut into 16 to 20 1½-inch pieces
1 green pepper, cut into 8 pieces
8 slices of onion, about 1½-inch squares
3 tablespoons soy sauce

3 tablespoons dry sherry
1 tablespoon brown sugar
1 egg, well beaten
¾ cup flour
1 tablespoon butter or margarine
2 tablespoons pure sesame oil

TOPPING SAUCE

2 tablespoons melted butter or margarine
2 tablespoons dry sherry

1 tablespoon soy sauce
1 tablespoon prepared horseradish

Thread skewers as follows: CHICKEN . green pepper . CHICKEN . onion . CHICKEN . green pepper . CHICKEN . onion . CHICKEN. Combine soy sauce, wine and brown sugar. Pour over kebobs in shallow plate. Let stand about 10 minutes, turning occasionally. Roll kebobs in beaten egg and then in flour, coating well. Heat oil and butter in skillet. Add kebobs and brown 5 minutes, turn and brown another 5 minutes. Cover. Cook slowly an additional 15 to 20 minutes until done. Combine and heat sauce ingredients and spread over each kebob before serving.

Indonesian Chicken Saté

BROIL: *Makes 5 6-inch skewers*

Saté is the Indonesian name for grilled pieces of meat—chicken, mutton, or pork—threaded on thin bamboo sticks about one foot long. Immediately upon removing from grill, the saté is dipped in a peanut or soy sauce in one of two ways. Either the pieces are removed one at a time with a fork and dipped individually in sauce, or the entire saté is dipped in the sauce and the meat is eaten right from the stick, the meat covering only the top half of stick, with space below for a firm hand grasp. According to Indonesians, the first way spoils the fun of it.

2 whole chicken breasts,
  skinned, boned, and cut into
  16 to 20 1½-inch pieces

MARINADE–BASTE

1 clove garlic, crushed
1 teaspoon sugar
3 tablespoons each of soy
  sauce, pure sesame oil,
  orange juice and lemon juice

PEANUT DIP SAUCE

⅓ cup crushed pineapple, well
  drained
2 teaspoons soy sauce
1 tablespoon dark molasses
2 tablespoons lemon juice
2 teaspoons grated lemon rind
⅓ cup peanut butter

¼ teaspoon each of chili
  powder, curry powder, and
  ground coriander
⅛ teaspoon each of ginger and
  garlic powder
1 tablespoon finely chopped
  onion

Three hours in advance: Combine marinade–baste ingredients in a bowl. Add chicken pieces. Cover. In a blender, combine dip sauce ingredients and blend until smooth. Put sauce in dip cups ready for use when serving.

Before serving: Thread chicken on skewers. Broil at 400° 4 to 5 inches from source of heat for 10 to 12 minutes, turn and baste with marinade–baste sauce, and broil another 8 to 9 minutes. If desired, grill on a small hibachi over medium-hot coals.

Indian Chicken Tikka

BROIL: *Makes 8 6-inch skewers*

In India and Pakistan, a popular kebob served as a snack or appetizer is *murgh tikka,* which refers to boned chicken (*murgh*) cut into bite-size pieces (*tikka*), marinated in a curry-spiced yogurt, threaded on skewers, and broiled or grilled over coals. It's frequently served with onion rings and a lime garnish.

4 whole chicken breasts, skinned, boned, and cut into 36 to 40 1½-inch pieces	8 slices of lime 8 slices of lemon

MARINADE

1½ cups plain yogurt
¼ cup finely grated cucumber
¼ cup finely chopped onion
1 teaspoon turmeric
1 teaspoon salt
½ teaspoon ground coriander

¼ teaspoon each of ground cinnamon, cardamom, cloves, and cumin
⅛ teaspoon ginger
3 bay leaves, crumbled

BASTE

5 tablespoons melted butter

3 tablespoons lime juice

Three hours in advance: Combine marinade ingredients in a bowl. Add chicken. Cover. Turn occasionally.

Before serving: Thread chicken on skewers as follows: CHICKEN . lime . CHICKEN . CHICKEN . CHICKEN . lemon . CHICKEN. Broil at 400° 4 to 5 inches from source of heat 10 to 12 minutes, turn and baste with baste sauce, and broil another 8 to 9 minutes. Baste generously before serving.

Variation: These are exceptionally good grilled. If you wish, grill on a small hibachi over a medium-hot bed of coals.

Chicken Kebobs Sicilian

BAKE: *Makes 6 10-inch skewers*

These are characterized by a cacciatore-like flavor. Serve with green noodles topped with grated Romano cheese. Garnish with parsley sprigs.

4 whole chicken breasts, skinned, boned, and cut into 36 to 40 1½-inch pieces

24 jumbo black pitted olives
18 large whole mushrooms, canned

MARINADE–BASTE

½ cup tomato sauce
½ cup dry sherry
¼ cup olive oil
3 cloves garlic, minced

1 teaspoon salt
½ teaspoon oregano
½ teaspoon basil

One and one-half hours in advance: Combine marinade–baste ingredients in a bowl. Add chicken pieces. Stir to coat well. Cover. Let stand at room temperature.

Before serving: Thread chicken on skewer, alternating with olives and mushrooms, beginning and ending with olives. Bake in preheated 350° oven for 15 minutes. Turn, baste, and bake an additional 10 to 15 minutes. Baste generously with sauce before serving.

Chicken Kebobs Spartan

BAKE: *Makes 6 10-inch skewers*

If you're familiar with Greek dishes, you'll find this tastes similar to Kapama. Serve with boiled macaroni topped with grated Kefalotiri cheese and melted butter, slightly burnt. Garnish plate with parsley. Accompany with side dish of Greek Salad, page 291.

4 whole chicken breasts, skinned, boned, and cut into 36 to 40 1½-inch pieces

24 onion wedges
18 pieces of lemon peel or lemon wedges

MARINADE–BASTE

½ cup tomato sauce
½ cup Chablis (or white Demestica wine)
¼ cup melted butter
2 tablespoons lemon juice
2 cloves garlic, minced

1 teaspoon onion, minced
1 teaspoon salt
½ teaspoon freshly ground black pepper
¼ teaspoon cinnamon

One and one-half hours in advance: Combine marinade–baste ingredients in a bowl. Add chicken pieces and stir. Cover. Let stand at room temperature.

Before serving: Thread chicken on skewer, alternating with onions and lemon pieces, beginning and ending with onions. Bake in preheated 350° oven for 15 minutes. Turn, baste, and bake an additional 10 to 15 minutes. Baste well before serving.

White Wine Poultry Kebobs

With this recipe, first decide which imported or domestic white wine you'd like to use as a beverage, and then use the same for cooking. You might select the heavier, aperitif kind of wine, dry vermouth. Or, perhaps you'd prefer Chablis, a dry table wine, or the sweeter Sauternes or Rhines; or, you might discern the difference in taste from wines named after one kind of grape, such as Pinot Chardonnay or Pinot Blanc, Dry Sémillon or Sauvignon Blanc; or Gewürztraminer, Johannisberg, Riesling, and so on. After you've determined the wine, select one of the marinade–bastes below and then also decide the fruit or vegetables that you'll want to thread on the skewer with the poultry; finally, choose whatever indoor or outdoor method of cooking kebobs is most convenient.

4 pounds boned chicken or turkey, dark or light meat
Companions for threading on skewer (fruit, vegetables, or none)
Salt, sprinkled or saturated to taste

Choice of Marinade–Bastes, three versions

VERSION I (*very simple*)

½ cup white wine

. . . OR . . .

VERSION II (*simple*)

½ cup white wine
⅓ cup melted butter

1 tablespoon paprika

. . . OR . . .

VERSION III (*sophisticated*)

Marinade:

½ cup white wine of your choice
¼ cup peanut oil
2 tablespoons lemon juice
2 tablespoons finely chopped onion
2 tablespoons soy sauce
2 tablespoons chopped parsley
1 clove garlic, minced

Baste:

⅓ cup clarified butter
1 teaspoon paprika

One hour in advance: Cut poultry into 1½-inch pieces. Combine marinade–baste ingredients of choice—very simple, simple or the marinade for the sophisticated version. Add poultry. Cover. Let stand at room temperature.

Before serving: Season poultry pieces with salt. Thread on skewer with selected companions. Broil or bake—or grill over coals outdoors.

Baste generously with marinade–baste. If you select the sophisticated version for basting, combine baste ingredients and brush kebobs with sauce as often as desired.

Chicken Kebobs à la Sauces and Crumbs

BAKE: *Makes 6 10-inch skewers*

Serve these baked kebobs as a snack with dip sauces. Before threading on skewer, coat pieces from each breast with a different sauce and cracker or bread crumb combination.

4 whole chicken breasts,
  skinned, boned, and cut into
  36 to 40 1½-inch pieces

SAUCES AND DRY BREAD CRUMBS

a) 2 tablespoons horseradish
  sauce
  3 to 4 tablespoons finely
  crumbled cracker crumbs
b) 2 tablespoons Sweet-Sour
  Dip Sauce (page 269)
  3 to 4 tablespoons finely
  crumbled graham-
  cracker crumbs

c) 2 tablespoons garlic
  dressing
  3 to 4 tablespoons
  Italian-seasoned bread
  crumbs
d) 2 tablespoons pizza sauce
  3 to 4 tablespoons French-
  bread crumbs

ACCOMPANIMENTS (on skewer)

For *a* and *b:* choice of mandarin oranges, water chestnuts, green pepper pieces, or pineapple chunks. For *c* and *d:* choice of pimiento pieces, black pitted olives stuffed with sharp cheese, cucumber slices, mushrooms, parboiled zucchini or eggplant chunks.

DIP SAUCES

For *a* and *b:* choice of soy sauce; Mustard Dip Sauces, page 269; Sweet-Sour Dip Sauce, page 269; or Sour Cream Dip Sauce, Sweet Accent, page 272. For *c* and *d:* choice of Spicy Cocktail Dip Sauces, pages 267–68.

Coat pieces of one breast (8 to 10 pieces) with one of the four sauce and bread crumb combinations. Dip pieces of breast in sauce and then coat well with crumbs. Repeat with the other breasts and coverings. Alternate the differently coated chicken pieces on one skewer, or for an Oriental-accented kebob thread "a" and "b" on skewers with choice of accompaniments, and for an Italian-accented kebob thread "c" and "d" on separate skewers with choice of accompaniments. Bake kebobs in preheated 350° oven on foil-lined baking pan for about 25 to 30 minutes. Serve with choice of dip sauces.

Variations: Marinate one hour in 4 tablespoons White Wine Marinade, Version III, page 182, and roll in 2 to 3 tablespoons seasoned breading mix; dip in 2 tablespoons melted butter mixed with 1 teaspoon anchovy paste and roll in 3 to 4 tablespoons French-bread crumbs.

LEFTOVER POULTRY

Use 6- or 10-inch skewers depending on how much poultry you have left over and how you want to serve the kebobs— for luncheon, snack, or appetizer.

Carrot and Poultry Kebobs

BAKE: *Makes assorted amounts*

Leftover cooked chicken or turkey (sliced or cubed)	1 teaspoon cinnamon
¼ cup melted butter or margarine	1 jar cooked whole carrots, cut into chunks

Dip leftover cooked poultry pieces in melted butter or margarine combined with cinnamon. Thread poultry on skewer alternately with carrots. Place skewers on foil-lined baking pan. Bake in preheated 350° oven until thoroughly heated, about 10 minutes.

Bamboo Shoots and Poultry Kebobs

BAKE: *Makes assorted amounts*

¼ cup melted butter or margarine
½ teaspoon freeze-dried chives
⅛ teaspoon ground nutmeg

Leftover cooked chicken or turkey (sliced or cubed)
1 can (6 ounces) bamboo shoots
Coarsely chopped cashew nuts

Combine butter, chives and nutmeg. Dip leftover cooked poultry in butter mixture. Thread poultry on skewers alternately with bamboo shoots. Place skewers on foil-lined pan. Bake in preheated 350° oven until thoroughly heated, about 10 minutes. Spread each kebob generously with cashew nuts and serve.

Variation: Dip poultry pieces in melted butter, dredge in Italian-bread crumbs, and thread on skewers alternately with bamboo shoots, pickles, and party salami, if you want a mixed meat kebob; omit nuts.

Apple and Poultry Kebobs

BAKE: *Makes assorted amounts*

Leftover cooked chicken or turkey (sliced or cubed)
¼ cup soy sauce
¼ cup melted butter (optional)
Pared and cored apple, cut into ¾-inch cubes

Mixture of 3 parts crushed potato chips to 1 part shredded sweetened coconut

Dip cooked poultry pieces in soy sauce. (For increased moisture, dip pieces in a combination of equal parts soy sauce and melted butter.) Thread poultry on skewer alternately with apple chunks. Place skewers on foil-lined baking pan and place in preheated 350° oven, about 10 to 12 minutes. Combine potato chips and coconut and spread mixture generously over each kebob.

Poultry Kebobs: Honey-Rum Accent

BAKE: *Makes assorted amounts*

Leftover cooked chicken or
    turkey (sliced or cubed)

Bananas, cut into 1-inch pieces
Green pepper

BASTE–TOPPING SAUCE

¾ cup honey
½ cup apple juice
2 tablespoons rum extract

2 tablespoons orange juice
¼ teaspoon allspice
¼ teaspoon nutmeg

Combine sauce ingredients in saucepan and simmer for about 5 minutes, stirring occasionally. Thread poultry on skewer alternately with green pepper and banana. Place on foil-lined baking sheet. Bake in preheated 350° oven, about 10 minutes. Baste often. Top with remaining sauce if desired.

Poultry Kebobs: Southern or Northern Style

BAKE: *Makes assorted amounts*

Leftover cooked chicken or
    turkey (sliced or cubed)

SOUTHERN VERSION

Accompaniments on Skewer

Sliced papaya or pineapple
    chunks

BASTE–TOPPING SAUCE

¾ cup orange juice

½ teaspoon cinnamon

⅓ cup apricot brandy

NORTHERN VERSION

Accompaniments on Skewer

Pimiento pieces, whole
    mushrooms, and black
    pitted olives

BASTE–TOPPING SAUCE

1 can (10¾ ounces) undiluted
    cream of mushroom soup

Chablis

Thread poultry on skewer, alternating with accompaniments. Bake in preheated 350° oven for about 10 minutes until heated thoroughly. Baste often. If you select the southern version, combine sauce ingredients in saucepan and stir over low heat. After using as a baste, thicken remaining sauce with 1 or 2 teaspoons cornstarch dissolved in water and serve as topping. If you select the northern version, fill empty can of soup with Chablis and combine with the soup in a saucepan. Stir over low heat. After basting, use as a topping.

12 · SHELLFISH AND FISH

WHAT TO CONSIDER BEFORE SKEWER-COOKING SHELLFISH AND FISH

In this section I have placed shellfish before fish because shellfish is easier to skewer-cook. However, both types of seafood share certain requirements for successful preparation. To start out, they must be fresh—and the fresher the better. It's best to patronize a market that sells fresh fish and shellfish daily, but where these are unavailable, use the frozen products, by all means. Second, when marinating seafood for more than three-fourths of an hour, keep it in the refrigerator. I usually put it there directly. And the third point is to avoid overcooking, which, of course, results in toughening and drying. Note, too, that broiled and baked kebobs generally won't require turning. If you do turn them, please do so carefully—only once, and allow at least half the total cooking time to elapse first, particularly with fish. Finally, the significance of salt. With seafood more than with any other food, I find the liberal use of this seasoning absolutely necessary for optimum flavor. And if lemon is called for in a recipe, the same applies to it. Do be generous, unless prohibited for medical reasons.

Most shellfish—shrimp, lobster, crab, oysters, scallops—make an impressive meal, snack, or appetizer for entertaining. And of this group, shrimp seems to lead in popularity. When cooking shrimp on 10-inch skewers, the large or jumbo size are indispensable both for appearance and taste. Small shrimp tend to dry out. Of course, small cooked shrimp served chilled on 6-inch skewers are perfectly inviting as part of an hors d'oeuvres assortment. When purchasing, remember that one pound in the shell provides about one-half pound shelled.

Oysters are the most challenging of the shellfish to skewer-cook because they're so slippery, but any trouble in spearing them seems insignificant once they are served and thoroughly enjoyed. Scallops, on the other hand, are the easiest of the shellfish to spear and cook. Basically, there are two kinds. The first—sea scallops—have a saucer-shaped shell and grow as large as 8 inches in diameter, with the muscle, or "eye" (the only part eaten in the United States), sometimes reaching 2 inches across. The other—bay scallops—are more grooved and the edges more serrated; these reach a maximum of 4 inches in diameter with the "eye" about 1½ inches across. Since scallops are shucked aboard ship as soon as they're caught, and then iced immediately, scallops don't appear in the marketplace with the shells. For skewer-cooking, I prefer the sea scallop but the bay, too, can be used. Try scallops on a skewer with fruits or vegetables, or, as in one recipe here, with shrimp.

At last, fish. It must be handled very gently for broiling or baking. In fact, many varieties can't be used because during cooking they crumble off the skewer. Which adapt best? I'd say those of rather firm flesh, such as halibut, salmon, swordfish, and Greenland turbot. And which adapt best to braising? Try perch, trout, or red snapper fillets. When you're cutting fish steaks into pieces, note that the combination of tender flesh with the tougher skin creates some difficulty. Simply alleviate the problem by using an extra-sharp knife. When cutting pieces of fish for use in broiling or baking, leave the skin on one side if you wish; and then when threading, spear the skewer through the skin or through the thin membrane next to it.

When threading strips of fish for braising, fold them in

half (skin side out) so that the skewer can be speared through the skin twice. Now for that task, you'll definitely need skewers with extra-sharp points. Allow half a pound boned fish per person.

Compared to shellfish, fish provides a more economical source of protein and minerals. In my opinion, it ranks as an excellent main dish feature, a refreshingly light change of pace to meat.

Lobster en Brochette

BROIL: *Makes 3 10-inch skewers*

1½ pounds lobster tails in the shell, thawed

1 lemon, cut into 6 wedges (or slices)

MARINADE

⅓ cup melted butter
⅓ cup dry sherry
2 tablespoons chopped parsley

2 tablespoons lemon juice
1 teaspoon salt
2 bay leaves

BASTE

¼ cup melted butter

Forty-five minutes in advance: Cut underside membrane of lobster tail around edges and remove shell. Cut lobster meat into 12 to 15 chunks. Combine marinade ingredients in a bowl. Add chunks of lobster, cover. Stir occasionally.

Before serving: Season lobster with additional salt if desired. Thread several chunks of lobster on skewer alternately with two lemon wedges per skewer. Broil at 425° 4 to 5 inches from source of heat for 7 to 10 minutes. Turn once and baste with melted butter, brushing generously just before serving. If desired, serve melted clarified butter in small cups for dipping.

Jumbo Shrimp Kebobs

BROIL: *Makes 8 10-inch skewers*

2 pounds raw jumbo shrimp,
  shelled and deveined (about
  25)
8 jumbo-size black pitted
  olives
1 green pepper cut into 8
  pieces

½ pound fresh mushrooms
  (about 16)
8 large pimiento-stuffed olives
8 cherry tomatoes

MARINADE–BASTE

⅔ cup vegetable oil
⅓ cup wine vinegar
2 tablespoons sherry
2 bay leaves

1 teaspoon Worcestershire
  sauce
¼ teaspoon fennel seed

One and one-half hours in advance: Combine marinade-baste ingredients in a large bowl. Mix well. Add shrimp. Cover and marinate in refrigerator, stirring occasionally.

Before serving: Thread each skewer as follows: SHRIMP wrapped around black olive . green pepper . mushroom . SHRIMP wrapped around pimiento olive . mushroom . SHRIMP wrapped around tomato. Broil at 425° 4 to 5 inches from source of heat for 12 to 15 minutes, turning once and basting often.

Variation: Substitute cucumber chunks for pimiento olive.

SHRIMP SELECTION:
Spiced • Sweet-Sour • Spiked

Spiced Shrimp Kebobs

BROIL: *Makes 4 10-inch skewers*

1 pound large raw shrimp,
  shelled and deveined (about
  25 to 27)

8 dill pickle cubes or slices
1 jar (4 ounces) pimientos,
  contents divided into 8 pieces

MARINADE–BASTE

⅓ cup vegetable oil
¼ cup ketchup
2 tablespoons lemon juice
1 tablespoon vinegar

½ teaspoon chili powder
½ teaspoon salt
⅛ teaspoon mild curry powder
½ clove garlic, minced

Two hours in advance: Combine marinade-baste ingredients in a bowl. Add shrimp. Cover. Let stand in refrigerator.
Before serving: Thread on skewer as follows: several SHRIMP . dill pickle . pimiento . several SHRIMP . dill pickle . pimiento . several SHRIMP. Broil at 425° 4 to 5 inches from source of heat about 5 to 6 minutes on each side, basting occasionally.

Sweet-Sour Shrimp Kebobs

BROIL: *Makes 4 10-inch skewers*

1 pound large raw shrimp, shelled and deveined (about 25 to 27)
1 green pepper cut into 12 pieces
½ small fresh pineapple, pared, cored, and cut into 8 chunks (about 1½-inch pieces)

1 teaspoon cornstarch dissolved in 2 teaspoons cold water

MARINADE–BASTE TOPPING

⅔ cup unsweetened pineapple juice
1 tablespoon soy sauce
1 tablespoon white vinegar
2 tablespoons lemon juice
3 tablespoons brown sugar

1 teaspoon prepared mustard
1 teaspoon salt
½ tablespoon celery flakes, crushed
⅛ teaspoon ginger

TOPPING MIXTURE

1 can (11 ounces) mandarin oranges, well drained and then finely chopped
1 can (6 ounces) water chestnuts, very well drained and then shredded

2 tablespoons imitation bacon bits or 4 slices crisp-cooked bacon, finely crumbled
2 tablespoons chopped parsley
1 teaspoon grated lemon peel

Forty minutes in advance: Combine marinade–baste topping ingredients in a bowl. Add shrimp. Cover. Set aside. In another bowl combine topping mixture, tossing well. Set aside.

Before serving: Thread shrimp on skewers, allowing 3 pieces of green pepper and 2 chunks of pineapple per skewer. Heat marinade in saucepan and add 1 teaspoon cornstarch dissolved in 2 teaspoons cold water to thicken. Broil kebobs at 425° 4 to 5 inches from source of heat about 5 to 6 minutes on each side, basting generously with sauce after turning. Apply remaining baste as a topping sauce, spread topping mixture on each kebob, and serve.

Spiked Shrimp Kebobs

BROIL: *Makes 4 10-inch skewers*

1 pound large raw shrimp, shelled and deveined (about 25 to 27)

8 whole boiled onions
4 pimiento-stuffed olives

MARINADE

⅓ cup dry sherry
⅓ cup peanut oil
2 tablespoons finely chopped parsley
1 teaspoon tarragon leaves
¼ teaspoon each of fennel seed and dill weed

1 clove garlic, crushed
1 teaspoon salt
1 teaspoon instant minced onion

BASTE

¼ cup melted butter   3 tablespoons dry sherry

One hour in advance: Combine marinade ingredients in a bowl. Add shrimp. Cover and let stand in refrigerator.

Before serving: Thread each skewer as follows: several SHRIMP . onion . SHRIMP wrapped around olive . onion . several SHRIMP. Broil at 425° 4 to 5 inches from source of heat about 5 to 6 minutes on each side. Combine baste ingredients and brush generously during cooking.

Variation: Begin and end skewer with green pepper pieces.

Skewered Shellfish Trio

BROIL: *Makes 5 10-inch skewers*

 1 pound king crab legs in shell
10 large raw shrimp in the shell
½ pound rock lobster tail in the shell, thawed
 5 pimiento-stuffed olives

5 boiled onions from jar
5 slices (¼ inch thick) cucumber, halved
1 large green pepper, cut into 10 pieces
¼ cup melted butter (optional)

MARINADES

Crab

2 tablespoons chopped celery
2 tablespoons chopped green onion
½ cup olive oil
2 tablespoons lemon juice

1 tablespoon minced parsley
1 teaspoon mint, crushed
½ teaspoon salt
3 tablespoons Madeira

Shrimp

⅓ cup salad oil
3 tablespoons red wine vinegar
¼ teaspoon Worcestershire sauce
2 tablespoons tomato juice

2 bay leaves, crushed
1 teaspoon tarragon leaves
1 clove garlic, crushed
½ teaspoon freshly ground black pepper

Lobster

¼ cup melted butter	2 tablespoons lemon juice
2 tablespoons chopped pimiento, drained (2-ounce jar)	1 teaspoon paprika
	1 teaspoon grated lemon rind
	¼ teaspoon salt

One and one-half hours in advance: Crack shell of crab at joints, carefully removing crab. Cut into 10 chunks. Combine crab marinade ingredients and add chunks. Cover. Refrigerate. Shell and devein shrimp. Combine shrimp marinade ingredients and add shrimp. Cover. Refrigerate.

Forty minutes before serving: With sharp knife, remove thin shell on underside of lobster tail. With fingers, carefully pull out lobster. Cut into 5 1-inch pieces. Combine lobster marinade ingredients and add pieces of lobster. Cover. Let stand at room temperature.

Before serving: Thread skewers as follows: cucumber . LOBSTER . green pepper . CRAB . SHRIMP wrapped around olive . CRAB . green pepper . SHRIMP wrapped around onion . cucumber. Broil 4 to 5 inches from source of heat at 425°, 12 to 15 minutes, turning once. If desired, baste with melted butter.

Skewered Scallops with Fruits or Vegetables

BROIL: *Makes 3 10-inch skewers*

Here on the skewer with scallops, you have a choice of accompaniments—vegetables or fruits. If you wish to serve both versions, remember to double the amount of scallops.

1 12-ounce package frozen scallops, thawed (bay or sea)	¼ cup soy sauce

VEGETABLE VERSION

12 cherry tomatoes
1 green pepper, cut into 9 pieces

¼ cup melted butter
2 teaspoons minced parsley

. . . OR . . .

FRUIT VERSION

6 thin strips bacon
9 pineapple chunks, canned or fresh
9 mandarin oranges, canned (or fresh orange cut into 9 wedges)

Orange peel cut into squares
6 maraschino cherries (optional)
Grated orange rind (optional)

Dip scallops in soy sauce. Drain on paper towel.

To prepare the skewer with vegetable accompaniments: Thread skewers as follows: tomato . SCALLOPS . green pepper . tomato . SCALLOPS . green pepper . tomato . SCALLOPS . green pepper . tomato . SCALLOPS. Combine melted butter with parsley and brush kebobs. Broil at 425° 4 to 5 inches from source of heat for 5 minutes. Baste with remaining butter and parsley. Turn and cook for 5 to 7 minutes longer until scallops are delicately brown, yet still moist.

Variation: Before serving, sprinkle with grated Romano cheese.

To prepare the skewer with fruit accompaniments: Thread skewers as follows, weaving bacon strips (2 per skewer) back and forth between scallops and fruit in a spiral effect: orange peel . SCALLOPS . pineapple . orange . SCALLOPS . pineapple . orange . SCALLOPS . pineapple . orange . orange peel. Broil at 425° 4 to 5 inches from source of heat for 12 to 14 minutes or until bacon is crisp. If more color and sweetness are preferred, substitute maraschino cherries for orange and sprinkle kebobs with grated orange rind.

Variation: Add or substitute for the above fruit: banana chunks dipped in beaten egg white and rolled in chopped nuts. If you want the fruit kebob cooked in less time, parboil bacon 3 to 5 minutes before threading on skewer.

Skewered Scallops and Shrimp

BAKE: *Makes 6 10-inch skewers*

12 large raw shrimp, shelled and deveined
 1 pound frozen sea scallops (about 16 to 18), thawed
½ cup French-bread crumbs

18 slices unpared cucumbers, ¼ inch thick
 6 bay leaves (optional)
12 small pimiento-stuffed olives

MARINADE–BASTE FOR SHRIMP

See Spiced Shrimp Kebobs, page 191

SAUCE FOR SCALLOPS

3 tablespoons melted butter
3 tablespoons orange juice
½ teaspoon dill weed

1 teaspoon freeze-dried chives
½ teaspoon each of orange and lemon rind

Forty minutes in advance: Combine marinade ingredients. Add shrimp. Cover.

Before serving: Combine melted butter, orange juice, dill weed, chives, orange and lemon rind. Add scallops and let stand five minutes. Dredge scallops in crumbs, coating well. Thread skewers as follows: SCALLOP . cucumber . SHRIMP curved around olive . bay leaf . SCALLOP . cucumber . SHRIMP curved around olive . cucumber . SCALLOP. Bake in preheated 400° oven for 12 to 15 minutes. Baste shrimp with remaining sauce.

Variation: An idea for appetizers—use ½ pound fresh bay scallops. Prepare one-half the butter sauce and roll scallops in ¼ cup dry bread crumbs. Thread on 6-inch skewers, alternating with olives and dill pickles.

Oyster Kebobs Parmesan

BROIL: *Makes 4 6-inch skewers*

If I know someone is keen on oysters, I serve these.

12 ounces fresh oysters
  (approximately 14 to 16)
Salt to taste
 1 egg, slightly beaten

½ cup grated Parmesan cheese
 1 small bunch green onions,
   the green part cut into 1-inch
   pieces

BASTE–TOPPING

½ cup Madeira
¼ cup melted butter
 1 teaspoon cornstarch
   dissolved in 1 tablespoon
   cold water

Drain oysters on paper towel. Season with salt to taste. Dip in slightly beaten egg. Roll in grated cheese. Thread on skewer as follows: several green onions . two OYSTERS . several green onions . two OYSTERS . several green onions. Allow 4 oysters per skewer. Broil at 425° 4 to 5 inches from source of heat 5 to 6 minutes on each side. Combine Madeira and melted butter, and baste kebobs. Before serving, heat sauce and add one teaspoon cornstarch dissolved in one tablespoon cold water and stir over heat until thickened. Spread generously over kebobs. Serve with toasted bread triangles.

Skewered Wrapped Oysters

BAKE: *Makes 3 10-inch skewers*

12 ounces fresh oysters
  (approximately 14 to 16)
 7 strips of bacon, halved
   crosswise

6 mushroom caps, canned or
   fresh
 1 green pepper, cut into 6
   pieces

Drain oysters on paper towel. Wrap each oyster in bacon. Thread skewers as follows: OYSTER . mushroom . OYSTER . green pepper . OYSTER . mushroom . OYSTER . green pepper . OYSTER. Bake in preheated 375° oven for 20 to 25 minutes or until bacon is crisp. (To bake oysters in less time, parboil bacon 3 to 5 minutes before wrapping.)

Variation: To make 7 6-inch skewers, make the following substitutions in the recipe above. Use two green peppers cut into 14 pieces and use 14 mushroom caps. Thread each skewer with two of the oysters wrapped in bacon alternately with two each of the green pepper pieces and mushrooms. Cook as above. If desired, top with Sauce Mornay, page 259. (Note, too, you may prefer to wrap only one of the two oysters on each kebob with bacon.)

FRESH FISH PLUS LEMONS

The most characteristic seasoning in Greek cooking is lemon. In fact, many Greeks squeeze it on nearly all their food—admittedly, at times the "lemoni" is overdone. Perhaps the only food where its lavish use is appreciated by everyone is fresh fish. Few would disagree here, I'm sure. Fresh fish plus lemons are simply a natural twosome.

Each of the following recipes has a lemon tang, yet each also has its own distinctive accent—domata (tomato), oregano, and curry. With each recipe, use two fresh lemons. Squeeze the lemon for juice as required in sauce. Remove peel and cut into pieces for threading. If this amount is too piquant for you, then squeeze only one lemon and cut the other into wedges or slices for threading on skewer. Select a firm-fleshed fish such as halibut, salmon, or Greenland turbot. Broil fish until done, or until fish flakes easily when touched with a fork.

Fish Kebobs: Lemon and Domata Accent

BROIL: *Makes 4 to 5 10-inch skewers*

1 pound firm-fleshed fish, cut
into about 20 1-inch pieces

8 pieces lemon peel
8 cucumber chunks

MARINADE–BASTE

⅓ to ½ cup freshly squeezed
lemon juice (2 lemons)
¼ cup tomato sauce
¼ cup olive oil
1 tablespoon finely chopped
parsley
½ teaspoon tarragon leaves
½ teaspoon celery flakes,
crushed

½ teaspoon dried mint,
crushed
¼ teaspoon freshly ground
black pepper
1 bay leaf
⅛ teaspoon ground cinnamon
1 clove garlic, crushed
1 teaspoon salt

Two hours in advance: Combine marinade-baste ingredients in a bowl. Stir well. Add fish. Cover. Refrigerate.

Before serving: Thread fish on skewer alternately with lemon peel and cucumber, beginning and ending with lemon peel. Baste. Broil at 425° 4 to 5 inches from source of heat 7 to 9 minutes, turn, and continue broiling an additional 7 to 9 minutes until done.

Variation: Substitute boiled onions, black pitted olives, or mushrooms for cucumbers.

Fish Kebobs: Lemon and Riganato Accent

BROIL: *Makes 4 to 5 10-inch skewers*

1 pound firm-fleshed fish cut
into about 20 1-inch pieces
4 bay leaves (optional)
1 14-ounce can whole artichoke
hearts (about 8 to 10)

1 large green pepper cut into
8 pieces
8 pieces lemon peel

MARINADE–BASTE

⅓ to ½ cup freshly squeezed
   lemon juice (2 lemons)
¼ cup olive oil
1½ teaspoons oregano leaves

2 bay leaves
1 teaspoon salt
1 clove garlic, minced
1 tablespoon finely chopped
   parsley

One hour in advance: Whip marinade–baste ingredients in a bowl. Add fish and cover. Refrigerate.

Before serving: Thread fish on skewer, allowing 1 bay leaf, 1 to 2 artichokes, 2 pieces green pepper and, of course, the lemon peel. Baste. Broil at 425° 4 to 5 inches from source of heat for 7 to 9 minutes, turn, and continue broiling about 7 to 9 minutes until done.

Variation: Substitute whole canned onions for artichokes.

Fish Kebobs: Lemon and Curry Accent

BROIL: *Makes 4 to 5 10-inch skewers*

1 pound firm-fleshed fish cut
   into about 20 1-inch pieces
1 green pepper cut into 8
   pieces

1 jar (4 ounces) whole
   pimientos, contents divided
   into 8 pieces
8 pieces lemon peel

MARINADE–BASTE

½ cup vegetable oil
⅓ to ½ cup freshly squeezed
   lemon juice (2 lemons)

1 teaspoon mild curry powder
1 teaspoon salt

Two hours in advance: Combine marinade–baste ingredients in a bowl. Add fish and cover. Refrigerate.

Before serving: Thread fish on skewers alternately with green pepper, pimiento pieces, and lemon peel. Begin and end with lemon. Baste with remaining sauce or melted butter. Broil at 425° 4 to 5 inches from source of heat for 7 to 9 minutes, turn, and continue broiling about 7 to 9 minutes until done.

Variations: Cut unseasoned fish, sprinkle with salt to taste, thread on skewers with lemon wedges, and baste with melted butter. Serve with Hollandaise sauce, page 261; cocktail or tartar sauces; or Clarified Butter, page 265.

Fish Kebobs Skordalia

BAKE: *Makes 6 10-inch skewers*

This is only for those fond of garlic (*skordo*).

3 cups Skordalia Sauce, page 264
2 pounds halibut, cut into 34 to 36 1-inch squares

2 lemons, each cut into 6 wedges
6 cloves garlic (optional)
6 cherry tomatoes

One hour in advance: Place 1½ cups of the Skordalia Sauce in a bowl. Add pieces of fish. Cover and refrigerate.

Before serving: Arrange fish on skewers, alternating with two lemon wedges and, if desired, a clove of garlic. Bake in preheated 350° oven for 15 minutes, turn, bake an additional 15 minutes. Place cherry tomato on tip of each skewer near end of baking. Use remaining 1½ cups of garlic sauce to top kebobs, or put it in bowl and serve for self-helpings. Accompany with side dishes of pickled beets and fried zucchini.

Variation: Alternate fish on a skewer with green pepper pieces.

Skewered Fish Plaki

BAKE: *Makes 6 10-inch skewers*

The response you should get from someone first entering your home while you're cooking the Greek Plaki sauce is this: "Hmmm—what smells so great!"

2 pounds halibut, cut into 34 to 36 1-inch pieces	Green onions, cut into 3-inch pieces, folded once
12 whole mushrooms, canned	1 lemon, cut into 6 wedges

PLAKI TOPPING SAUCE

¼ cup olive oil	½ teaspoon dill weed
2 medium onions, finely chopped	1 teaspoon salt
½ cup chopped green onions	⅛ teaspoon freshly ground black pepper
3 cloves garlic, minced	½ cup golden raisins
½ cup tomato puree	½ cup chopped parsley
1 cup Chablis	

In a skillet, sauté onions and garlic in oil until onions are tender and slightly brown. Add tomato puree, wine, dill, salt and pepper. Stir and simmer until liquid is reduced to one-third the original amount. Add raisins and parsley. Remove from heat. Cover and put aside. Salt fish to taste and thread on skewers alternately with mushrooms, green onion, and lemon wedges until skewer is filled. Pour Plaki Sauce over skewers. Bake in preheated 350° oven for 20 minutes, turn, bake an additional 10 to 15 minutes. Accompany with mashed potatoes, fresh fruit salad, and snow peas with almonds.

Skewered Salmon

BROIL: *Makes 4 10-inch skewers*

2 pounds salmon steaks (about
  4 1-inch salmon steaks, each
  boned and cut into 4 pieces)
1 small eggplant, cubed

1 teaspoon salt
2 tomatoes, each cut into 4
  wedges

MARINADE–BASTE

½ cup Rhine wine
⅓ cup vegetable oil
2 teaspoons minced parsley
½ teaspoon tarragon leaves

½ teaspoon salt
¼ teaspoon celery salt
¼ teaspoon dill seed

One and one-half hours in advance: Combine marinade–baste ingredients in a bowl. Add pieces of fish. Cover. Let stand in refrigerator.

Thirty minutes in advance: Sprinkle eggplant with 1 teaspoon salt and let stand in a bowl, tossing occasionally.

Before serving: Drain eggplant and dry. Thread salmon on skewers alternately with tomato and eggplant. Broil at 425° 4 to 5 inches from source of heat for 6 to 8 minutes, turn, baste with remaining sauce, and broil an additional 6 to 8 minutes. If you prefer, use melted butter for basting. Accompany with corn soufflé, lettuce-and-spinach salad.

Trout Kebobs

BRAISE: *Makes 2 8-inch skewers*

According to the responses in one taste sampling thus far, this very moist kebob was voted "unexcelled" (for fish, that is).

1 pound trout fillet
Salt to taste
½ teaspoon celery salt
¼ cup all-purpose flour
¼ cup cracker meal
¼ cup Italian-bread crumbs
1 large egg, well beaten

Green onions (10 pieces, about
    4 inches long, folded once)
1 large whole canned pimiento,
    cut into 4 pieces
2 tablespoons melted butter
1 tablespoon olive oil
1 lemon, halved

TOPPING MIXTURE

⅓ cup shredded mozzarella
    cheese
⅓ cup shredded green pepper

2 tablespoons chopped celery
2 tablespoons chopped parsley
¼ teaspoon dill weed

Fifteen minutes in advance: Cut trout into 12 strips, about
1 x 3 inches. In a bowl, season trout with salt and celery salt,
rubbing and tossing into fish well. In another bowl, combine
ingredients for the topping mixture. Set aside.

Before serving: In a bowl, combine flour, cracker meal, and
Italian-bread crumbs. Dip trout pieces into beaten egg and
then dredge with bread coating mixture. To thread each
fish strip on skewer, fold once so that skin is on outside
and the skewer can be speared through the skin twice.
(Note: Expect some difficulty if you don't have skewers with
sharp points. You might want to use a pick or needle to
assist making a hole in skin.) Thread skewers tightly as
follows: Green Onion . TROUT . Pimiento . TROUT . Green
Onion . TROUT . Green Onion . TROUT . Pimiento . TROUT
. Green Onion . TROUT . Green Onion. (In other words, for
each skewer allow 5 pieces of green onion, 6 pieces of trout—
½ pound fish—and 2 pieces of pimiento.) In skillet, heat
butter and olive oil. Add kebobs. Cover skillet and cook 5
minutes. Turn kebobs. Cover and cook an additional 5 minutes. Turn kebobs. Cover and cook 8 to 10 minutes more.
Squeeze ½ lemon over each kebob and spread generously
with topping mixture. Serve immediately—one trout kebob
per person.

Skewered Red Snapper

BRAISE: *Makes 3 8-inch skewers*

1 pound red snapper fillet
5 tablespoons all-purpose flour
5 tablespoons yellow corn meal
1 egg, well beaten
1 can (8 ounces) unsweetened
   pineapple chunks
1 small green pepper cut into
   6 pieces

2 tablespoons peanut oil
1 tablespoon melted butter
1 can (8 ounces) crushed
   unsweetened pineapple, very
   well drained
½ teaspoon rum extract
4 to 6 tablespoons chopped
   cashews or macadamia nuts

MARINADE

3 tablespoons Chablis
1 tablespoon soy sauce
2 tablespoons unsweetened
   pineapple juice (reserved
   from unsweetened pineapple
   chunks)

1 teaspoon salt
⅛ teaspoon dry mustard
⅛ teaspoon ginger
⅛ teaspoon garlic powder

Twenty minutes in advance: Combine marinade ingredients
in a bowl. Cut red snapper into 12 to 15 strips, 1 x 3 inches.
Add fish strips to marinade and toss well. Cover.

Before serving: In a bowl, combine flour and corn meal.
Drain fish strips, dip into beaten egg, and then dredge in
flour and corn meal mixture. (Note: To thread fish strips on
skewer, fold them once so that skin is on the outside and
the skewer can pierce through the skin twice.) Thread
skewer tightly as follows: Pineapple . RED SNAPPER .
Green Pepper . RED SNAPPER . Pineapple . RED SNAP-
PER . Green Pepper . RED SNAPPER . Pineapple . RED
SNAPPER. (In other words, for each skewer allow 5 pieces
of fish, 3 chunks of pineapple, and 2 pieces of green pepper.)
In skillet, heat oil and butter. Add kebobs. Cover. Cook 4 to
5 minutes. Turn kebobs. Cover. Cook an additional 4 to 5

minutes. Turn kebobs again. Cover. Cook 8 to 10 minutes more. In a small bowl, sprinkle drained crushed pineapple with rum extract and toss. Spread each kebob first with crushed pineapple and then top with chopped nuts to taste.

13 · VEGETABLES, FRUITS, CHEESE

WHAT TO CONSIDER BEFORE SKEWER-COOKING VEGETABLES, FRUITS, CHEESE

When these foods alone are threaded on skewers, in some instances, you might consider serving them as a main dish, especially the versatile eggplant. In other instances, these foods on a skewer become the focus of a main dish salad. But, for the most part, consider them accompaniments—a side dish of salad or vegetable, an appetizer, snack—even dessert. To menus which otherwise lack inviting color, a kebob accompaniment provides just the polishing touch.

There really is no limit to what you can do to arrange fruits and vegetables on skewers for serving without cooking. To cook them, however, is another matter. Obviously, some aren't suitable, and those that are often require delicate handling. Basically, remember two things: first, select slightly underripe produce; and second, undercook rather than overcook. Green-tipped bananas, for example, retain their shape far better under heat than ripe ones. To skewer-cook most fruits and vegetables, attend carefully to timing, particularly when the source of heat is direct. A minute too long for some is the point at which the pulp or cellulose tissue disintegrates . . . and then, all is lost, not only from a nutritional point of view—goodbye heat-soluble vitamins—but also from the aesthetic point of view. When fruits and vegetables cook alternately on a skewer with meat, however, that is something else. Here, any objection to a possible loss of texture is, in my opinion, outweighed by a gain in flavor achieved when foods cook next to one another.

Since certain vegetables require longer cooking than others, you could parboil or precook some if you wanted all vegetables on a skewer to arrive at the same stage of doneness simultaneously. Or, combine certain cooked canned varieties with fresh vegetables. Still another way is to add the fast-cooking ones such as tomatoes on the tips of skewers near the end of cooking. Note, too, that under heat, whole cherry tomatoes usually retain their shape far better than wedges or slices of the larger varieties. In many instances, how you thread and cook vegetables is a matter of personal preference. For example, when cooking green pepper, if a soft texture is desired, parboil before threading; for crispiness, thread it raw. The same is true of onions. When you have a choice whether or not to peel certain foods, that too is usually a question of individual liking, although generally more can be said in favor of not removing the skins.

If you wish to marinate vegetables, avoid wine as a predominant liquid in the marinade and instead use other acids such as wine vinegar or lemon juice. You'll be far happier with the results.

Apples, bananas, and avocados are some of the fruits that turn slightly brownish when peeled and left to stand. To prevent this, coat them with acids such as orange, grapefruit, or lemon juice.

Now for cheese. Like vegetables and fruits, it can be speared in numerous ways to serve without cooking. But when cooked, kebobs with cheese need extra-careful attention. Heat long enough for the cheese to melt; and of course, the harder the cheese, the longer it generally takes to reach the melting point.

Mushrooms en Brochette

BROIL: *Makes 4 6-inch skewers*

Place two 6-inch skewers on a lettuce leaf and serve as a vegetable side dish to a meat course.

12 large fresh mushrooms (about ½ pound)
 1 green pepper cut into 8 pieces

1 4-ounce jar whole pimiento, contents divided into 12 pieces

BASTE

¼ cup melted butter
 1 tablespoon lime juice

2 teaspoons minced parsley

Remove stems from mushrooms and reserve for other uses. Wipe mushroom caps with a cloth dampened with a little vinegar and water. Thread skewers as follows: green pepper . pimiento . mushroom cap . pimiento . mushroom cap . pimiento . mushroom cap . green pepper. Combine baste ingredients and baste kebobs before and during cooking, and generously just before serving. Broil 4 to 5 inches from source of heat about 4 to 6 minutes on each side until delicately brown.

CHILLED VEGETABLE KEBOBS

Consider these when you want a color and temperature complement to a main dish. They're convenient at serving time when all you have to do is reach into the refrigerator and place them on the table.

Skewered Hearts of Palm

Makes 3 6-inch skewers

1 can (14 ounces) hearts of
palm, drained
¾ cup Vinaigrette Variation,
page 263
6 large black pitted olives

Sharp cheese for stuffing olives
2 whole canned pimientos, cut
into 6 pieces
3 lettuce leaves

Three hours before serving: Cut hearts of palm into nine 1½-inch pieces and place in bowl. Pour vinaigrette dressing over them, cover, and place in refrigerator.

One hour before serving: Stuff pitted olives with sharp cheese. Thread on skewer as follows: stuffed black olive . palm . pimiento . palm . pimiento . palm . stuffed black olive. Place on lettuce leaves and refrigerate until ready to serve.

Cucumber and Tomato Kebobs

Makes 4 8-inch skewers

3 slices (about ¼ inch thick)
sharp Cheddar or caraway
cheese, 2 inches square
6 slices (¼ inch thick)
unpeeled cucumber, about
2 inches in diameter

2 medium firm tomatoes, each
cut into 8 wedges
4 small black pitted olives
1 cup Guacamole, Version II:
Golden, page 271

Sandwich one slice cheese between two slices cucumber. Cut in half and trim cheese to round edge of cucumber. Cut in half again into triangle shapes. Thread 4 tomato wedges (skin side toward handle) alternately with 3 cucumber-cheese sandwiches, beginning and ending with tomato. Garnish tip of skewer with olive. Place on a platter and keep in refrigerator until ready to serve. Fill 4 dip-sauce cups with

Golden Guacamole Dip. Place on platter next to kebobs and serve. Vegetables are removed from skewer a piece at a time and dipped in sauce.

Skewered Artichokes

BAKE: *Makes 2 8-inch skewers*

These skewer-cooked canned vegetables promise a very pleasant surprise.

1 can (14 ounces) artichoke hearts, drained
4 medium black pitted olives
2 medium pimiento-stuffed olives
2 tidbits of sharp cheese

6 bay leaves (optional)
½ large green pepper, quartered
2 tablespoons grated Parmesan cheese

SAUCE

¼ cup melted butter
¼ cup tomato sauce
1 tablespoon lemon juice
2 teaspoons minced parsley

¼ teaspoon dill weed
¼ teaspoon mint flakes, crushed

Dip artichokes in sauce, handling carefully and coating thoroughly. In center of each artichoke, embed either black pitted olive, pimiento-stuffed olive, or tidbit piece of cheese. When threading skewer, spear and secure artichoke through center of stuffing. For each skewer arrange 4 stuffed artichokes alternately with 3 whole bay leaves, beginning and ending each skewer with green pepper. Sprinkle ½ tablespoon grated cheese on the artichokes with the black olives. Place on foil-lined baking pan with tips of skewers suspended on edge of pan. Heat in preheated 350° oven about 8 to 10 minutes until cheese melts. If desired, serve with Skordalia Sauce, the Greek garlic topping, page 264.

SWEET POTATO KEBOBS, SWEET AND NONSWEET

Sweet potatoes are not only a delicious accompaniment to most meats, they are also abundant in vitamin A. You'll find these go especially well with chicken and pork. One version is noticeably sweet, and the other, interestingly, is not.

Sweet Potato—Canned Vegetables and Fruits

BAKE: *Makes 3 6-inch skewers*

1 can (1 pound) sweet potato halves, drained, cut into 12 to 14 chunks

6 black pitted olives (or 6 seedless grapes or 3 each of olives and grapes)

6 slices spiced apple rings, well drained

1 slice canned pineapple ring, cut into 3 pieces

3 large leaves of lettuce or cabbage

BASTE

¼ cup melted butter

2 tablespoons Triple Sec (orange liqueur)

2 tablespoons apricot preserves

2 tablespoons orange marmalade

⅛ teaspoon ground cloves

Combine baste ingredients and carefully dip potatoes, coating them well. Place olives inside center of apple rings to spear skewer through olive. Thread skewers as follows: sweet potato . olive with apple ring . sweet potato . pineapple . sweet potato . olive with apple ring . sweet potato. Brush kebobs with sauce. Heat on foil-lined baking pan in preheated 325° oven for 6 to 8 minutes until thoroughly warmed. Spread generously with sauce before serving. Place kebobs on lettuce or cabbage leaf, since the juice from apple ring may run.

Nonsweet Sweet Potato—Fresh Vegetables

BROIL: *Makes 4 6-inch skewers*

3 small sweet potatoes (about 1½ x 4 inches)
1 large green pepper, cut into 12 pieces

12 1-inch slices from a medium onion
Thyme to taste

MARINADE

⅓ cup olive oil
3 tablespoons tomato juice
2 tablespoons lemon juice

¼ teaspoon freshly ground black pepper
½ teaspoon leaf thyme

BASTE

¼ cup melted butter

One hour in advance: Place potatoes in boiling water for 8 to 10 minutes. Peel and cut crosswise into ½-inch slices, about 5 to 6 per potato. Combine marinade ingredients and add potatoes, coating well.

Before serving: Thread skewers as follows: green pepper . sweet potato . onion . sweet potato . green pepper . onion . sweet potato . green pepper . onion . sweet potato. Broil 4 to 5 inches from source of heat for 4 to 5 minutes, baste with butter, turn, broil additional 6 to 8 minutes. The tips of potatoes should be charred. In Greek this is referred to as *xero psimeno,* meaning burnt-cooked. Brush with butter before serving. Sprinkle with thyme to taste.

SKEWERED EGGPLANT
FROM THE SKILLET

Present the following recipes in one of two ways—served as an accompaniment, or as the entree, perhaps with the addition of leftover meats. As accompaniments, the eggplant and zucchini go well with roast or broiled lamb, the pineapple version with pork, and the Avgolemono with beef and lamb. The latter, truly an elegant dish, can even stand alone served with a side dish of fruit salad.

Zucchini and Eggplant Kebobs

BRAISE: *Makes 4 8-inch skewers*

8 chunks (1 x 1½ inches) unpared eggplant (about ½ pound)
1 egg, well beaten
⅓ cup Italian-seasoned bread crumbs
4 slices (1½ inches) unpared cucumber, halved

1 large green pepper, cut into 8 pieces
4 slices unpared zucchini, about 1 medium, 1½-inch diameter
2 tablespoons olive oil
4 tablespoons grated Parmesan cheese

SKILLET SAUCE

½ cup tomato sauce
⅓ cup Chablis
2 tablespoons dry sherry
1 tablespoon lemon juice
2 tablespoons water

½ teaspoon sweet basil leaves
¼ teaspoon dried mint, crushed
1 clove garlic, crushed
½ teaspoon salt

Combine skillet-sauce ingredients and set aside. Dip eggplant chunks in beaten egg, and roll in crumbs, coating well. Thread skewers as follows: cucumber (curved side toward skewer handle) . eggplant . green pepper . zucchini . eggplant . green pepper . cucumber (flat side toward skewer handle).

In large skillet, heat oil and add kebobs. Cover. Simmer about 3 to 4 minutes, turn, simmer 2 to 3 minutes more. Add skillet sauce. Cover. Cook 5 minutes, turn, scooping sauce over kebobs. Cover and cook an additional 4 to 6 minutes until tender. Sprinkle one tablespoon cheese over each kebob and serve.

Pineapple and Eggplant Kebobs

BRAISE: *Makes 4 8-inch skewers*

12 chunks (1 x 1½ inches) unpared eggplant, about ¾ pound	1 large green pepper, cut into 8 pieces
8 chunks (1 x 1½ inches) fresh pineapple	2 slices bacon
	½ cup shredded sharp Cheddar cheese

MARINADES

For Eggplant

⅓ cup orange juice	2 bay leaves, crumbled
⅓ cup tomato sauce	½ teaspoon dried tarragon, crushed
½ teaspoon celery salt	
1 clove garlic, crushed	

For Pineapple

¼ cup ruby Port	1 tablespoon lemon juice
1 tablespoon Kirsch	

One hour in advance: Combine marinade ingredients in a bowl and add eggplant, mixing well. Cover. Refrigerate. In another bowl, combine marinade ingredients, add pineapple and stir. Cover. Refrigerate.

Before serving: Thread skewers as follows: eggplant · green pepper · pineapple · eggplant · green pepper · pineapple · eggplant. In large skillet, fry bacon until crisp and remove from skillet. Use crumbled bacon as a garnish if you wish. Place kebobs in hot bacon fat and cook, covered, over low heat for 3 to 4 minutes, turn, simmer an additional 3 to 4 minutes. Add 2 tablespoons of the marinade from pineapple to that remaining from the eggplant and pour this mixture over kebobs. Cover and cook an additional 8 to 10 minutes or until eggplant is tender. Sprinkle shredded Cheddar cheese on top of each kebob.

Eggplant Kebobs Avgolemono

BRAISE: *Makes 5 6-inch skewers*

1 medium unpared eggplant (about 1 pound), cut into 18 to 20 chunks, about 1 x 1½ inches
1 teaspoon salt
5 pieces (about 1 inch) each of pickled sweet pepper, green pepper, and celery
¼ cup milk
¼ cup orange juice, freshly squeezed

1½ teaspoons almond extract
¾ cup flour
2 eggs, well beaten
1½ tablespoons butter
1½ tablespoons olive oil
Grated orange rind from 1 orange
1 cup Avgolemono Sauce, page 262
5 tablespoons sliced blanched almonds

Sprinkle eggplant with salt and let stand 20 minutes. Drain and wipe dry. Thread skewers as follows: eggplant . pickled pepper . eggplant . green pepper . eggplant . celery . eggplant. Combine milk, orange juice, and almond extract, and dip skewers in this mixture. (Don't be surprised if the milk curdles—it will!) Let stand about 8 to 10 minutes, turning kebobs often. Twist and turn kebobs in flour, coating well, then dip in egg and again twist and turn in flour. In large skillet, heat butter and oil and add kebobs. Cook, covered, over low heat 3 to 4 minutes, turn, cook additional 3 to 4 minutes, turn and cook 8 to 10 minutes more until tender. Sprinkle each kebob with grated orange rind, spread with generous amount of Avgolemono Sauce (prepare sauce while kebobs cook, or have ready in advance and just heat) and sprinkle 1 tablespoon almonds on each kebob.

Variation: Instead of Avgolemono, you might want to try Sauce Mornay, page 259, or Skordalia (Greek garlic sauce), page 264.

VEGETABLE AND FRUIT KEBOB COOKOUT

Here are two kinds of kebobs for skewer cooking outdoors: one, a stuffed version; and the other, chunks.

Stuffed Vegetables and Fruits, Picnic Style

GRILL

Prepare the Night Before . . . a, b, c and d!

a) STUFFED RED ONION AND CUCUMBER SHELLS

4 medium red onions
1 cucumber, unpared, cut into 4 1½-inch chunks

8 firm cherry tomatoes
1½ cups Vinaigrette Variation, page 263

Carefully remove center of onion, leaving a shell of 2 or 3 layers of onion. (Retain center for use in recipes wherever chopped onion is needed.) Scoop out center seed-flesh of cucumber, leaving the firm white part. Make certain the tomatoes fit into the center of onions and cucumbers, then wrap them in foil and put in refrigerator. Place onions and cucumber shells in container and pour Vinaigrette sauce over them. Cover. Refrigerate.

b) STUFFED SWEET PEPPERS

4 medium-to-large sweet peppers (long, light green in color)

Potato Stuffing

½ cup stiff mashed potatoes, salt and pepper to taste
2 strips crumbled crisp bacon (or equivalent imitation bacon chips)

Place peppers in boiling water 2 to 3 minutes. Cool. Cut off stem from pepper and remove seeds. Combine potatoes with bacon, mixing well. Lightly squeeze the pepper while filling it with potato mixture. Replace tops securely. Refrigerate.

c) STUFFED TOMATOES

4 medium firm tomatoes

Zucchini Stuffing

5 medium zucchini, unpared and cut in half crosswise	¼ teaspoon ground cinnamon
2 tablespoons finely chopped onion	1½ teaspoons salt
1 tablespoon melted butter	3 tablespoons grated Parmesan cheese
1 egg, well beaten	2 tablespoons chopped tomato pulp (scooped from tomatoes)
½ cup soft bread crumbs	
¼ teaspoon dill weed	
¼ teaspoon dried mint, crushed	

Heavy-duty aluminum foil (4 8 x 10-inch pieces)

Cut tops of tomatoes and scoop out centers, reserving 2 tablespoons for use in stuffing (and save the rest for some other recipe, such as a sauce). Cook zucchini in boiling salted water for 10 minutes until tender. Drain well. Mash in bowl, and combine with remaining stuffing ingredients, mixing thoroughly. Fill tomato shells with mixture and replace tops. Wrap each tomato in heavy-duty foil, folding ends top-side-up by the cut part of tomato. Refrigerate.

d) STUFFED LEMONS AND ORANGES

3 large thick-skinned lemons	1 cup granulated sugar
4 medium thick-skinned oranges	¼ teaspoon nutmeg
3 cups water	¾ teaspoon ground allspice
1 cup cider vinegar	½ teaspoon ground clove

Bean Stuffing for Lemons

1 can (8 ounces) butter beans (baby limas), drained and mashed
1 can (2 ounces) flat fillet of anchovies, drained and finely chopped

1 tablespoon ketchup
1 clove garlic, crushed

Sweet Potato Stuffing for Oranges

1 cup stiff mashed sweet potatoes, salt and pepper to taste
3 tablespoons drained pineapple tidbits

⅛ teaspoon cinnamon
⅛ teaspoon nutmeg
2 tablespoons brown sugar

Heavy-duty aluminum foil
(7 8 x 10-inch pieces)

Grate away all the rind from the oranges and lemons (if desired, use it for seasoning in other recipes). Cut one slice off stem end of fruit. Cut and scrape out seed and pith completely, being careful not to tear skins. In order to remove lemon centers thoroughly, you may have to cut a slice off both ends. In a pot, bring water, vinegar, sugar, and spices to a boil. Add lemon and orange shells. Cover. Boil until tender, about 20 to 25 minutes. Cool. In separate bowls, combine ingredients for bean and sweet potato stuffings, mixing well. Fill lemon shells with bean stuffing and orange shells with sweet potato mixture. Wrap each in foil, twisting ends of foil by the cut side of fruit shell. Refrigerate.

Day of serving—at the grill: On long skewers, thread as follows until filled: red onion with cherry tomato in center (spear skewer only through tomato) · cucumber shell with cherry tomato in center (spear skewer through cucumber and tomato) . stuffed sweet pepper (spearing through center of pepper). Use the Vinaigrette marinade to baste the skewers during cooking. On other long skewers, thread the foil-wrapped items (don't remove foil during cooking) : tomatoes (spearing skewer through center, folded side of foil away from grill) . lemons and oranges (spearing skewer through center smooth part, away from twisted foil ends). Grill 4 inches away from glowing coals until heated thoroughly, the skewers without foil-wrapped items about 5 to 8 minutes and the others, 10 to 14 minutes. This could serve from 6 to possibly 12, depending on your picnickers' attitude toward vegetables, the general size of their appetite (that is, outdoor-type appetite) and the size of the rest of the meal.

Chunks of Vegetables and Fruits

GRILL

1 medium eggplant, unpared, about 1 pound, cut into 18 to 20 chunks, about 1 x 1½ inches
2 large thick-skinned, unpeeled oranges, each cut into 8 wedges

1 large cucumber, unpared, cut into 8 to 10 ½-inch slices
2 large green peppers, each cut into 8 pieces
3 zucchini, unpared, cut into 10 to 12 1½-inch chunks

MARINADES

For Eggplant

⅔ cup salad oil
¼ cup red wine vinegar
½ teaspoon sweet basil
¼ teaspoon leaf marjoram
1 clove garlic, crushed

2 bay leaves, crumbled
1 teaspoon salt
¼ teaspoon ground black pepper

For Oranges

⅓ cup ruby Port
2 tablespoons Kirsch

1 tablespoon lemon juice

BASTE–TOPPING SAUCE

Tomato Barbecue Sauce, Sweet-Sour Variation, page 266

One hour in advance: In a bowl, toss eggplant with combined marinade ingredients. Turn occasionally. In another dish, toss oranges with combined marinade ingredients, turning several times.

Before serving: On long skewers thread until filled as follows: cucumber . green pepper . eggplant . zucchini . and oranges. Grill 5 inches away from glowing coals, basting with baste-topping sauce for about 12 to 16 minutes until eggplant and zucchini are cooked through. Place skewer point side down on platter and with fork push vegetables off skewer. Serve immediately. Serves 4 to 5.

Variation: Include with the above a few skewers of the following: 16 fresh medium-size mushroom caps marinated in Vinaigrette Variation, page 263, for 1 hour in refrigerator, covered. Thread two mushrooms alternately on skewer with one cherry tomato. Grill until lightly brown, turning once. Top with Sauce Mornay, page 259.

MAIN COURSE SALADS WITH
ETHNIC HIGHLIGHTS

What is a main course salad? For certain, it's not a tossed green salad served in a large bowl. That should be labeled what it is—a side dish. Nor is it—and I cringe here—a combination of syrupy canned fruits topped with a flavorful high-calorie dressing. A main-course salad, in my opinion, is this: it's served on one plate—either luncheon or dinner size—but it must be substantial. It should be satisfying and include protein-rich foods such as eggs, nuts, cheese, beans, fish, meat.

The following salads consist basically of three parts—the salad bed, the dressing, and the kebobs which are placed on top. The idea is contrast—in seasonings, in texture, and in temperature (hot kebobs with cold bed of salad). As the kebob chunks are removed from the skewer one at a time and eaten, the dressing and salad are also eaten. For some tastes, this kind of salad might be too unusual. But for the adventurous, it should be just right: something filling (enough to satisfy a hearty appetite), fun to eat, and slightly extravagant (these aren't inexpensive).

The Scandinavian Salad

Makes 3 main-dish salads

SEAFOOD SALAD BED

1 jar (8 ounces) fillet of herring in wine sauce, drained and chopped very fine

1 can (2 ounces) smoked salmon, drained, cut into small pieces

1 can (7½ ounces) red sockeye salmon, drained and flaked

2 medium unpared apples, cored and diced

1 cup crushed potato chips

1 teaspoon dill weed

½ cup dairy sour cream

LINGONBERRY DRESSING

⅓ cup preserved lingonberries

2 tablespoons orange juice

1 tablespoon Kirsch

THE BROILED KEBOBS (3 8-inch skewers)

Ham Rolls

4 slices imported boiled ham (4 x 6 inches) cut lengthwise into 12 strips

¼ pound Nokkelost (Norwegian caraway cheese) cut into 9 1 x 1½-inch squares

2 ounces Danish blue cheese, cut into 3 1 x 1½-inch squares

⅓ cup melted butter

¼ teaspoon ground cardamom

1 can (8 ounces) whole onions, drained

6 slices (¼ inch thick) unpared cucumber

3 cherry tomatoes (optional)

3 hard-cooked eggs, sliced

Combine herring, both kinds of salmon, and apples, mixing well. Stir in potato chips. Add the dill to sour cream and toss well with fish mixture. Chill. In a bowl, combine lingonberries, orange juice and Kirsch, stirring well. Set aside. Wrap 9 chunks of Nokkelost cheese with 9 strips of ham; use remaining strips of ham to wrap blue cheese chunks. Add cardamom to butter and dip onions in mixture, coating well. Halve cucumber slices. Thread skewers as follows: ham wrapped around Nokkelost . onion . cucumber (speared through white, not seed, part) . ham wrapped around blue cheese . onion . cucumber . two ham rolls wrapped around Nokkelost. Tip skewer with tomato if desired. Broil 4 to 5 inches from source of heat about 6 to 8 minutes until cheese begins to melt. Baste skewers with butter and cardamom used to coat onions. Remove seafood salad from refrigerator and scoop a generous portion onto three luncheon plates. Pour Lingonberry Dressing over salad in strip-layer fashion and top with broiled kebobs. Garnish each plate with one egg, sprinkling each slice with cardamom.

The Polynesian Salad

Makes 4 main-dish salads

TROPICAL SALAD BED

1 can (1 pound) hearts of palm, drained, cut into thin slices, crosswise
1 can (6 ounces) bamboo shoots, drained
1 can (4½ ounces) cooked medium shrimp, drained
1 tablespoon each of chopped green onion, cucumber, and green pepper
1 can (1 pound) bean sprouts, drained

1 jar (2½ ounces) whole mushrooms
3 tablespoons sesame seeds, toasted
1 tablespoon sugar
1 tablespoon wine vinegar
1 tablespoon soy sauce
¼ teaspoon garlic juice

Parsley sprigs

THE BAKED KEBOBS (4 8-inch skewers)

12 preserved kumquats
1 can (2¼ ounces) deviled ham
1½ teaspoons dry bread crumbs
1 can (4½ ounces) boned chicken, drained and finely chopped

8 chunks papaya
1 slice (1 inch) fresh pineapple, cut into 4 chunks
8 maraschino cherries
⅓ cup melted butter
2 tablespoons light rum
⅔ cup ground macadamia nuts

AVOCADO DRESSING

1 ripe avocado	¼ teaspoon Worcestershire
½ cup sour cream	sauce
1 tablespoon lemon juice	1 tablespoon dry sherry
1 teaspoon lemon rind	

Combine the first 7 salad ingredients, mixing well. Blend the next 4 ingredients and toss with vegetable mixture. Chill. Split kumquats and remove seeds. Remove flesh, chop and add to salad bed mixture. Mix deviled ham with bread crumbs and stuff 6 kumquats. Stuff remaining 6 kumquats with boned chicken. Thread on skewer as follows: kumquat . cherry . papaya . pineapple . kumquat . papaya . cherry . kumquat. Gently roll filled skewer in butter mixed with rum and then roll in nuts, coating thoroughly. Place on foil-lined baking pan and bake in preheated 350° oven for 6 to 8 minutes until thoroughly heated. Blend dressing ingredients thoroughly. Remove salad from refrigerator and scoop a generous portion onto 4 luncheon or dinner plates. Add avocado dressing in strip-layer fashion. Top with baked kebobs. Garnish plates with parsley sprigs.

The Mexican Salad

Makes 3 main-dish salads

THE BEAN SALAD BED

1 cup pinto beans, drained and rinsed	¼ cup chopped cucumber
1 cup dark red kidney beans, drained well	2 cups shredded cabbage
½ cup chopped celery	1 tablespoon prepared mustard
½ cup jumbo pitted black olives, halved	½ teaspoon chili powder
¼ cup chopped onion	2 tablespoons sweet relish
	2 tablespoons crumbled crisp bacon (or equivalent imitation bacon chips)

HOT SAUCE DRESSING

1 tablespoon finely chopped
 onion
1 tablespoon butter
1 tablespoon flour

½ cup tomato juice
¼ cup canned tomatoes and
 jalapeño pepper sauce
1 tablespoon Burgundy or
 other dry red wine

THE BRAISED KEBOBS (3 8-inch skewers)

Skillet Sauce

½ cup dry sherry
½ teaspoon leaf marjoram
¼ teaspoon leaf thyme

1 clove garlic, crushed
½ teaspoon chili powder
3 tablespoons water

4 small zucchini, cut into
 12 1½-inch chunks
1 red pepper, cut into 9 pieces
6 pieces sweet pickled peppers
 (sweet banana variety)

⅓ cup flour
1 egg, well beaten
2 tablespoons olive oil

BEEF-TACO GARNISH ROLLS

¼ cup (2 ounces) processed
 cheese, room temperature
2 tablespoons tomato sauce
¼ teaspoon oregano
1 teaspoon chopped canned
 green chilies

1 cup crushed taco-flavored
 tortilla chips
3 slices thin roast beef, halved

Combine the first 7 salad ingredients, mixing well. Blend
the remaining 4 ingredients and toss with bean mixture.
Chill. Sauté onion in butter 2 to 3 minutes. Remove from
heat. Gradually add flour, stirring constantly until foamy.
Over low heat add tomato juice and the tomato and jalapeño
pepper sauce, stirring constantly until thickened. Stir in
Burgundy. Combine skillet-sauce ingredients. Dip zucchini
chunks in beaten egg and dredge with flour. Thread zucchini
on skewers alternately with red and yellow pepper, allowing
4 zucchini per skewer. In large skillet, heat oil and add
kebobs. Cook over low heat 5 minutes, turn, cover and cook
5 minutes more. Add skillet sauce and cook, covered, until

tender, 10 to 12 minutes. In a bowl, blend soft cheese, tomato sauce, and oregano. Stir in green chilies and tortilla chips, mixing very well. Divide mixture into 6 portions, scooping onto beef slices. Roll. On 3 luncheon or dinner plates, place generous scoop of bean salad from refrigerator. Top with hot sauce dressing, pouring sauce in a strip fashion. Place kebobs over dressing. Garnish each dish with two beef-taco rolls.

Calorie Counter's Side-Dish Salad

Makes 3 6-inch skewers

Select the kind of cottage cheese to use according to your daily calorie quota. Note: ½ cup cottage cheese (curd pressed down), creamed style, 130 calories; uncreamed, 85 calories; and low fat, about 93 calories. Since cottage cheese is an excellent source of protein—½ cup = 15 grams—more so than other cheese, this salad could double as a very light main dish.

1 carton (1 pound) cottage cheese	3 large leaves of lettuce, washed, dried, and chilled
¼ teaspoon dill weed	1 large ripe pear, unpared, cored, sliced into 6 wedges
½ teaspoon dried mint, crushed	
2 tablespoons green pepper, finely chopped	1 medium-size ripe mango, cut into 9 to 12 chunks

DRESSING FOR COTTAGE CHEESE

⅓ cup orange juice	½ teaspoon rum extract
⅓ cup unsweetened pineapple juice	¼ teaspoon ground nutmeg
1 tablespoon lemon juice	2 eggs
2 tablespoons water	1 tablespoon cornstarch

In a bowl, mix cottage cheese with dill, mint, and green pepper. Arrange lettuce leaves on salad plates and scoop cheese mixture on each leaf. Thread 3 6-inch skewers with pears (skin side toward handle) and mangoes, allowing two pear slices per skewer. In saucepan, heat orange, pineapple and lemon juices, water, rum extract, and nutmeg. In a bowl, beat eggs with mixer until foamy. Stir in cornstarch. Slowly add several tablespoons at a time of the warmed mixture to eggs, stirring constantly with wooden spoon. Pour in saucepan and continue stirring until sauce thickens. Scoop sauce over mounds of cottage cheese and place skewers of fruit on top of dressing.

Stinger Fruit Kebobs

BAKE: *Makes 4 8-inch skewers*

Serve as a hot fruit salad accompaniment to pork, ham, lamb, chicken. They double well as a dessert, too.

3 slices (½ inch thick) fresh pineapple
3 tablespoons white crème de menthe
8 chunks (about 1½ inches) cantaloupe or honeydew melon
2 tablespoons brandy
8 chunks (1½ inches) banana
1 egg white, beaten until foamy
¾ cup coarsely chopped walnuts
1 package (3 ounces) cream cheese, room temperature

Two hours in advance: Pare, core and cut pineapple into 12 chunks. Place in bowl and add crème de menthe, mixing well. In another dish, add brandy to melon and stir, turning occasionally.

Before serving: Thread skewers as follows: pineapple . melon . banana . pineapple . melon . banana . pineapple. Dip skewers into egg white and then roll in chopped nuts, coating well. Place on foil-lined baking pan and bake in preheated 425° oven for 8 to 10 minutes until heated thoroughly. In saucepan over low heat, gradually blend one to two tablespoons each of the remaining crème de menthe and brandy marinades into the cream cheese, stirring until smooth to desired sauce consistency. Spread sauce over kebobs and serve immediately.

Continental Fruit Kebobs

BAKE: *Makes 2 6-inch skewers*

The crisp sesame coating gives these fruit kebobs distinction. Serve them as a dessert in the Continental fashion or as fruit accompaniment to lamb, chicken or beef.

2 slices (½ inch) medium-size eating oranges (cut crosswise), peeled
1 tablespoon Kirsch
2 freestone peaches (about same size as orange)
4 Bing cherries, halved and pitted
2 tablespoons Madeira
2 ripe pears

4 seedless grapes
2 pieces caraway cheese (about ½-inch cubes)
2 Italian plums, halved and pitted
2 tablespoons melted butter
¼ cup sesame seeds, toasted
1 package (3 ounces) cream cheese, room temperature

One hour in advance: Pour Kirsch over orange slices and let stand. Halve and pit peaches. Cut ½-inch slices from each peach half, using only the center slices. Combine peach slices and cherries and pour Madeira over them. Let soak, stirring occasionally.

Before serving: Cut each pear crosswise into 3 ½-inch slices. Cut away core. Fit grapes into 4 pear slices and cheese into remaining pear centers. Embed cherries in center of peach slices. Thread skewers as follows: plum . peach with cherry . pear with grape . orange . pear with cheese . peach with cherry . pear with grape . plum. Push fruits together. Dip kebobs in melted butter and roll in sesame seeds, coating well. Bake in preheated 350° oven in foil-lined baking pan for 10 to 12 minutes. In saucepan, thin cream cheese by adding 1 to 2 tablespoons of the remaining Madeira mixture, stirring until smooth to sauce consistency. Spread over kebobs.

SKEWERED DESSERTS

For myself, there is nothing more ruinous (more devastating, really) to a meal than an elaborate pastry served immediately after the main dish. It's like giving the main dish an insult. For many others, however, a meal is simply not complete unless they consume some refined sweet . . . and for them, the sweeter the better. Since every sincere host or hostess desires only to please, I hope these meet your sweet needs. See also the Ice Cream Bakes, pages 295–98.

Slightly Sweet: Fresh Fruit Delight

BROIL: *Makes 4 6-inch skewers*

These contrasting textures are sure to invite compliments.

8 chunks (1 x 1½ inches) watermelon, seeds carefully removed
¼ cup ruby Port
4 dried apricots
1 tablespoon Kirsch
1 tablespoon orange juice
2 medium nectarines, pitted, cut into 8 wedges

1 large banana cut into 4 1½-inch chunks
¼ cup melted butter
⅓ cup cornflake crumbs or graham-cracker crumbs
¼ cup coarsely chopped walnuts

TOPPING SAUCE

1 (3 ounce) package cream cheese, room temperature
4 to 5 tablespoons orange juice

1½ tablespoons Triple Sec
2 teaspoons grated orange rind

One hour in advance: Soak watermelon chunks in Port. In small cup, combine Kirsch with orange juice and add apricots to soak.

Before serving: In saucepan over low heat, thin cream cheese by blending in Triple Sec and orange juice, stirring until smooth to sauce consistency. Add orange rind. Thread skewers as follows: nectarine . watermelon . banana . dried apricot . watermelon . nectarine. Dip skewers in melted butter and roll in crumbs, coating well. Broil 4 to 5 inches from source of heat for 6 to 8 minutes until heated through. Top kebobs with sauce and sprinkle one tablespoon of nuts over each kebob.

Sweet: Cherry and Cake à la Mode

BAKE: *Makes 8 6-inch skewers*

There is a difference between cherry brandy and cherry-flavored brandy. The first, a high-proof liquor called Kirsch (Kirschwasser), is dry, whereas the second, a liqueur, is sweet. Both are very flavorful.

1 can (1 pound) pitted dark sweet cherries, drained, reserving 2 tablespoons syrup
1 tablespoon Kirsch
1 tablespoon Triple Sec
16 1-inch cubes slightly dry pound cake
¼ cup melted butter
3 tablespoons cherry-flavored brandy
1 tablespoon lemon juice
½ cup sweetened coconut
8 chunks (1½ inches) bananas (about 2 large)
1 egg white, beaten
1 cup coarsely ground walnuts
2 pints vanilla ice cream

One hour in advance: Combine two tablespoons syrup, the Kirsch and Triple Sec, add to cherries, and toss. Let stand, stirring occasionally. Combine butter, cherry-flavored brandy, and lemon juice, dipping cake chunks in mixture and then rolling in shredded coconut. Refrigerate.

Before serving: Dip bananas in beaten egg and roll in nuts, coating well. Thread skewers as follows: cherry . cake . cherry . banana . cake . cherry. Heat in foil-lined pan in preheated 350° oven for 8 to 10 minutes until coconut is toasted. Scoop ⅓ to ½ pint ice cream into center of dessert dish, placing kebobs on each side. Spoon one tablespoon sauce from cherries over ice cream. Top with cherry. Place dish on underliner and serve. This dessert requires a spoon as well as a cocktail fork for removing sweets from skewer. Makes 4 portions, two 6-inch skewers per serving.

Very Sweet: A Confection from the Skillet

BRAISE: *Makes 6 6-inch skewers*

You might consider serving this around the holidays.

18 dried Calamata string figs
    (about ¾ pound)
¼ cup bourbon
2 tablespoons water

3 tablespoons Triple Sec
2 tablespoons orange juice
12 dried peaches

12 water chestnuts
1 tablespoon butter or
    margarine
½ cup coarsely chopped walnuts

DATE BALLS

½ cup seedless raisins or
    currants
½ cup pitted dates
½ cup chopped walnuts
2 tablespoons bourbon

1 teaspoon grated lemon rind
1 teaspoon grated orange rind
⅓ cup sifted confectioners'
    sugar

SKILLET SAUCE

½ cup Burgundy
3 tablespoons lemon juice
¼ cup orange juice
2 tablespoons water

Two hours in advance: Cut stems from figs. Combine bourbon and water in a small bowl and add figs. In another bowl, combine Triple Sec and orange juice and add peaches, turn often. In electric blender, add all ingredients for date balls except confectioners' sugar. First, stir to combine well and then chop. Form into ten 1-inch balls and roll in confectioners' sugar. Put to side.

Before serving: Thread 6 skewers as follows: water chestnut . fig . peach . fig . peach . fig . water chestnut. Combine skillet-sauce ingredients. Melt butter in skillet. Add kebobs and simmer for 3 to 4 minutes. Add skillet sauce, cover, cook over low heat for 4 to 5 minutes, turn kebobs, cook an additional 4 to 5 minutes. Scoop sauce over them often. Place kebobs on individual serving dishes and garnish tip of each skewer with a date ball. Serve remaining date balls in a dish. Top each kebob with 1 to 2 tablespoons of chopped nuts. Serve immediately.

SKEWERED CHEESE CANAPÉS

Here are cheese treats—one served chilled and the other hot. The first is ideal for entertaining and the other suits for snacking.

A Speared Centerpiece of Cheese

Makes 12 6-inch skewers speared into an Edam or Gouda cheese

FOR ACCOMPANIMENTS ON SERVING TRAY

½ pound Calamata string figs
⅓ cup bourbon
2 medium apples, unpared, cored and cut into 24 thin wedges
½ cup sweet vermouth
12 dried prunes, pitted (or 12 preserved kumquats, seeded and pulp removed)

3 tablespoons cheese spread, bacon-flavored
Assorted crackers and cheese biscuits

FOR THE SPEARS

4 ounces blue cheese, shaped
  into 6 balls and rolled in
  chopped parsley
3 ounces cream cheese, shaped
  into 6 balls and rolled in
  chopped nuts
1 2 x 3-inch piece Cheddar
  cheese (8 ounces), cut into 12
  1-inch cubes

1 (2 ounces) package of
  processed Gruyère cheese
  triangles (6 2-inch triangles
  to a package)

A choice of foods to thread alternately on skewer with cheese: pickles, pimiento-stuffed olives, maraschino cherries, peppers, anchovies rolled in capers and stuffed in jumbo black pitted olives, banana chunks, oranges, cocktail onions, pineapple tidbits, mushrooms—and so on

THE CENTERPIECE BASE

1 9-ounce Edam or Gouda
  cheese

One hour in advance: Cut stems from figs. Let soak in bourbon. Place apples in sweet vermouth and let stand in refrigerator. Stuff prunes or kumquats with cheese spread and chill. Chill the blue cheese and cream cheese balls. Halve the cheese triangles lengthwise into twelve 1-inch triangles. Assemble the foods for threading on skewer with cheese. Each skewer will have 3 pieces of cheese and 2 accompaniments. Plan on variety—have some skewers with salty accents, others sweet, spicy, sweet-sour, depending on imagination, preferred tastes, and what's available.

Before serving: On large tray, place Edam or Gouda cheese in center. Thread 12 skewers with one piece each of Gruyère and Cheddar cheese and one cheese ball. Alternate on skewer with chosen accompaniments. Spear skewers into cheese base. Surround centerpiece with crackers and fruit, placing apples and figs in decorative serving cups. After the kebobs are eaten, cut into the cheese base to serve with crackers.

Griddled Cheese and Rye Kebobs

BROIL (*griddle-broil*): *Makes 4 8-inch skewers*

9 thin slices rye or
pumpernickel bread (5 x 5
inches)
10 ounces (2½ inches thick)
caraway cheese, cut into 24
thin slices

8 large pimiento-stuffed olives
2 medium tomatoes, cut into
8 wedges
1 tablespoon butter

Cut pumpernickel slices into four squares. Make a double-decker sandwich with two thin slices of cheese and three slices of bread. Thread 3 double-decker sandwiches per skewer alternately with tomatoes and olives. (Pierce skewer through each tomato wedge twice.) Melt 1 tablespoon butter on griddle. Heat skewers 4 to 5 minutes, turning several times until cheese begins to melt. Remove skewers and serve.

Variations: Thread 6-inch skewers with various cheeses: cubes of sharp cheese, cream cheese balls mixed with freeze-dried chives and rolled in nuts or toasted sesame seeds, cheese sandwiches with dark or light bread. Thread with: pineapple chunks, cucumbers, orange slices (peeled), canned mushrooms, pickled sweet or hot peppers, and so on.

Spiedini Mozzarella Special

BRAISE: *Makes 6 6-inch skewers*

This dish, of Italian origin, is one adaptation of the many fried and baked *spiedini* (skewered) dishes. Serve as an appetizer or anytime you want something special to accompany a beverage.

½ loaf Italian bread (about
½ pound), crust removed,
cut into 8 slices about ¾
inch thick
½ pound mozzarella cheese,
cut into 7 slices, each ¼
inch thick
12 medium black pitted olives
1 4-ounce jar pimiento,
contents divided into 12
pieces

¾ cup milk
1½ teaspoons almond extract
⅔ cup flour
2 eggs, slightly beaten
3 tablespoons olive oil
3 tablespoons butter

TOPPING SAUCE

1 can (2 ounces) flat fillet
anchovies, well drained
⅓ cup melted butter
3 tablespoons dry sherry

1 tablespoon lemon juice
2 teaspoons grated lemon rind
2 tablespoons minced parsley

Quarter bread slices into 32 squares. Quarter cheese slices into 28 squares. Thread skewers as follows: olive . bread . cheese . pimiento . bread . cheese . bread . cheese . pimiento . bread . cheese . bread . olive. (In other words, thread each skewer with 5 pieces of bread, 4 cheese, 2 pimiento and 2 olives.) You'll have a few extra pieces of bread and cheese remaining, either to thread on skewers or, if no one is looking, to snack on. Push together on skewer. Combine milk and almond extract. Dip and turn skewers in milk mixture just enough to moisten. Avoid sogginess. Dredge with flour, turning and twisting, coating well; next dip and turn in egg and then again in flour. In large skillet, heat butter and oil. Add kebobs. Fry slowly, turning often, until all sides are golden brown. Slide off skewers, spoon sauce over them, and serve immediately.

To prepare sauce: Mince anchovies and add to melted butter in saucepan. Stir in remaining sauce ingredients and heat.

Convenience tip: If you wish to make a double recipe or simply time these for serving with something else, place cooked *spiedini* on a cookie sheet and keep warm in a 225° oven.

Skewered Feta Sandwiches

BAKE: *Makes 12 6-inch skewers*

Slightly on the salty side, these make perfect accompaniments with favorite beverages. Certainly colorful . . . and very appropriate as appetizers.

4 frankfurter rolls	24 firm cherry tomatoes, even size
¼ cup melted butter	24 anchovy fillets rolled in capers (2 2-ounce cans, drained)
½ pound feta cheese, crumbled (1 cup)	
1 tablespoon brandy	
2 green peppers, cut into 24 pieces	

One hour in advance: Brush 2 tablespoons melted butter on one side of 4 split rolls. Spread ¼ cup crumbled feta cheese on one side of each roll. Combine 1 tablespoon brandy with remaining 2 tablespoons butter and brush over crumbled cheese. Cover rolls. Wrap in foil. Refrigerate.

Before serving: Cut off tops of tomatoes and scoop out centers. Fill tomato shells with anchovy and replace tops. Take rolls from refrigerator and cut each crosswise into 6 1-inch sandwiches. Thread on skewers as follows: green pepper . feta sandwich . tomato . feta sandwich . green pepper . tomato. Place on foil-lined baking pan in preheated 350° oven for 6 to 9 minutes until cheese begins to melt. Serves 8 to 10 for appetizers, 5 for snacks.

Convenience tip: Thread in advance and keep refrigerated until serving time and then just pop into the oven.

14 · MIXED MEATS

WHAT TO CONSIDER BEFORE
SKEWER-COOKING MIXED MEATS

Before trying a recipe in this section, and particularly before creating your own mixed meat kebobs, first try several of the single meat recipes. This should help sharpen your skills for cooking and serving a variety of different meats on one skewer. Then, when you're all enthused and eager to express your very own idea for kebobs of mixed meats, write it down and do it. Just make certain the different fresh meats require the same cooking time. You wouldn't, for example, combine fresh pork with fish. As for spearing a variety of precooked meats on a skewer, the possible combinations are infinite. And that's it. If you're happy with the result, do it again, refining it even more. If it's not perfect according to your standards, then revise the recipe or begin fresh with another idea. Above all, whether you prefer to follow the recipes here or create your own, remember that the idea of skewer cooking is—to enjoy.

Enjoy!

Lamb, Veal, and Pepperoni Kebobs

BRAISE: *Makes 4 8-inch skewers*

If you like anchovies, you might want to garnish the kebobs with the crunchy topping mixture. But even without the topping, this dish stands on its own beautifully.

4 rib lamb chops, 1 inch thick
12 slices (¼ inch each) pepperoni sausage, about ⅓ pound
8 whole canned mushrooms

1 pound veal cutlet cut into 12 strips, folded once
Green onions, the green part cut into 1-inch pieces (about 16)
2 tablespoons olive oil

SKILLET SAUCE

½ cup chicken bouillon (1 cube dissolved in hot water)
⅓ cup dry sherry
2 tablespoons Southern Comfort

1 clove garlic, finely minced
¼ teaspoon leaf thyme
¼ teaspoon sweet basil

ANCHOVY CRUNCH TOPPING MIXTURE (optional)

1 cup shredded mozzarella cheese (4-ounce package)
½ cup coarsely chopped salted cashew nuts

1 can (2 ounces) flat anchovies, drained well
1 tablespoon French-bread crumbs

Trim lamb from bone, keeping some fat. (Note: Use bones, if you wish, for soup stock.) Remove casing from pepperoni. Thread skewers as follows: mushroom . LAMB . PEP-PERONI . VEAL . PEPPERONI . VEAL . 4 pieces of onion . PEPPERONI . VEAL . mushroom. Combine skillet-sauce ingredients. Heat oil in skillet. Add kebobs and brown 6 to 8 minutes, turning often. Pour skillet sauce over kebobs. Cover. Simmer 10 minutes, turn, scooping sauce over kebobs. Cover and simmer an additional 10 to 12 minutes. Spoon sauce over kebobs and serve. If you wish, combine crunch topping mixture and garnish kebobs.

Mixed Meat Kebobs, German Accent

BRAISE: *Makes 6 6-inch skewers*

Serve with drop noodles (spätzle) and a side dish of beets.

1 slice (1 inch thick) veal bologna, cut into 12 chunks
6 thin slices boiled ham (4 x 6 inches), halved and folded twice
1 large green pepper, cut into 12 pieces

1 pound veal cutlet, cut into 18 pieces, folded once
6 square pieces of onion
2 strips of bacon

SKILLET SAUCE

⅓ cup tomato sauce
½ cup ruby Port
1 tablespoon red wine vinegar
1 tablespoon lemon juice
1 bay leaf, crushed
¼ teaspoon ground allspice
¼ teaspoon ground cloves

¼ teaspoon sweet basil
½ teaspoon celery flakes, crushed
⅛ teaspoon garlic powder
1 cup dairy sour cream

Thread skewers as follows: BOLOGNA chunk . HAM . green pepper . VEAL . onion . HAM . BOLOGNA chunk . VEAL . green pepper . VEAL. Fry bacon in skillet to get 2 tablespoons drippings. Remove bacon strips (and if desired crumble and use as a seasoning in salad). Brown kebobs in bacon fat about 5 minutes, turning often. Combine skillet-sauce ingredients except the sour cream and 2 tablespoons Port. Pour skillet sauce over kebobs and cover. Simmer 10 minutes. Turn kebobs. Scoop sauce over kebobs and simmer an additional 10 minutes. Transfer kebobs to warm platter. Combine sour cream and 2 tablespoons Port. Stir this mixture into skillet, heat, but do not boil. Spoon sauce over kebobs and serve immediately.

Skewered Veal and Ham Wraparounds

BRAISE: *Makes 4 8-inch skewers*

½ pound chicken livers cut into 8 pieces
Powdered sage
4 boiled ham slices, halved lengthwise
½ pound veal cutlet cut into 8 strips

Grated Romano cheese
8 pimiento-stuffed olives
4 small boiled onions
1 green pepper, cut into 8 pieces
2 tablespoons margarine or butter

SKILLET SAUCE

½ cup beef bouillon (bouillon cube dissolved in ½ cup hot water)
½ cup dry vermouth
¼ cup finely chopped parsley

2 tablespoons ketchup
¼ teaspoon nutmeg
⅛ teaspoon freshly ground black pepper

Sprinkle chicken livers with powdered sage. Wrap each liver with slice of ham. Sprinkle veal cutlet generously with Romano cheese and fold once. Thread on skewer as follows: olive . VEAL CUTLET strip . onion . LIVER wrapped with HAM . green pepper . VEAL CUTLET strip . LIVER wrapped with HAM . green pepper . olive. Combine skillet-sauce ingredients, stirring well. Melt butter or margarine and brown kebobs 4 to 5 minutes. Pour skillet sauce over kebobs. Cover. Simmer for 10 minutes. Turn kebobs and spoon sauce over them. Simmer an additional 10 to 12 minutes, occasionally turning kebobs and spooning sauce over them.

CHICKEN AND HAM COMBINATIONS

This series offers various seasonings and kebob cookery methods for combining chicken, chicken livers, and ham.

Examine the recipes closely. If they don't strike you as particularly appealing, perhaps one of them will inspire your own creation. Refer, also, to the sections on variety meats, chicken, and ham.

Plain Chicken Livers and Ham Kebobs

BROIL: *Makes 4 10-inch skewers*

1 pound chicken livers, about
   24 pieces
Salt to taste
12 small whole cooked carrots
   (1-pound jar)

4 slices boiled ham, halved
   lengthwise
8 pimiento-stuffed olives
4 strips bacon, halved
   crosswise

BASTE

⅓ cup claret

Season livers with salt. Thread on skewers as follows: LIVER . carrot . HAM wrapped around LIVER . olive . BACON wrapped around LIVER . carrot . HAM wrapped around LIVER . olive . BACON wrapped around LIVER . carrot . LIVER. Broil 4 inches from source of heat for 7 to 8 minutes, turn, baste, and broil an additional 6 to 7 minutes.

Polynesian-Style Chicken and Ham Kebobs

BAKE: *Makes 4 10-inch skewers*

½-pound ham slice (cook-before-
   eating), cut into 8 1-inch
   cubes
1 whole chicken breast,
   skinned, boned, and cut into
   8 1½-inch pieces
6 ounces chicken livers, about
   8 pieces

4 strips bacon, each halved
   crosswise
8 chunks papaya or pineapple
1 lime, cut into 8 slices
4 maraschino cherries
¼ cup chopped macadamia nuts

MARINADE FOR CHICKEN AND HAM

⅓ cup dry sherry
2 tablespoons each of orange
  juice, apricot nectar,
  pineapple juice and soy sauce

1 clove garlic, minced
¼ teaspoon ground ginger

BASTE

⅓ cup melted butter

One hour in advance: Combine marinade ingredients in a bowl. Add ham and chicken pieces. Cover. Let stand at room temperature.

Before serving: Wrap chicken livers with bacon. Thread skewer as follows: papaya . lime slice . HAM cube . CHICKEN . CHICKEN LIVER wrapped with bacon . HAM cube . CHICKEN . CHICKEN LIVER wrapped with bacon . lime slice . papaya. Place on foil-lined baking pan and bake in preheated 350° oven for 10 to 15 minutes, turn, baste with butter, and bake additional 10 minutes. Baste generously with butter and garnish each skewer with one tablespoon of chopped nuts.

Variation: Omit chicken livers with bacon. Instead of one chicken breast, use two and cut into 16 pieces.

Chicken and Ham Kebobs, Mediterranean Style

BRAISE: *Makes 4 8-inch skewers*

8 medium black pitted olives
1 green pepper, cut into 8
  pieces
1 whole chicken breast,
  skinned, boned, and cut into
  8 1½-inch pieces
8 ounces chicken livers, about
  12 pieces
1 jar (4 ounces) pimientos,
  contents divided into 8 pieces

½-pound ham slice (cook-
  before-eating) cut into 8
  1-inch cubes
2 tablespoons olive oil
2 tablespoons grated Parmesan
  cheese
2 tablespoons grated Romano
  cheese

SKILLET SAUCE

½ cup tomato sauce
⅓ cup dry vermouth
2 teaspoons finely chopped
  parsley

¼ teaspoon oregano leaves
1 clove garlic, minced

Thread skewers as follows: olive . green pepper . CHICKEN . several pieces LIVER . pimiento . HAM . LIVER . HAM . pimiento . CHICKEN . green pepper . olive. Combine skillet-sauce ingredients. Heat oil in skillet and brown kebobs 4 to 5 minutes. Pour skillet sauce over kebobs. Cover. Simmer for 10 minutes. Turn kebobs. Simmer an additional 10 to 12 minutes, occasionally turning kebobs and spooning sauce over them. Combine cheeses and sprinkle one tablespoon over each kebob. (If desired, thread on 6-inch skewers to serve as snacks.)

Skewers of Coated Mixed Meats

BAKE: *Makes 8 6-inch skewers*

2 whole chicken breasts,
  skinned, boned, and cut into
  16 1½-inch pieces
1-pound ham slice (cook-
  before-eating) cut into 16
  1-inch cubes
16 pineapple chunks

2 strips bacon, each cut
  crosswise into 4 pieces
8 medium black pitted olives
1 egg, beaten
2 tablespoons milk
⅓ cup cornflake crumbs

MARINADE FOR CHICKEN

⅓ cup Chablis
⅓ cup pineapple juice
¼ cup lemon juice

2 tablespoons soy sauce
1 clove garlic, minced

Two hours in advance: Combine marinade ingredients. Add chicken pieces. Cover. Let stand at room temperature, stirring occasionally.

Before serving: Thread skewers as follows: HAM . pineapple chunk . CHICKEN . BACON . black olive . CHICKEN . pineapple chunk . HAM. Dip skewers and roll in beaten egg combined with milk and then roll in cornflake crumbs. Place on foil-lined baking pan and bake in preheated 350° oven for 20 to 25 minutes, turning once.

Variations: Use leftover roast meats instead of fresh. If desired, add favorite precooked sausages on the skewer. Also, instead of cornflake crumbs, you might prefer to use Italian-seasoned crumbs, or you might coat some skewers with one mixture and others with another.

Chicken, Pork, and Sausage Kebobs

BRAISE: *Makes 4 8-inch skewers*

16 slices (¼ inch each) smoked Polish sausage (½-inch diameter, about ½ pound)

1 pound boneless pork loin chops, ½ inch thick, cut into 16 pieces

2 whole chicken breasts, skinned, boned, and cut into 16 1½-inch pieces

12 slices (½ inch thick) unpared cucumber, diameter of slices about 1½ inches

2 tablespoons olive oil

SKILLET SAUCE

½ cup beer
¼ cup tomato sauce
2 tablespoons orange juice
1 tablespoon lemon juice

1 clove garlic, minced
¼ teaspoon freeze-dried chives
½ teaspoon celery flakes, crushed

TOPPING MIXTURE

4 tablespoons grated Parmesan cheese

2 teaspoons grated orange rind

Thread skewers as follows: SAUSAGE . PORK . CHICKEN . SAUSAGE . cucumber . CHICKEN . PORK

. SAUSAGE . cucumber . CHICKEN . PORK . SAUSAGE . CHICKEN . cucumber . PORK. Combine skillet-sauce ingredients. Heat oil in skillet. Brown kebobs in covered skillet about 5 to 7 minutes. Add skillet sauce, cover and simmer 10 minutes. Turn kebobs, scooping sauce over them, cover and cook an additional 12 to 15 minutes. Combine topping mixture and garnish each kebob.

Pork, Ham, and Salami Kebobs

BRAISE: *Makes 8 6-inch skewers*

8 wedges cocktail oranges
   (1 10-ounce jar)
1 tablespoon brandy
1 center slice fully cooked
   ham, ½ inch thick, cut into
   24 pieces
12 thin slices hard salami,
   about ¼ pound, halved,
   folded once

1 pound boneless pork loin
   chops, about ½ inch thick,
   cut into 16 pieces
8 square pieces onion

SKILLET SAUCE

½ cup Rhine wine
3 tablespoons Curaçao
2 tablespoons brandy
2 tablespoons tomato paste

2 tablespoons water
⅛ teaspoon cinnamon
⅛ teaspoon tarragon leaves

TOPPING MIXTURE

1 package (4 ounces) shredded
   Cheddar cheese
½ cup shredded dill pickle (1
   dill pickle in vacuum
   package, about 8 ounces)

Toss oranges with brandy. Thread skewers as follows: HAM . SALAMI . PORK . orange . HAM . SALAMI . PORK . SALAMI . onion . HAM. Combine skillet-sauce ingredients. Cook kebobs in covered skillet 5 to 6 minutes. Add skillet sauce. Cover. Simmer 10 minutes. Turn. Scoop sauce over kebobs. Cover and cook additional 12 to 15 minutes. Combine topping mixture and garnish each kebob.

Skewered Beef, Lamb Kidney, and Pork Sausage Links

BROIL: *Makes 8 10-inch skewers*

1 sirloin steak, 1½ inches thick (3 to 4 pounds), trimmed and cut into 16 to 18 cubes
6 lamb kidneys
2 tablespoons butter
2 tablespoons finely chopped onion

8 pork sausage links
8 small chunks cucumber
1 green pepper, cut into 8 pieces
5 ounces Canadian bacon, sliced and cut into 1-inch pieces
Salt to taste

MARINADE

3 tablespoons olive oil
1 clove garlic, crushed

10 peppercorns, crushed

BASTE

½ cup melted butter

One hour in advance: Toss beef cubes with marinade in a bowl. Cover. Let stand at room temperature.

Before serving: Wash kidneys and remove outer covering. Split in half lengthwise, removing fat and tubes. Cut each kidney into 4 pieces and sauté in butter and onions for 4 to 5 minutes. Place link sausages in pan of boiling water and cook 5 to 7 minutes. Thread skewers as follows: BEEF . SAUSAGE LINK wrapped around cucumber . green pepper . KIDNEY . bacon pieces . KIDNEY . BEEF . bacon. Allow 3 pieces of kidney per skewer. For medium doneness, broil 4 inches from source of heat for 10 or 11 minutes; for well done, 4 to 5 inches from source of heat for 12 to 15 minutes. Season steak and kidneys with salt to taste before turning kebobs halfway through cooking. Baste generously with butter.

Beef Rib-Eye and Oyster Kebobs

BROIL: *Makes 8 6-inch skewers*

These are very special appetizers.

16 medium fresh mushroom caps, about ½ pound
2 tablespoons olive oil
2 tablespoons lemon juice
½ teaspoon dried mint, crushed
½ teaspoon dried chervil
12 ounces fresh oysters, about 16

2 tablespoons grated Parmesan cheese
4 slices bacon, halved crosswise
1 rib-eye steak (about 13 ounces), 1 inch thick, cut into 16 cubes

BASTE–TOPPING SAUCE

½ cup sweet vermouth
¼ cup melted butter
1 teaspoon cornstarch dissolved in 1 tablespoon water

One hour in advance: In a bowl, toss mushrooms with a combination of oil, lemon juice, mint, and chervil. Cover.
Before serving: Toss 8 oysters with Parmesan cheese. Wrap each of the remaining 8 oysters with a piece of bacon. Thread skewers as follows: BEEF . OYSTER with cheese . mushroom . OYSTER with bacon . BEEF . mushroom. Combine sweet vermouth with butter. Broil kebobs 4 inches from source of heat 6 or 7 minutes, turn and baste, broil an additional 8 or 9 minutes or until bacon is cooked. Add cornstarch mixture to baste, heat, and stir until thickened. Spread over kebobs and serve.

Variation: To serve beef on the rare side, omit bacon and broil a total of 10 or 11 minutes. Or, if preferred, partially cook bacon in skillet several minutes before threading.

Skewered Ham and Lamb

BROIL: *Makes 4 10-inch skewers*

1½ to 1¾ pounds boned leg of lamb, cut into 16 1½-inch pieces
1 pound ham steak, cut into 16 1-inch cubes

2 green peppers, cut into 16 pieces
4 cherry tomatoes

MARINADE–BASTE

½ cup olive oil
½ cup dry sherry
3 tablespoons soy sauce
⅛ teaspoon freshly ground black pepper

1 large onion sliced and separated into rings

Two hours in advance: Combine olive oil, sherry, soy sauce and pepper in a bowl. Mix well. Add onions and stir. Add lamb and ham cubes and cover. Let stand at room temperature, turning meat occasionally.

Before serving: Thread lamb and ham alternately with green pepper. Allow four pieces green pepper per skewer. Broil 4 inches from source of heat about 10 minutes, turn and broil an additional 7 to 9 minutes. Baste often. Garnish tips of skewers with cherry tomato near the end of broiling time.

Lamb and Beef Kebobs, Picnic Style

GRILL

2½ pounds boned leg of lamb, cut into 1½-inch pieces

2½ pounds top sirloin, cut into 1½-inch cubes

MARINADE

1¾ cups Italian salad dressing
½ cup sweet vermouth
¼ cup lemon juice

2 medium onions, sliced and
separated into rings
2 bay leaves

Night before picnic: Combine the ingredients of this piquant-tasting marinade in a very large container. Add lamb and beef. Cover. Refrigerate overnight, turning meat occasionally.

Morning of picnic: Place container of meat with marinade in a refrigerator box or ice chest.

At picnic site: Thread long-handled skewers with meat until filled. Allow space between meat cubes for even cooking. Grill about 3 to 4 inches over glowing coals until cooked to desired doneness. Turn often. Serves from 8 to 10 persons.

Variations: Substitute ham for lamb or use all beef. Or use CHOICE or PRIME quality sirloin tip or top round, if preferred; or use lower-grade tip and top round with instant meat tenderizer, following directions on label. And if you prefer a less tangy marinade, use one of the tomato barbecue sauces on pages 265–67.

Brunch Kebobs

BRAISE: *Makes 4 6-inch skewers*

To get the meat for these kebobs, you'll need to stop at a delicatessen.

¼ pound sliced ham (about 5 slices, 4 x 6 inches)
1 smoked Thuringer sausage (about ¼ pound)
¼ pound sliced white meat chicken roll, about 8 slices
¼ pound sliced roast beef (about 5 to 6 slices, 4 x 6 inches)

1 can (8¾ ounces) peach halves, contents very well drained
⅔ cup buckwheat pancake mix
½ cup milk
1 egg, slightly beaten
3 tablespoons melted margarine

TOPPING SAUCE

⅔ cup preserved lingonberries   4 teaspoons lemon juice
2 tablespoons orange juice

Stack ham slices and cut into 8 square stacks. Cut Thuringer into 8 slices, about ½ inch thick. Divide chicken roll slices into two stacks of 4 slices and cut each stack into quarters. Stack slices of beef and cut into 8 square stacks. Cut peach halves into 12 pieces. Thread skewer as follows: HAM stack . smoked THURINGER slice . CHICKEN stack . peach . BEEF stack . CHICKEN stack . HAM stack . peach . BEEF stack . peach . smoked THURINGER slice. In a bowl, combine pancake mix, milk, and egg and one tablespoon of melted margarine. Place thick batter in a large scooped-edged dish. Use a large spoon to assist in completely covering kebobs with batter (this is a little messy). Heat remaining melted margarine in skillet. Add kebobs and cover. Cook for 5 minutes. Turn kebobs only with a spatula. Cover and cook for additional 5 minutes. Uncover and cook 8 to 10 minutes more, turning kebobs several times to brown on all sides. Combine topping-sauce ingredients and spread over each kebob.

Skewered Chicken Livers and Pork Sausage Links

BROIL: *Makes 4 10-inch skewers*

Serve as a hearty snack, or if you wish, a main dish accompanied with German or Greek potato salad.

8 pork sausage links (8-ounce   4 large pimiento-stuffed olives
  package)   1 green pepper, cut into 8
½ pound chicken livers, about   pieces
  12 pieces, drained   4 large black pitted olives
16 large mushroom caps

MARINADE–BASTE

½ cup Rhine wine
¼ cup salad oil
2 tablespoons finely chopped
   onion

½ teaspoon salt
½ teaspoon paprika

One hour in advance: Precook sausage links in boiling water about 4 minutes. Drain and pat dry, using paper towel. Combine marinade–baste ingredients in a bowl. Add liver and sausage. Cover. Let stand in refrigerator.

Before serving: Thread skewer as follows: mushroom . SAUSAGE LINK wrapped halfway around pimiento olive . mushroom . green pepper . several LIVERS . green pepper . mushroom . SAUSAGE LINK wrapped around black olive . LIVER . mushroom. Baste generously. Broil 4 to 5 inches from source of heat for 10 to 15 minutes, basting and turning several times.

Wiener and Burger Kebobs

BROIL *(griddle-broil)*: *Makes 4 10-inch skewers*

Serve these whenever you want a dressed-up, bunless presentation of the everyday favorites—hamburgers and hot dogs.

BURGER KEBOBS

½ pound ground round steak
¼ cup dry bread crumbs
1 teaspoon soy sauce

¼ teaspoon Tabasco
⅛ teaspoon Worcestershire
   sauce

2 small pimiento-stuffed olives
3 jumbo-size all-beef wieners
   (6 to 1 pound)
4 black pitted olives
Tidbits of sharp cheese

4 pickled cucumber slices
4 pineapple chunks
4 pieces green pepper
2 tablespoons butter or
   margarine (optional)

Combine burger kebob ingredients in a bowl. Shape into 4 log shapes and 2 balls. Embed pimiento-stuffed olive in center of each ball, rolling several times. Chill. Cut wieners into 4 log shapes and 2 small chunks. Stuff black olives with cheese. Thread two skewers as follows: black pitted olive . WIENER log . cucumber pickle . stuffed BURGER KEBOB ball . cucumber pickle . WIENER log . black pitted olive. Thread remaining two skewers as follows: pineapple chunk . BURGER KEBOB log . green pepper . WIENER chunk . green pepper . BURGER KEBOB log . pineapple chunk. Melt butter or margarine on griddle if desired. Griddle-broil kebobs about 10 to 14 minutes until done, turning several times. Serve with Mustard Dip Sauce, Variation I, page 269, or Tomato Barbecue Sauce, Version II: Uncooked, page 266.

Variation: If you prefer oven-broiling to griddle-broiling, use the range broiler and baste with a tomato barbecue sauce.

Snack Tray of Mixed Meat Kebobs

BROIL: *Makes 14 6-inch skewers*

16 medium shrimp in the shell, about ½ pound
16 anchovy-stuffed olives
1 package (5 ounces) cocktail-size smoked sausage links (16 sausages)
8 pieces *Senf Gurken* (mustard pickle)
1 center slice fully cooked ham (¾ inch thick) cut into 26 pieces
2 tablespoons Dijon-style mustard
¼ cup coarsely chopped walnuts

1 large green pepper, cut into 12 pieces
¼ pound sliced pastrami, stacked and quartered into about 1-inch pieces
Whole pimiento, cut into 6 1-inch pieces
¼ pound sliced hard salami, stacked and quartered into about 1-inch pieces
¼ pound roast beef slices, stacked and cut into 1-inch pieces

BASTE

½ cup melted butter

CHEESE TOPPING SAUCE (1⅓ cups)

2 packages (4 ounces)
whipped Cheddar-flavored
cheese
2 tablespoons dry sherry
2 tablespoons chopped
pimiento, well drained

2 tablespoons shredded
cucumber
2 tablespoons shredded onion
½ teaspoon celery flakes,
crushed

TOPPING SAUCE

1 cup Tomato Barbecue Sauce,
Version II, page 266

Shell and devein shrimp. Thread 8 skewers as follows:
SHRIMP wrapped around olive . SAUSAGE LINK . *Senf
Gurken* . HAM cube . SHRIMP wrapped around olive .
SAUSAGE LINK. Toss remaining cubes of ham with mustard and coat with nuts. Thread 6 skewers as follows: green
pepper . HAM cube . PASTRAMI slices . pimiento . SALAMI
slices . HAM cube . ROAST BEEF slices . green pepper .
HAM cube. Broil the 14 kebobs 5 inches from source of heat 7
to 8 minutes, turn and baste generously with butter and broil
additional 6 to 7 minutes. Heat cheese-sauce ingredients and
pour in server. Add Tomato Barbecue Sauce in another server
and place both sauces in the center of a large tray, about
13 inches in diameter. Place kebobs around the tray, handle
side near rim, skewer points radiating from center. Place
this tray on food warmer and include spoons for each of the
sauces.

Variations: If desired, include skewers of a favorite burger
kebob selection, appetizer-size balls. Or, if preferred, select
other topping or dip sauces to accompany the kebobs.

MORE MIXED MEAT
KEBOB SUGGESTIONS

The following suggestions are for those of you who have by now tried many recipes in this book and have acquired the simple knack of skewer cooking and don't need many details written in a recipe format.

Braised Kebob Ideas

Veal and Ham, Italiano: Follow the recipe for Veal Kebobs Italiano, page 94, and include ham.

Veal and Pork Kebobs: Follow the recipe for On-the-Range Pork Kebobs, page 123. Instead of the 1½ pounds boned pork loin, substitute 1 pound pork and ½ pound veal.

Baked Kebob Ideas

Cooked Mixed Meats on a Skewer: Thread cooked chicken or turkey pieces and precooked sausage alternately on a skewer with roast beef or ham cubes and pieces of green pepper and mushrooms. Dip filled skewer in melted butter and roll in Italian-seasoned bread crumbs, or dip in beaten egg and then roll in cornflake crumbs. Place kebobs on foil-lined baking pan and bake in preheated oven until brown, about 10 minutes. Accompany with topping sauces, Hollandaise, page 261, or Sauce Supreme, page 259, or Thin Sweet-Sour Sauce, page 264. Or, if you prefer, serve with dip sauces, such as a selection from the Horseradish Dip Sauces, pages 268–69, or the Cheddar, Anchovy, and Sweet versions of the Sour Cream Dip Sauces, pages 272–73.

Broiled Kebob Ideas

Pork, Lamb, and Veal Kebobs, Latholemono: If you enjoyed the Lamb Kebobs Latholemono, page 100, then you'll undoubtedly find the mixed meat version interesting, too. Follow the Latholemono recipe, using 2 pounds boned lamb and 1 pound each of boned pork loin and veal, instead of all lamb. Cook longer since pork must be cooked until well done. If you like your lamb pink, perhaps you'd better consider broiling the meats separately. Thread 8 10-inch skewers as follows: two cubes of LAMB, one each of VEAL and PORK alternately with green peppers, mushrooms and bay leaves. Baste generously with Latholemono marinade-baste (and you may want to double the amount of it).

Skewered Mixed Meat Snacks: • Thread skewer as follows: black pitted olive . boiled HAM strip wrapped around banana chunk . dilled tomato . ready-to-eat SAUSAGE . boiled HAM strip wrapped around pineapple or papaya fruit . dilled tomato . ready-to-eat SAUSAGE . black pitted olive. Broil 4 inches from source of heat until heated thoroughly. Accompany with the Cheddar Accent version of the Sour Cream Dip Sauces, page 272.

• Thread skewer as follows: green pepper . boiled HAM strip wrapped around chunk of sharp cheese . bell pepper . smoked SAUSAGE link . boiled HAM strip wrapped around chunk of sharp cheese . green pepper. Baste with melted butter combined with dill weed. Broil 4 to 5 inches from source of heat until cheese begins to melt. Sprinkle top of each kebob with grated Parmesan or Romano cheese and crumbled crisp cooked bacon. Place kebob on French bread, slide off skewers, and serve.

Griddle-Broiled Kebob Ideas

Mixed Meat Kebob Snacks: Place filled skewers on lightly greased griddle and cook until thoroughly heated, turning kebobs often. Serve with an assortment of dip sauces, such as Guacamole, pages 270–71, Spicy Cocktail Dip Sauces, pages 267–68, Sweet-Sour Dip Sauce, page 269, and the Sour Cream Dip Sauces, pages 272–73. Accompany with pretzels, chips, and crackers. Thread 6-inch skewers in some of the following ways:

* Canned LUNCHEON MEAT chunk . green pepper . pineapple chunk . water chestnut . BURGER KEBOB . dried apricot.
* Canned cocktail SALAMI pieces . pickled or dilled Brussels sprouts . black pitted olives stuffed with cheese . boiled HAM strip wrapped around pimiento-stuffed olive.
* Cocktail FRANKS . cherry peppers . cocktail onion . LUNCHEON MEAT chunks . pimiento . sweet midget pickle.
* HAM slice wrapped around blue cheese ball rolled in chopped nuts . papaya chunk . fully cooked SAUSAGE . partially cooked BACON piece . orange section . apple chunk.
* Cooked SHRIMP . KNACKWURST chunk . pickled cauliflower . boiled HAM strip wrapped around Swiss cheese chunks . boiled onion . pickled watermelon rind.
* Mushroom cap . HAM chunk . CHICKEN LIVER . green pepper . chunks of cooked sweet potato.
* Leftover roast MEAT cubes (dipped in melted butter and dredged in bread crumbs) . fully cooked SAUSAGE . orange section . cucumber piece . black pitted olive.

15 · SAUCES

Béchamel

Here is a convenient rather than classic version of white sauce. By itself, it makes a fine topping for vegetable kebobs. Its most frequent use, however, is as a base to prepare more elaborate sauces.

2	tablespoons butter	$\frac{1}{8}$	teaspoon ground white
2	tablespoons flour		pepper
$1\frac{1}{4}$	cups milk, warmed	$\frac{1}{8}$	teaspoon nutmeg
$\frac{1}{4}$	teaspoon salt		

Melt butter in heavy saucepan. Add flour and cook over low heat, stirring constantly with wooden spoon about 3 minutes until foamy. Remove from heat. Very gradually add milk, stirring briskly with a wire whisk. Add salt, pepper, and nutmeg. Cook over low heat, stirring constantly until sauce thickens and comes to a boil, about 4 to 5 minutes. Cook over low heat 1 or 2 minutes more. Note: This must be stirred constantly after liquid is added. Makes 1 cup medium sauce.

Variations in thickness: For thinner sauce, use 1 tablespoon each of flour and butter for $1\frac{1}{4}$ cups milk; for a thicker sauce, use 3 to 4 tablespoons each of flour and butter.

Variations in seasoning: Add 1 medium minced onion and 1 bouquet garni (parsley, thyme, and bay leaf) or $\frac{1}{4}$ teaspoon dried bouquet garni, crushed. If desired, add 1 small minced onion to butter and cook until soft before adding flour.

Sauce Mornay

This is a cheese sauce with Béchamel as the base. Makes an excellent topping for fish, veal, and poultry kebobs.

1 cup Béchamel sauce, page 258
2 tablespoons grated Gruyère or Swiss cheese
2 tablespoons grated Parmesan cheese

1 tablespoon softened butter (optional)

In a heavy saucepan, combine warmed Béchamel sauce with cheeses. Stir over low heat just until cheeses melt. Add butter if desired. This sauce should not boil. Makes 1 cup.

Sauce Supreme

Although this sauce is known as Sauce Supreme, it seems to me a misnomer. It's terribly rich and in my opinion not very exciting in taste.

2 tablespoons butter
2 tablespoons flour
1¼ cups canned chicken broth, warmed

¼ cup whipping cream
¼ teaspoon salt
⅛ teaspoon ground white pepper

Melt butter in heavy saucepan. Add flour, stirring with wooden spoon until smooth, about 2 minutes. Remove from heat. Gradually add warmed broth, stirring constantly with wire whisk. Place over heat and cook about 4 to 5 minutes, stirring constantly until thickened. Stir in cream and seasonings. This sauce is commonly served with baked chicken kebobs. Makes 1¼ cups.

Quick Brown Sauce

A basic sauce used to make other sauces.

2 tablespoons butter
2 tablespoons flour
1¼ cup (10½-ounce can)
   beef consommé

1 tablespoon tomato paste
Salt and freshly ground black
   pepper to taste

Melt butter in a heavy saucepan. Blend in flour and stir briskly with a wire whisk until light brown, about 3 to 4 minutes. Remove from heat. Very slowly add about two-thirds of the consommé, stirring with whisk until thickened. Place over low heat and continue gradually adding consommé, stirring briskly. Bring to boil, reduce heat, and simmer for 10 minutes. Stir in tomato paste and simmer about 5 minutes. Add salt and pepper to taste. Makes 1 cup.

Brown Sauce I

Here is an example of Brown Sauce used to prepare another sauce. Sauce Chasseur, page 65, is another example.

¼ cup finely chopped onion
¼ cup finely chopped green
   onion
1 clove garlic, minced
1 tablespoon olive oil
1 tablespoon butter
⅓ cup white (dry) Port

3 sprigs parsley, 1 sprig thyme
   and 1 bay leaf (or 1 teaspoon
   dried bouquet garni
   seasoning)
1 cup Quick Brown Sauce,
   above

Sauté onions and garlic in oil and butter until lightly brown, about 5 minutes. Add wine and herbs. Simmer until liquid is reduced to half. Stir in Quick Brown Sauce. Simmer about 10 minutes. Makes ¾ cup.

Brown Sauce II

And here is another sauce using the Brown Sauce as a base. It's near enough to the Bordelaise to serve as a simple substitute.

⅔ cup dry red wine
2 tablespoons chopped green onion
1 tablespoon finely chopped parsley

1 cup Quick Brown Sauce, page 260
Freshly ground black pepper to taste

Boil wine, onion, and parsley until liquid is reduced to one-third cup. Strain if desired. Stir in Brown Sauce and bring to a boil again. Let sauce simmer 3 to 4 minutes. Add pepper to taste. Makes about 1⅓ cups.

Hollandaise

Stir continuously and briskly . . . add ingredients gradually . . . never let water in lower pan of double boiler touch upper section and don't allow water to boil. If you think the temperature is getting near the danger point, just temper it by adding more cold water. And if by some chance, the mixture does curdle, add about 1 tablespoon of boiling water drop by drop to rebuild emulsion, beating constantly.

6 tablespoons softened butter
½ tablespoon lemon juice
½ tablespoon tarragon vinegar
½ teaspoon salt

¼ teaspoon ground white pepper
3 egg yolks
2 tablespoons heavy cream

In top of double boiler, melt one tablespoon of softened butter with lemon juice and vinegar, salt and pepper over hot water. Add yolks, stirring briskly with wire whisk until blended well and eggs are thick and foamy. Add second tablespoon of butter, beating constantly. Add remaining pieces of butter one at a time, blending each thoroughly before adding remaining tablespoons, stirring, of course, all the while, until sauce is thickened and coats spoon. Remove from heat. Add one tablespoon cream and stir until blended and then add the other tablespoon in the same fashion. Continue to beat with whisk for two to three minutes. Makes ¾ cup.

Sauce Béarnaise

A highly seasoned Hollandaise.

3 tablespoons tarragon vinegar
3 tablespoons dry white wine
1 tablespoon minced green onion
1 tablespoon freshly chopped tarragon (or 1 teaspoon dried)
1 tablespoon freshly chopped chervil (or 1 teaspoon dried)
¼ teaspoon salt
⅛ teaspoon ground white pepper
¾ cup Hollandaise, page 261

In a small heavy skillet, cook all ingredients, except Hollandaise, until reduced to one-half of the original volume. Strain mixture if desired. Add cooled mixture to the Hollandaise.

An even quicker version: To ¾ cup Hollandaise add 1 tablespoon tarragon vinegar and 2 teaspoons each of parsley flakes and dried tarragon and 1 teaspoon freeze-dried chives.

Avgolemono Sauce

Try this tangy sauce instead of Hollandaise—it has far less fat, keeps better, and is much less difficult to prepare.

3 large eggs (room temperature)
1 tablespoon cornstarch
½ cup freshly squeezed lemon juice (about 2 large lemons)
1 cup beef bouillon (bouillon cube dissolved in 1 cup hot water)

Beat eggs in bowl with mixer until foamy. Add cornstarch and lemon juice. Very slowly add hot bouillon, stirring constantly with wooden spoon. Pour slowly into saucepan and continue stirring over low heat until sauce thickens and coats spoon. This takes a while, from 8 to 10 minutes, so don't become impatient. The result is worth the wait and effort. Makes 1½ cups. Note: For a less tangy sauce, use juice from 2 small lemons—¼ to ⅓ cup.

Basic Vinaigrette

This is a basic oil and vinegar dressing referred to as either Vinaigrette or French dressing. (The Greeks call it Latho-xithi.) Use it as a marinade for fruits and vegetables or cold cooked meats.

¼ cup red wine vinegar	¼ teaspoon freshly ground
½ teaspoon salt, or more to taste	black pepper
	½ cup olive oil

In a bowl, beat vinegar with salt and pepper. Very slowly add oil, beating continuously. Beat or shake before using. Makes ¾ cup.

Vinaigrette Variation

2 tablespoons freshly squeezed lemon juice	2 teaspoons minced onion
2 tablespoons red wine vinegar	½ teaspoon tarragon leaves
1 teaspoon salt	¾ teaspoon dried mint, crushed
¼ teaspoon freshly ground black pepper	1 tablespoon chopped canned pimiento
½ teaspoon dry mustard	½ teaspoon grated lemon rind
1½ teaspoons minced fresh parsley	9 tablespoons olive oil

In an electric blender, add above ingredients and blend at high speed a few seconds. Makes ⅔ cup.

Skordalia Sauce

This is a strong garlic sauce. So if you like garlic (and it likes you), go get the blender and let's get started.

⅓ cup olive oil
⅓ cup freshly squeezed lemon juice
2 cups cold mashed potatoes
1 cup chicken bouillon (bouillon cube dissolved in 1 cup hot water)

5 cloves garlic, sliced
½ teaspoon salt (more or less to taste)

In a blender, add ingredients and blend thoroughly at high speed, stopping to stir down occasionally. Makes 3 cups.

Thin Sweet-Sour Sauce

Use this tangy sauce as a baste and topping for chicken or pork kebobs.

1 cup canned crushed pineapple
⅓ cup granulated sugar
⅓ cup white wine vinegar
⅓ cup dry sherry
2 teaspoons celery flakes, crushed
2 tablespoons finely chopped canned pimiento

2 tablespoons finely chopped green pepper
⅛ teaspoon garlic powder
1 teaspoon salt
2 tablespoons soy sauce
2 teaspoons cornstarch

Combine all ingredients except cornstarch in saucepan and heat slowly 5 minutes. Mix cornstarch and 4 teaspoons water and add to sauce, stirring until smooth, clear and bubbly. Makes 2 cups.

Clarified Butter

Drawn butter, ghee, and clarified butter—all mean the same: a clear butter with the salts and milk solids removed. It doesn't burn or spatter—no matter how hot it gets.

To clarify, simmer butter about 10 minutes until the milk curd and salt separate. There will be a white milky foam on top and brown specks on bottom of pan. Do not brown. Let stand a few minutes and strain to carefully get clear yellow butter. This can be stored in refrigerator and seasoned if desired. Use it as a baste combined with other seasonings such as spices and wine. I should add, however, that many prefer melted butter that hasn't been clarified, since it retains a richer flavor.

Tomato Barbecue Sauce, Version I: Cooked

Barbecue sauce made with fresh tomatoes has a distinctively good taste.

¼ cup finely chopped onion	½ cup Burgundy
3 tablespoons minced green onion	¼ cup dark brown sugar, firmly packed
1 clove garlic, sliced	2 tablespoons prepared mustard
2 tablespoons butter or margarine	1 tablespoon Worcestershire sauce
2 tablespoons tomato paste	
¼ cup salad oil	1 tablespoon salt
2 cups diced tomatoes, peeled and pulp removed (about 4 medium)	½ teaspoon ground black pepper

In a large saucepan or skillet, sauté onions and garlic in butter until soft and transparent, not brown. Add tomato paste, oil and tomatoes. Cover. Cook over low heat for 8 to 10 minutes. Add wine, sugar, mustard, Worcestershire sauce, salt, and pepper. Cover. Simmer 10 to 15 minutes. Stir occasionally. (Strain if desired.) Makes 2 cups.

Tomato Barbecue Sauce, Version II: Uncooked

A barbecue sauce in a jiffy—just shake in a jar and stir.

1 cup (8-ounce can) tomato sauce
½ cup ketchup
⅓ cup chili sauce
3 tablespoons brown sugar
1 teaspoon dry mustard
1 tablespoon red wine vinegar
2 tablespoons lemon juice

2 tablespoons salad oil
¼ teaspoon garlic powder
1 tablespoon soy sauce
1 teaspoon Worcestershire sauce
¼ teaspoon ground black pepper

Combine all ingredients and mix thoroughly. Makes 2 cups.

Basic (Mild) Tomato Barbecue Sauce with Variations

Variations are . . . sweet-sour/sweet glaze/herb/hot.

3 tablespoons finely chopped onion
3 tablespoons finely chopped green onion
2 whole cloves garlic, sliced thin
4 tablespoons salad oil
3 tablespoons tomato paste
1 cup tomato sauce

½ cup ketchup
2 tablespoons soy sauce
1 teaspoon dry mustard
¼ teaspoon ground black pepper
2 tablespoons brown sugar
1 tablespoon wine vinegar
1 tablespoon lemon juice
¼ teaspoon celery salt

In large saucepan or skillet, sauté onions and garlic in oil until tender and translucent, but not brown. Stir in remaining ingredients and simmer for 8 to 10 minutes. Serve warm or cold. Makes 2 cups.

Sweet-Sour Variation: Follow basic sauce recipe. When stirring in ingredients, add an additional 2 tablespoons brown sugar; ¼ cup crushed pineapple, drained; 2 tablespoons wine vinegar; 2 tablespoons orange juice; ¼ teaspoon ground ginger.

Sweet Glaze Variation: Follow basic sauce recipe. When stirring in ingredients, add 2 tablespoons each of orange marmalade, honey, molasses, and water.

Herb Variation: Follow basic sauce recipe. When stirring in ingredients, add 2 teaspoons each of parsley flakes, basil, and tarragon; ½ teaspoon ground thyme; 2 bay leaves, finely crumbled; 2 tablespoons dry white wine.

Hot Variation: Follow basic sauce recipe. When stirring in ingredients, add 1 teaspoon chili powder; 2 tablespoons finely chopped pickled sweet banana pepper; 1 hot pepper minced or ⅛ to ¼ teaspoon cayenne pepper to taste; 1 teaspoon Worcestershire sauce; 2 tablespoons lemon juice; 1 teaspoon grated lemon rind.

Spicy Cocktail Dip Sauce, Version I: Mild and Different

¼ cup chili sauce
3 tablespoons tomato paste
¼ cup ketchup
2 tablespoons Burgundy

1 tablespoon whipping cream
1 teaspoon brown sugar
1 teaspoon lemon juice

Combine all ingredients and mix thoroughly. Good with sausage, lightly seasoned burger kebobs, veal, or fish. Makes ¾ cup.

Spicy Cocktail Dip Sauce, Version II: Hot and Familiar

⅓ cup chili sauce
⅓ cup ketchup
½ teaspoon Dijon-style
   mustard
1 teaspoon soy sauce
1 teaspoon Worcestershire
   sauce

½ teaspoon onion juice
1 teaspoon lemon juice
2 drops Tabasco sauce
2 teaspoons bourbon

Combine all ingredients and mix thoroughly. Chill. To make a cocktail dip just for seafood kebobs, add 2 teaspoons drained prepared horseradish. Makes ¾ cup.

Horseradish Dip Sauces—3 Variations

These sauces go particularly well with cooked sausage, ham or cold beef.

VARIATION 1: *Lemon Highlight*

1 cup mayonnaise
¼ cup prepared horseradish,
   drained
¼ teaspoon ground nutmeg

½ teaspoon Worcestershire
   sauce
1 teaspoon lemon juice
1 teaspoon grated lemon rind

Mix thoroughly. Chill. Makes 1¼ cups.

VARIATION 2: *Touch of Tomato*

½ cup dairy sour cream
2 tablespoons prepared
   horseradish, drained

1 tablespoon chili sauce
½ teaspoon salt
2 to 3 drops Tabasco

Combine above ingredients, stirring and mixing thoroughly. Chill. Makes ¾ cup.

VARIATION 3: *Tangy*

2 tablespoons prepared
  horseradish
2 tablespoons dry sherry
1 tablespoon Worcestershire
  sauce

1 tablespoon lemon juice
2 tablespoons whipping cream
2 3-ounce packages softened
  cream cheese, halved

In a blender, add ingredients and blend thoroughly at high speed, stopping to stir down if necessary. Chill. Makes 1 cup.

Sweet-Sour Dip Sauce

Serve this thick sauce chilled or at room temperature with sausage, pork, ham, or luncheon meat kebobs.

1½ tablespoons cornstarch
¼ teaspoon dry mustard
¼ cup brown sugar, firmly
  packed
2½ tablespoons red wine
  vinegar

½ cup canned chicken broth
¼ cup orange juice
⅓ cup apricot preserves
2 tablespoons finely chopped
  canned pimiento

In saucepan blend cornstarch, mustard and brown sugar. Stir in vinegar, broth and orange juice and heat, stirring constantly. Add apricot preserves and stir until mixture comes to a boil and thickens. Add pimiento. Cook a few minutes more. Makes 1 cup.

Mustard Dip Sauces—2 Variations

VARIATION 1: (*Sweet-sour; served chilled*)

½ cup mayonnaise
½ tablespoon tarragon vinegar
½ tablespoon granulated sugar
1 tablespoon dry mustard

1 tablespoon pineapple juice
⅛ teaspoon turmeric
¼ teaspoon salt

Stir ingredients until thoroughly mixed. Chill. Good with cold cooked beef. Makes ⅔ cup.

VARIATION 2: (*Mild; served warm*)

3 tablespoons red wine vinegar
2 tablespoons butter
½ teaspoon salt
2 teaspoons dry mustard
⅛ teaspoon turmeric
2 tablespoons crushed
 pineapple

1 tablespoon granulated sugar
½ teaspoon instant minced
 onion
1 egg, well beaten

Mix vinegar and butter in the top of a double boiler over hot water. Heat until butter melts. Add salt, mustard, turmeric, pineapple, sugar and minced onion. Mix well. Remove from heat. Add small amount of hot mixture to beaten egg to prevent curdling. Add egg mixture to hot sauce, stirring constantly until thickened. Makes ½ cup.

Guacamole, Version I: Traditional

2 medium (about ½ pound
 each) ripe avocados, peeled,
 pitted, and sliced
1 medium tomato, peeled and
 diced
1 clove garlic, sliced
½ teaspoon salt
1 tablespoon lemon juice

1 tablespoon olive oil
2 tablespoons chopped parsley
2 tablespoons chopped green
 pepper
2 tablespoons chopped green
 onion
1 to 2 teaspoons chili powder
 to taste

In electric blender, add above ingredients. Stir to combine ingredients and then blend at high speed until smooth, occasionally stopping to stir down. Chill. Leave pit in guacamole until ready to serve to prevent browning. Makes about 1 cup.

Guacamole, Version II: Golden

1 medium avocado, peeled, pitted, and sliced
1 14-ounce can whole artichoke hearts, well drained (absorb moisture in paper towel)
1½ tablespoons anchovy paste
¼ cup dry sherry
2 tablespoons lemon juice
⅓ cup coarsely grated Romano or Parmesan cheese

1 tablespoon olive oil
1 4-ounce jar pimiento, well drained and chopped
2 tablespoons chopped cucumber
1 clove garlic
¼ cup chopped onions
½ to 1 teaspoon chili powder to taste

In electric blender, add ingredients. Stir to combine. Blend at high speed, stopping and stirring occasionally, until smooth. Chill. Makes about 2 cups.

Chick-pea Dip

Although this Middle Eastern dip, called "hummos," is typically eaten with flat bread or crackers, it also can be used as a dip with plain lamb kebobs.

1 can (15 ounces) chick-peas (Mexican garbanzos) with juice drained to the level of peas

1 tablespoon tahini (ground hulled sesame seed)
2 cloves garlic, sliced
3 tablespoons lemon juice

In blender, add ingredients and blend thoroughly at high speed, stopping to stir down occasionally. Chill. Makes 1 cup.

Sour Cream Dip Sauces—4 Variations

VARIATION 1: *Cheddar Accent*

⅔ cup dairy sour cream
1 tablespoon lemon juice
2 tablespoons ruby Port
1 6-ounce package pasteurized
  processed cheese food
  (sharp Cheddar flavor)

2 tablespoons finely chopped
  cucumber
1 tablespoon chopped green
  onion
¼ teaspoon dill weed

In an electric blender, add ingredients and blend at high speed until smooth, stopping to stir down if necessary. Makes 1⅓ cups.

Optional: Add 2 to 3 tablespoons coarsely grated aged Cheddar.

VARIATION 2: *Anchovy Accent*

⅔ cup dairy sour cream
1½ tablespoons anchovy paste
1 teaspoon garlic juice
2 tablespoons chopped onion
¼ cup chopped canned
  pimiento

½ cup coarsely grated
  Romano cheese
1 6-ounce package cream
  cheese

In electric blender, add ingredients and blend at high speed until smooth. Makes 1¾ cups.

VARIATION 3: *Sweet Accent*

2 tablespoons chopped onion
2 tablespoons crushed
  pineapple
2 tablespoons orange juice
1 6-ounce package pasteurized
  processed cheese food (sharp
  flavor)

⅓ cup dairy sour cream
⅓ cup apricot nectar

In electric blender, add ingredients and blend thoroughly at high speed until smooth. Serve with ham. Makes 1 cup.

VARIATION 4: *Mild and Different*

1 cup crumbled feta cheese
¾ cup dairy sour cream
1 3-ounce package cream
   cheese
1 tablespoon lemon juice

¼ cup Mavrodaphne wine
1 tablespoon minced parsley
1 teaspoon crushed mint flakes
2 tablespoons chopped green
   onion

In electric blender, add ingredients and blend at high speed until smooth, stopping to stir down if necessary. Chill. Serve as a dip sauce with broiled, unseasoned lamb kebobs. Excellent, too, with leftover cold beef or lamb. Makes 1¼ cups.

Low-Calorie Dip Sauce

1 cup low-fat cottage cheese
2 tablespoons low-calorie
   Roquefort dressing
¼ teaspoon dry mustard
2 tablespoons finely chopped
   green onion

⅛ teaspoon garlic powder
⅛ teaspoon ground white
   pepper

In electric blender, add ingredients and blend at high speed until mixture reaches smooth sour-cream consistency and an inviting mint color. Stop occasionally to stir down. Chill. Makes 1 cup.

Greek Fondue Dip

Serve this dip in a fondue pot, with broiled Kefte Burger Kebobs. Guests remove the meat from skewer with cocktail fork and dunk into the fondue.

THE KEBOBS

Prepare half the recipe of Kefte Burger Kebobs, page 76; shape 1 pound meat into 30 appetizer balls. Thread 10

6-inch skewers as follows: 3 chilled burger balls, 2 pieces of green pepper and 1 large pimiento-stuffed olive. Broil 4 to 5 inches from source of heat for 4 to 6 minutes, turn and broil an additional 4 to 5 minutes. Baste with Mavrodaphne wine. Serve burger kebobs on small individual trays. For beverage, serve the remaining Demestica white wine used in the fondue or, for contrast, Demestica dry red wine.

THE DIP

½ pound Kasseri* cheese, coarsely shredded
1½ tablespoons flour
1 clove garlic, cut in half
2 tablespoons butter
2 tablespoons chopped onion
½ teaspoon dried mint flakes, crushed
1 cup Demestica white wine

1 tablespoon lemon juice
¼ teaspoon salt
⅛ teaspoon freshly ground black pepper
⅛ teaspoon ground nutmeg
⅛ teaspoon ground cinnamon
⅛ teaspoon ground allspice
1½ tablespoons Metaxa brandy

Dredge cheese with flour. Rub ceramic fondue pot (or a chafing dish) well with cut side of garlic. Melt butter and sauté onions about a minute. Add mint flakes. Pour in wine and lemon juice and heat slowly until bubbles begin to rise to the surface, just before reaching the boiling point. Do not boil. Then, very gradually, add the cheese by small handfuls, stirring constantly with a wooden spoon in one direction. Melt each handful of cheese before adding the next, stirring all the while until fondue thickens. Add salt, pepper, nutmeg, cinnamon and allspice. When fondue starts to bubble, stir in brandy until blended. Serve immediately. Keep warm. Note: This cheese does not melt as readily as Swiss Gruyère. As with all fondues, keep it just warm to maintain the right consistency but never cook further. If mixture becomes too thick as cheese absorbs wine, add heated—not cold—wine to thin.

* Kasseri—a firm, mild-flavored cheese made of goat's milk—is available in stores specializing in Greek and Italian imported foods.

16 · SUGGESTED ACCOMPANIMENTS

Feta and Cream Cheese Balls

About Feta: Feta is a semisoft white cheese made from sheep's or goat's milk and sometimes both. Compared to cottage cheese and Italian ricotta, feta is firmer, saltier, and sharper. When purchased in a can or sealed cellophane container, it usually has little or no brine, and thus tends to become dry. To keep moist, make a *salamoora* (brine) by boiling milk, water, and salt. For 1 pound feta combine 1 cup water, ¼ cup milk, and 1 teaspoon salt. Let cool. Add cheese and store in covered container in refrigerator.

1 cup crumbled feta cheese
1 package (3 ounces) cream cheese

Finely chopped parsley

In a large bowl, add crumbled feta and cream cheeses. Use an electric mixer to beat the cheeses until thoroughly mixed and smooth. Shape into balls and roll in finely chopped parsley. Chill. These go especially well with appetizer or snack kebobs. Makes 4 2-inch balls or 8 1-inch balls.

Tiganita Tirakia (Fried Cheeses)

Although some might consider this heresy, I feel there is really no need to insist on using Greek cheese for this recipe.

VERSION I: *Gruyère Cheese*

1 4-ounce package processed
  Gruyère cheese (available as
  6 ½-inch-thick triangle
  pieces wrapped in foil)
1 beaten egg

3 tablespoons Italian-seasoned
  bread crumbs
3 tablespoons cornflake crumbs
2 tablespoons butter
1 lemon, cut into quarters

Halve the pieces of cheese lengthwise to make a total of 12 triangles. Dip in beaten egg. Dredge 6 pieces in Italian-seasoned bread crumbs and 6 in cornflake crumbs, coating well. In a large heavy skillet, heat butter until slightly brown. Briskly fry cheese pieces until brown on each side, turning once. This semisoft cheese melts quickly, and thus heating takes only a few minutes. Remove from pan with spatula and place on cheese serving board. Squeeze lemon juice generously over all the pieces. Serve immediately. Makes 12 1-inch triangles.

VERSION II: *Parmesan Cheese*

½-pound piece Parmesan
  cheese, ½ inch thick
2 tablespoons flour
2 tablespoons brandy

2 tablespoons lemon juice
1½ tablespoons butter
1½ tablespoons olive oil

Cut cheese into 8 pieces, about 2 x 1 inches. Dust with flour. Combine brandy and lemon juice in cup and set aside. In a large heavy skillet, heat butter and oil. Fry 4 or 5 pieces of cheese at a time, allowing ample space between them. When the sides show signs of melting, turn, fry a few more minutes. The outside will be brown and crisp and the inside soft. Remove from pan with spatula. Place on cheese serving board. Pour lemon-brandy mixture over them. Note: Parmesan is harder and saltier than Gruyère, and will thus take more heat before it begins to melt. Makes about 8 2 x 1-inch pieces.

Taramasalata (Fish Roe Dip)

This is Greek caviar, a dip served as an appetizer with sesame crackers or toast tips. Tarama, the red roe of cod, is usually available in 10-ounce jars. Unused portion keeps well if sealed tightly and refrigerated.

4 slices white bread, crusts trimmed
¼ cup water
5 ounces tarama
2 tablespoons finely chopped onion

1 clove garlic, crushed
½ teaspoon dill weed
1 egg yolk
½ cup olive oil
⅓ cup freshly squeezed lemon juice, about 1½ lemons

Soak bread in water until water is absorbed. Put tarama, onion, and garlic in blender and blend until pureed. Add dill, bread and egg yolk and blend at medium speed. Pour oil and lemon alternately in small amounts while blender is on lowest setting until mixture becomes pale pink, light, and fluffy. Chill. Makes about 1½ cups.

Dolmathes (Stuffed Grape Leaves)

Serve as a first course to a kebob entree or make it the entree with kebobs as appetizers.

Although stuffed grape leaves are popular in many Middle Eastern countries, Avgolemono Sauce is unique to the Greek version. The following recipe has been served as a tradition in our family, adapted by each generation. Cook it on top of the range in one pot. And by all means, encourage guests to use their bread to dip in the sauce.

FOR THE STOCK

2 pounds lamb stew meat with bone (or lamb necks)
7 cups water

1 tablespoon salt
1 can (16 ounces) tomatoes

FOR THE MEAT FILLING AND LEAVES

2 pounds ground round steak
1½ cups finely chopped onion
(about 2 onions)
½ tablespoon salt
¼ teaspoon freshly ground
black pepper

1 teaspoon finely crushed
dried mint
¼ cup uncooked rice
1 tablespoon olive oil
1 jar (16 ounces) grapevine
leaves

FOR THE AVGOLEMONO SAUCE

5 eggs
½ cup freshly squeezed lemon
juice (about 2 lemons)

1. Prepare meat stock in 2-quart heavy pot: Bring the salted water and lamb stew meat to a boil. Skim off the scum. Mash tomatoes and add to stock. Cover. Simmer for 45 minutes. Set aside. (1 hour)

2. Prepare meat filling in a bowl: Mix ground beef with onions, salt, pepper, and mint. Combine rice with olive oil and add to meat mixture. Add ¾ cup meat stock from pot. The meat should have a loose consistency. (15 minutes)

3. Stuff grape leaves: Drain leaves and rinse well with water to remove any excess brine. Blanch leaves for 2 to 3 minutes in boiling water. Place under cold running water. Drain. Remove stems and gently open and flatten each leaf. Place a heaping tablespoon of meat filling in center of leaf, dull side up. Carefully fold over sides of leaf to cover meat like an envelope. Makes about 40 dolmathes. (Note: If leaves are small or torn, use two leaves.) (45 minutes)

4. Cook stuffed leaves: Place dolmathes on top of cooked lamb in pot that was set aside after preparation of stock. Arrange them folded side down in layers. Place a heavy plate over them to keep them in place and prevent unwrapping. Cook over low heat about one hour. To test doneness, remove one dolmathe and cut with fork to check tenderness of leaf. (1 hour)

5. Prepare Avgolemono Sauce with Dolmathes: Beat eggs

in large bowl until foamy and gradually add lemon juice. Add warm stock very slowly by spoonfuls from the pot. Stir continuously to prevent curdling. Do this until most of the stock is used up. With one hand, pour entire mixture back into pot while gently shaking it left to right with the other hand. Let stand 5 minutes, uncovered. Serve. (About 15 minutes)

Suggested alternatives for preparation: Prepare step 1 the night before and steps 2 through 5 the day of serving. Or prepare steps 1 through 3 in the morning and 1½ hours before serving do steps 4 and 5. Or prepare steps 1 through 4 in the morning and 15 minutes before serving heat dolmathes and do step 5.

Note on reheating: If you've any leftovers, reheat only in a double boiler to prevent curdling of egg-lemon sauce.

Note on servings: As first course, allow 3 to 4 dolmathes per person; as an entree, 6 to 8.

Note on grape leaves: The most tender leaves are, of course, those hand-picked from the vine. According to my grandmother, they are best picked in June, at least in the Midwest. For dolmathes, if you pick and use leaves the same day, boil for about 10 minutes before stuffing them. Drain and let sit in salt for another 10 minutes, then rinse and drain. To prepare dry leaves—a garland—thread 40 to 60 of them on a string, using a needle and Number 8 thread. Spear needle in center of leaf. Hang the string of grape leaves to dry, allowing space between each leaf. In about two weeks, gently tie each string of dried grape leaves into garlands. Cover with plastic to protect them from dust. Hang individual garlands on hooks to avoid their crumbling. Store several months or as long as you wish. Before using for dolmathes, dip the garland in boiling water for about 10 minutes.

Flaked Salmon Salad

Serve this as part of an appetizer assortment.

1 cup beer
2 tablespoons lemon juice
¼ cup lime juice
2 bay leaves
4 whole allspice
3 whole peppercorns
¼ teaspoon dill seed
1 tablespoon salt

2 pounds fresh salmon,
trimmed and boned
2 tablespoons olive oil
½ cup chopped green pepper
½ cup finely chopped onion
1 cup chopped green onion
⅓ cup chopped canned pimiento
1 lime

In a pan, add beer, lemon and lime juice, bay leaves, allspice, peppercorns, dill, and salt. Bring to a boil. Add salmon. Poach 10 to 12 minutes. Remove from liquid and let fish cool. Use fork to flake. Chill thoroughly. Keep in refrigerator until ready to serve. Add oil, green pepper, onions, and pimiento to salmon and toss lightly. Serve on platter, garnished with slices of lime. Makes about 4 cups salad.

Flaked Kippered Herring Salad

Here is another fish salad to use as part of an appetizer assortment. I always keep several cans of kippered herring on the shelf to meet quick needs.

1 can (7 ounces) kippered
herring
1 lemon, halved
1 jar (2 ounces) sliced
pimiento, well drained

½ medium green pepper,
coarsely chopped
½ medium onion, finely chopped

In a bowl, drain fish, using paper towel. Use fork to flake. Squeeze one lemon half and add pimiento, green pepper, and onion. Toss lightly. Slice other lemon half in thin wedges for garnish. Makes 2 cups salad.

Chicken Soup Avgolemono

I call this soup the "curdle hurdle" because it's just that! If you can prevent the curdling of the eggs, then you've got it made—a masterpiece. Here, I strongly suggest you curb any urge to add a little more of one ingredient or less of another because of the sensitive combination of acids, eggs, and heat. Constant stirring and gradual additions are extremely important.

Serve this soup with Skewered Chicken, Soup-Inspired, page 176. Cut the roaster chicken in half crosswise, reserving the breast part for kebobs and the rest for the soup.

1 roaster chicken, 4 to 5 pounds
1 tablespoon salt
3 chicken bouillon cubes
½ to ¾ cup manestra* or orzo (soup pastas)

4 large eggs, separated (room temperature)
⅓ cup freshly squeezed lemon juice (2 small lemons)

Rinse whole chicken. Cut in half crosswise, removing whole breast from top portion. Cut off wings, neck, and back. Wrap skinned breast in wax paper and refrigerate for use as kebobs. Place wings, neck, back and lower portion of bird in kettle with about 10 to 11 cups water. Add salt to taste, about 1 tablespoon. Cover and simmer over low heat, about 50 minutes. Remove cooked chicken and refrigerate if desired for use as sandwiches the next day. Strain broth. Add bouillon cubes and manestra or orzo to broth and boil about 20 minutes until tender.

In a large bowl, beat egg whites with electric beater until soft peaks form. Add yolks one at a time and continue beating. Gradually add lemon juice while continuing to beat. With

* Rice may be substituted.

one hand, slowly add a large spoonful of hot broth from kettle to the egg-lemon mixture in the bowl, stirring constantly with a ladle in the other hand. Add another spoonful or two. Continue adding the hot broth gradually until about three-fourths of the broth has been added to the egg-lemon in bowl. Slowly pour this mixture into remaining broth in kettle and stir gently. Let stand 5 minutes, uncovered, until thickened. Serve. Note: This soup can be heated but never boiled. It will curdle when boiled and then all will be in vain. Makes about 8 cups soup.

Variation: Rather than halve the chicken, cook it whole. Use leftover boiled meat for kebobs.

Sautéed Onions, Mushrooms, and Green Pepper

Serve with Beef and Burgundy Kebobs, page 58.

12 whole boiled onions, canned
 1 large red onion, sliced
 ¼ cup Burgundy
 2 tablespoons granulated sugar
 2 tablespoons butter
 ¼ cup marinade-baste for Beef and Burgundy Kebobs

 1 green pepper, cut into julienne strips
 1 4½-ounce jar jumbo mushrooms, drained

One hour in advance: Combine Burgundy and sugar and pour over onions.
 Before serving: Drain onions and sauté in butter until partially soft. Heat marinade-baste to boiling point and add to onions. Stir. Add green pepper and mushrooms, stirring well. Add more marinade–baste if desired. Cook until onions are soft. Arrange on plate next to Beef and Burgundy Kebobs. Makes about 1½ cups.

Sautéed Pea Pods, Water Chestnuts, and Bamboo Shoots

Use the marinade-baste from the Beef and Bourbon Kebobs, page 60, to prepare this accompaniment. Serve with those kebobs.

2 tablespoons chopped onion
¼ cup chopped green onion
1 clove garlic
2 tablespoons olive oil
1 package (6 ounces) combination frozen pea pods, water chestnuts, bamboo shoots

2 tablespoons marinade–baste for Beef and Bourbon Kebobs
1 tablespoon soy sauce

In skillet, sauté onions and garlic in olive oil. Add frozen package of vegetables. Cook at high temperature for 2 to 3 minutes, stirring constantly. Add marinade–baste sauce combined with soy sauce. Stir briskly and cook vegetables until tender. Place servings on plate next to Beef and Bourbon Kebobs. Makes about 1 cup.

Vegetable Verve

2 tablespoons margarine
½ cup chopped onion
½ teaspoon salt
⅛ teaspoon freshly ground black pepper
1 teaspoon dried mint, crushed

1 tablespoon finely chopped parsley
⅓ cup tomato sauce
⅓ cup dry sherry
⅓ cup beef bouillon (bouillon cube in ⅓ cup hot water)
2 packages (10 ounces) frozen peas or beans

In a saucepan, sauté onion in margarine until lightly browned. Add salt, pepper, mint, parsley, tomato sauce, sherry, and broth. Bring to boiling point. Add frozen vegetables. Cover. Cook until tender, 8 to 10 minutes. Makes 6 ½-cup servings.

Sweet and Sour Vegetables

2 tablespoons vegetable oil
1 large onion, cut into thin slices and separated into rings
1 medium green pepper, cut into thin strips
1 carrot, sliced thin
⅓ cup coarsely chopped celery
1 can (11 ounces) mandarin oranges, drained
1 can (13¼ ounces) pineapple chunks, drained (reserve ½ cup syrup)

1 can (16 ounces) chow mein vegetables, drained
1 can (4 ounces) whole mushrooms, drained
2 tablespoons each of soy sauce and ketchup
3 tablespoons granulated sugar
2 tablespoons cornstarch
2 tablespoons white wine vinegar

Heat oil in large skillet. Sauté onion, green pepper, carrot, and celery about 3 to 4 minutes. Add oranges, pineapple chunks, syrup, chow mein vegetables, and mushrooms. Simmer several minutes. Mix together soy sauce, ketchup, and sugar, and add to skillet. Combine cornstarch with about 2 to 3 tablespoons of cold water to make a paste. Add to skillet with wine vinegar, stirring constantly until thickened. Makes about 4 cups.

Spanakopetes (Spinach Squares)

This makes a delightful, different kind of side dish to go with kebobs. Spanakop*eta* is a dish of spinach filling between phyllo sheets, baked, and then cut and served in square shapes. However, if serving kebobs as part of an appetizer or snack menu, you might prefer Spanakopet*akia,* individual appetizers, consisting of phyllo wrapped entirely around the spinach filling. Either way, you could prepare these a day or two in advance and serve warm or cold.

FOR THE SPINACH FILLING

½ cup chopped dry onion
1 cup chopped green onions
⅓ cup olive oil
4 packages (10 ounces) frozen chopped spinach, thawed and drained
2 tablespoons butter or margarine
2 tablespoons flour
1 cup milk, warmed
4 eggs, separated

1 cup finely crumbled feta cheese
¼ cup chopped parsley
1 teaspoon salt
⅛ teaspoon freshly ground black pepper
1 tablespoon dried mint, crushed
¼ teaspoon cinnamon
¼ teaspoon nutmeg

FOR THE PHYLLO LAYERS (for bottom and top of pan)

½ pound phyllo pastry sheets (available in 1-pound packages in Greek specialty shops)

¼ pound butter or margarine, melted

1. Prepare spinach filling: In 4-quart pan, sauté onions in oil until soft. Add spinach. Stir. Cook over medium heat a few minutes. In saucepan, melt butter and gradually add flour until mixture is brown, then slowly add warm milk. Stir until smooth. Add this sauce to spinach mixture. Combine cheese with beaten egg yolks, parsley, salt, pepper, mint, cinnamon, and nutmeg. Add to spinach mixture. Fold in egg whites beaten to soft peaks. Set aside.

2. Prepare baking pan (9 x 13 x 2½ inches): Brush pan with melted butter. Use half the phyllo sheets as a base. Refrigerate remaining phyllo until ready to use. Layer sheets individually, brushing each generously with melted butter. Add spinach filling and spread evenly. The sheets overlapping the sides of pan may be folded inward. Place remaining pastry sheets over spinach filling. Brush melted butter on each sheet. Use scissors or razor to cut sheets overlapping sides of pan. Spear top with toothpick every one and a half inches to prevent filling and phyllo from separating. Sprinkle a little water on top to prevent pastry from curling.

Bake in preheated 375° oven for 10 minutes. Bake an additional 20 minutes at 350° until crust is golden brown. Remove from oven and let cool slightly. Cut into 12 squares. Unused portions can be wrapped in foil and frozen for future use.

Madeira-Topped Potato Mounds

Serve with Beef and Madeira Kebobs, page 57.

1 package (3 ounces) instant whipped potatoes (plus ingredients indicated in directions, such as butter, salt, water, and milk)	1 teaspoon minced parsley 12 small pimiento-stuffed olives 1 tablespoon Madeira 3 tablespoons clarified butter, melted

Follow directions on package except use ⅓ cup less water for stiff potatoes. Stir in parsley. Let cool slightly. Shape potatoes into 4 balls and then flatten at base to form a mound. Cut 12 small pimiento-stuffed olives in half and press 6 of them on top of each mound to form a strip design. Place on same pan to be used for heating. Chill until needed. Bake in 325° oven for 10 to 12 minutes or until warmed through. With a wide spatula, transfer mound onto plate next to kebob. Combine Madeira with butter, thickened slightly with cornstarch dissolved in water if desired. Top each mound. Makes 4 Madeira-topped potato mounds.

Instant Potato Balls

1 package (3 ounces) instant whipped potatoes (plus ingredients indicated in directions, such as butter, salt, water, and milk) ½ teaspoon parsley flakes	½ teaspoon freeze-dried chives ½ teaspoon instant minced onion ¼ teaspoon ground nutmeg ⅓ cup cornflake crumbs

Follow directions on package to prepare *stiff* mashed potatoes. This means using more flakes or less than half the amount of milk. Add parsley, chives, onion, and nutmeg. Let cool. Shape potatoes into balls. Dredge in cornflake crumbs. Place potato balls on a long sheet of foil, folding once to cover. Refrigerate until needed. Before serving, bake uncovered in preheated 325° oven for 12 to 15 minutes or until thoroughly heated. Makes 14 to 16 balls (about 1½ inches each).

Picnic Potato Salad

This cold Greek potato salad, I think, makes a perfect accompaniment to kebobs served at a picnic. (Also it could be served hot, a nice accompaniment to cold meats.)

5 pounds red potatoes, about 13 medium	1 tablespoon salt
	1 teaspoon oregano leaves
¾ cup olive oil	1 large onion, finely chopped
⅓ cup cider vinegar	

Boil potatoes with jackets until cooked, approximately 40 minutes. Drain. Peel while hot. Break up potatoes with fork and add oil. Mix well. Add vinegar, salt, oregano and onion. Mix well again. Place in large covered bowl or pan in refrigerator. Makes 9 cups.

My Mother's Pastitsio

Pastitsio is a truly special baked dish of layered macaroni with meat filling and a cream sauce topping. Serve either as a side dish with an entree such as Special Beef Souvlakia, page 42, or as the entree with a side dish of vegetable kebobs, such as Eggplant Kebobs Avgolemono, page 217. Preparation time is 1 hour 20 minutes; baking time: 35 minutes; cooling time: 30 minutes.

FOR THE MEAT FILLING

¼ cup butter or margarine
4 medium onions, finely chopped, about 2 cups
2 cloves garlic, minced
2½ pounds ground round steak
1 tablespoon salt
1 can (6 ounces) tomato paste

¾ cup water
1 tablespoon ground allspice
1 tablespoon ground nutmeg
1 teaspoon ground cinnamon
¾ teaspoon ground cloves
¼ teaspoon freshly ground black pepper

FOR THE MACARONI LAYERS

1 pound macaroni
1¼ cups grated Romano cheese (4 ounces)
1¼ cups grated Parmesan cheese (4 ounces)

¾ cup melted butter or margarine (1½ sticks)
6 eggs, beaten well
¾ cup milk

FOR THE CREAM SAUCE TOPPING (Crema)

½ cup melted butter or margarine (1 stick)
6 tablespoons flour, sifted
4 cups hot milk
½ teaspoon ground nutmeg

¼ cup grated Parmesan cheese
4 eggs, unbeaten
Salt to taste (about ¼ teaspoon)

2 tablespoons melted butter
2 tablespoons cracker meal

3 tablespoons grated Parmesan cheese

1. Prepare meat filling in a heavy pot: Sauté onions and garlic in margarine or butter until transparent. Add meat and cook until most of the liquid is absorbed. Add salt and tomato paste thinned with ¾ cup water. Cover. Simmer for about 30 minutes, stirring occasionally and adding water if necessary. Add allspice, nutmeg, cinnamon, cloves and pepper. Continue to simmer for about 15 minutes. Remove from heat and set aside.

2. Prepare macaroni layer in a pot: Cook macaroni according to package directions. Do not overcook. Transfer cooked macaroni to colander; rinse with cool water and drain well. Return to dried pot. Combine cheeses and add to macaroni, mixing thoroughly. Stir in melted butter. Combine milk and beaten eggs and add to macaroni. Mix well and set aside.

3. Prepare topping sauce in a saucepan: Add flour to melted butter and stir until foamy. Gradually add hot milk and cook over low heat, stirring constantly. Add remaining topping-sauce ingredients. Continue stirring until thick and smooth.

4. Prepare pan of pastitsio (11 x 16 x 2½ inches) : Brush bottom and sides of pan with melted butter. Sprinkle with cracker meal and 1 tablespoon Parmesan cheese. Pour one-half of macaroni mixture into pan and spread evenly. Follow with layer of meat filling, using entire amount. Cover with remaining macaroni. Spread topping sauce over macaroni layer and sprinkle with remaining Parmesan cheese.

Bake in preheated 350° oven for 35 minutes until golden. Cool at least 30 minutes before slicing into squares. This is important to maintain shape. Cut into 15 squares.

Note: This reheats well. If you wish, wrap in foil and freeze any remaining portions.

Mariam's Pilaf

¼ pound (1 stick) butter
1 cup uncooked vermicelli noodles
2 cups uncooked white rice (long-grained)

¼ teaspoon salt
Freshly ground black pepper to taste
2 teaspoons bouillon powder
4 cups water

In a heavy pan, sauté noodles in butter until golden brown. Remove from heat. Wash and drain rice and then add to noodles. Stir in salt, bouillon powder, and pepper. Add water. Cover and cook at medium heat 20 to 25 minutes until liquid is absorbed. Makes 11 ½-cup servings.

Bulgur

Bulgur, a highly nutritious processed wheat, is parboiled, dried, and partially debranned, and then either cracked or used in whole-grain form. With its toasty appearance and nutlike flavor, it makes a nice change of pace from rice.

2 tablespoons vegetable oil
2 tablespoons each of minced onion, celery, green pepper
1 clove garlic, sliced
1 cup bulgur
1 cup chicken bouillon (1 cube dissolved in 1 cup hot water)

⅔ cup water
⅓ cup Burgundy
1 teaspoon dried mint, crushed
1 teaspoon sweet basil
¼ teaspoon freshly ground black pepper

Sauté onion, celery, green pepper and garlic in oil until golden. Add bulgur and stir to coat all grains, browning very lightly. Combine remaining ingredients and add to bulgur. Cover tightly. Bring to a boil. Reduce to very low heat and cook about 15 minutes until liquid is absorbed and bulgur is fluffy. Makes 6 ½-cup servings.

Variation: Before serving, stir in 2 tablespoons each of grated Parmesan cheese and of chopped pimiento.

Wild Rice and Mushrooms

1 box (6 ounces) seasoned long-grain and wild rice
½ pound fresh mushrooms
2 tablespoons each of finely chopped onion, green onion, parsley, and green pepper

1½ tablespoons olive oil
1½ tablespoons butter
3 tablespoons sweet vermouth

Cook rice according to package directions. Wipe mushrooms with cloth dampened with vinegar and water. Slice lengthwise. In skillet, sauté onions in oil and butter until transparent. Add parsley, pepper, and mushrooms, and simmer until lightly brown, about 5 minutes. Stir in sweet vermouth. Toss rice with mushrooms until evenly distributed. Makes 8 ½-cup servings.

Greek Salad, Salata

1 head Boston lettuce	1 clove garlic
Leaf lettuce or Romaine	16 Greek olives, Calamata kind
Endive (a small handful)	(pit them)
2 tomatoes, quartered	½ pound feta cheese (½ cup
6 green onions, cut into pieces	crumbled, remainder cut into
½ cucumber, thinly sliced	chunks for garnishing
2 tablespoons chopped parsley	individual servings)

DRESSING

Salt to taste	¼ to ⅓ cup olive oil
Freshly ground black pepper,	3 to 4 tablespoons red wine
to taste	vinegar

GARNISH

Chunks of feta cheese	Choice of oregano, thyme, or
Anchovy fillets	dried mint (optional)
Greek pitted olives	

Wash greens thoroughly under cold running water. Discard bruised leaves. Drain and dry well. Chill until crisp, at least an hour. For instant crispness, shortly before using, add one tray of ice cubes to greens. Cut one clove of garlic in half and rub large wooden salad bowl. Remove greens from refrigerator. If necessary, use paper towels to absorb moisture. Greens should be dry for dressing to adhere. In a large bowl, tear greens into pieces and toss with tomatoes, onions, cucumbers, parsley, olives and crumbled cheese. Season with salt and pepper. Slowly pour olive oil over greens and toss together until coated. You may prefer to use less or more oil depending on taste and actual volume of salad. The objective is to coat, not immerse, with seasonings. Pour wine vinegar over salad and toss again, gently.

Arrange on individual salad plates or bowls. Top each serving with chunks of feta cheese, 2 anchovy fillets, and 2 or 3 olives. Serve oregano, thyme, or dried mint as optional seasonings. Makes 3 to 4 side-dish salads.

Simple version: Cut one cleaned and chilled medium head lettuce into pieces and season with salt, freshly ground pepper (about ¼ teaspoon), olive oil (about 2 tablespoons), red wine vinegar (about 1½ tablespoons) and ½ teaspoon freshly ground coriander seed. The coriander, you'll find, gives salad a distinctive flavor. Makes 2 to 3 side-dish salads.

Convenience tip: You may want to keep a pepper mill filled with coriander seed for ready use in salads.

Angouro Salata

In Greek, *angouro* is the word for cucumber. This salad is best served after chilled at least one hour.

2 medium cucumbers (about ½ pound each), pared, cut into ¼-inch slices
1 medium red onion, thinly sliced
¼ cup olive oil
3 tablespoons white wine vinegar
¼ teaspoon dried mint, crushed
¼ teaspoon celery flakes, crushed
1 teaspoon minced parsley
Salt
Freshly ground black pepper

Halve the cucumber slices and combine with onion slices in a large bowl. Combine oil, vinegar, mint, celery, and parsley and season to taste with salt and freshly ground pepper. Add to vegetables. Toss well. Chill. Makes 3 to 4 side-dish salads.

Variation: For contrast you might want to add chunks of tomato to this salad—then it becomes Angouro-Domata Salata.

A Tropical Drink

Serve with Tropicana Frank Kebobs, page 154.

1 can (13¼ ounces) pineapple syrup (½ cup) and pineapple chunks, reserving 8 for Frank Kebobs

2½ cups ginger ale*

½ cup orange juice
2 tablespoons maraschino cherry juice
2 to 3 jiggers rum (optional)
Maraschino cherries

In a blender, add pineapple syrup, pineapple chunks, ginger ale, orange juice, and cherry juice, plus rum if desired. Blend. Pour in tall glasses filled with ice. Spear cherries on cocktail spears and place in beverage as a garnish. Makes 4 cups.

Mediterranean Mists

Serve as an after-dinner drink with or without dessert.

DRY VERSION

Crushed ice
2-ounce jigger dry (*secco*) Orvieto (Italian white wine)

1-ounce jigger brandy
1 slice lemon

Half fill Old-Fashioned glass with crushed ice. Combine wine and brandy and pour over ice. Garnish with lemon slice. Makes 1 after-dinner drink.

* Or 1½ cups quinine tonic and 1 cup ginger ale.

SWEETER VERSION

Crushed ice
1-ounce jigger each of brandy,
  Mavrodaphne wine, and
  Cointreau

1 slice lime

Half fill Old-Fashioned glass with crushed ice. Combine brandy, wine and Cointreau and pour over ice. Garnish with lime. Makes 1 after-dinner drink.

Molasses Oatmeal Cookies

These are what I call my picnic cookies—always included in my picnic menus. Stir in one bowl and drop—it's simple. And you can vary their texture—moist and chewy, or crisp and crunchy. (I might add, men seem to favor the first version unanimously; children lean toward the second.)

1 cup raisins
1 cup butter (2 sticks)
½ cup (1 stick) vegetable
  shortening
1 cup light brown sugar
¼ cup granulated sugar
2 medium eggs
½ cup dark molasses
3½ teaspoons ground cinnamon
1 teaspoon ground nutmeg
¼ teaspoon ground ginger

¼ teaspoon ground clove
1 teaspoon each of baking
  powder, baking soda, salt
  and vanilla extract
1 tablespoon water
2 cups all-purpose flour,
  unsifted
5 cups quick-cooking oats
  (uncooked)

In advance: Preheat oven to 350°. Soak raisins in warm water. Remove butter from refrigerator to soften for easier mixing. Grease two cookie sheets lightly (you'll finish sooner using two sheets; while one is in oven, prepare the other).
Before baking: In one large bowl, cream butter, shorten-

ing, and both sugars. Add eggs and molasses and beat well. Stir in spices, baking powder, baking soda, salt, vanilla, water, and raisins which have been drained and patted dry. Add flour and oats and mix thoroughly. This takes just a bit of elbow grease. Drop mixture by rounded teaspoons on greased cookie sheet, placing about two inches apart, approximately 12 to 15 per sheet.

Bake 8 to 13 minutes. If you want them moist and chewy, leave them in about 8 to 10 minutes. They will be soft and light brown. If you want them crisp and crunchy, leave them in about 11 to 13 minutes or until golden brown.

Remove from pan with spatula and place on cake wires to cool. Although quite soft when first removed from oven, cookies firm up quickly as they cool. Place cooled cookies on platter or in cookie jar. Store in a tight container, if you wish, to keep fresh. Makes 8 to 9 dozen.

Chocolate-Bourbon Ice Cream Bake

When serving kebobs hot as an entree, I like to plan for a cold dessert, and my selection is nearly always ice cream. I find it's the most versatile and well-liked dessert. (Of course, I should add that I grew up in a home where the freezer was at all times stacked with the homemade kind—Dad owned a confectionery.) Actually, an adaptation of Baked Alaska, this recipe does something special to ice cream, just as skewer-cooking does to meat.

The ice cream bake is essentially made of four parts : crust, filling, meringue and sauce. Prepare the first three ahead of time. The only preparation the day of serving is the sauce. Makes 1 9-inch pie.

CRUST

9-inch ready-to-use graham-
    cracker crust

FILLING

Ice Cream Layer

3 pints French vanilla ice
  cream*

Bourbon-Chocolate Layer

1 cup finely grated chocolate
  (4-ounce package of
  bittersweet chocolate)
1 cup chopped walnuts
½ cup confectioners' sugar

3 tablespoons bourbon
1 tablespoon milk
¼ teaspoon each of cinnamon,
  cloves, and nutmeg

MERINGUE

4 medium egg whites

½ cup granulated sugar

SAUCE

⅓ cup chocolate syrup

1 tablespoon bourbon

The day or week before: Prepare crust, filling, meringue.
Preheat oven to 400°. Remove ice cream from freezer and
let it soften a little to make it easier to scoop. In a ready-to-
use crust (or if you prefer, bake your own), spread and
pack ice cream evenly and carefully. Place in freezer for at
least 15 minutes until ice cream is firm. In a bowl, combine chocolate, nuts, sugar, bourbon, milk, and spices. Remove
crust with ice cream from freezer and spread chocolate mixture, covering ice cream completely. Place in freezer until
ready for meringue. Beat egg whites with electric mixer
until foamy. Add sugar gradually. Continue beating at high
speed until the meringue forms glossy stiff peaks. Spread
meringue over Ice Cream Bake, making certain the entire
ice cream surface is covered to protect from heat. Bake in
oven 3 to 4 minutes until meringue peaks are golden. Place
in freezer immediately.

  * Note on French ice cream: If you prefer, substitute regular vanilla
ice cream. The French has fuller flavor as well as a firmer, smoother
texture.

Before serving: Heat chocolate syrup and add bourbon to your liking. I prefer the ratio of 1 part bourbon to 3 parts chocolate. Cut slices of Ice Cream Bake and pour hot sauce over individual servings.

Variations of Ice Cream Bake—with heated sauces:

· Chocolate-Mint Ice Cream Bake:
  Filling: 3 pints chocolate ripple ice cream; brush mint extract over ice cream before spreading meringue
  Sauce: ¾ cup chocolate topping, 2 teaspoons pure mint and peppermint extract

· Rum Ice Cream Bake:
  Filling: 3 pints vanilla ice cream or butterscotch twirl; brush rum extract over ice cream before spreading meringue
  Sauce: ¾ cup butterscotch topping, 2 teaspoons rum extract

· Other Combinations:
  Filling: 2 pints pistachio-nut ice cream, 1 pint orange sherbet; brush Cointreau or Curaçao liqueur before spreading meringue
  Sauce: almond- or orange-flavored

  Filling: 3 pints maraschino cherry (New York cherry) ice cream
  Sauce: ⅓ cup cherry topping with 2 tablespoons cherry-flavored brandy

  Filling: 3 pints chocolate ripple; spread 1 cup grated chocolate before spreading meringue
  Sauce: crème de menthe topping

  Filling: 3 pints black walnut ice cream; top with ¾ cup chopped nuts
  Sauce: hot fudge or brandy-flavored

Variations of Ice Cream Bake—without sauce

. A few starter ideas
   Berry ice cream, topped with coconut before spreading
      meringue
   Vanilla ice cream, topped with ½ cup pineapple preserves
   Butter pecan ice cream, topped with chopped nuts

PART THREE

And Here Are Entertaining Ideas

17 · MENUS

WHAT TO CONSIDER
BEFORE USING THESE SUGGESTED MENUS

If you believe that the key to a perfect menu is combining the beverage and foods in a way that is compatible in the eyes of those you're serving, then you'll understand the dilemma I experienced with this section. I find it difficult to write a menu without first knowing specifically for whom, when and where. Obviously, a menu published on some printed pages couldn't possibly intrigue or fill the need of everyone for every situation. The perfect menu—the timely menu—must be personalized.

With the strictly skewered meals, for the most part, you won't have to be overly concerned about coordinating dishes, at least not to the same degree that you would if planning an entire menu to be eaten in a relatively short time. Please, too, don't interpret the term *strictly skewered* literally. You can—and should—complete menus with accompaniments that are not skewered.

In the menus that follow, the asterisked dishes are those for which recipes appear in the earlier part of the book.

FOR LATE RISERS ON THE WEEKEND

Honeydew Melon Wedges with Fresh Strawberries

*Brunch Kebobs**

Parsley-Sprinkled Scrambled Eggs,
a Plain Omelette or
Poached Eggs

Coffee
(Pitchers and Pitchers of It)

Variation: For a formal brunch, serve champagne or a champagne punch with a side dish of salted almonds. For an after-party gathering approaching dawn, you might prefer to serve only the Brunch Kebobs with coffee.

MIDDAY MENUS

MIDDAY MENU I

Chilled Tomato Juice with Lemon Twist
Celery Sticks, Carrot Curls, Green Pepper Rings
Cubed Luncheon Meat Kebobs*
Salad of Cottage Cheese with Berries
Sesame Breadsticks
Coffee   *Milk*

MIDDAY MENU II

Bouillon Seasoned with Sherry
or
Warmed Apple Juice
The Scandinavian Salad*
Rye Crackers   *Butter*
Coffee

MIDDAY MENU III

Baked Grapefruit
The Polynesian Salad*
Hot Biscuits   *Butter*
Iced Tea

MIDDAY MENU IV

A Tray of Assorted Finger Foods:
Strips of Hard Salami   *Cherry Tomatoes*   *Black Olives*
Sardines or Smoked Salmon on Crackers
Wedges of Gouda Cheese

Chablis (Pinot Chardonnay)

Zucchini and Eggplant Kebobs* or
Eggplant Kebobs Avgolemono*

Hard Crust Rolls

Mint Sherbet   *Coffee*

MIDDAY MENU V

Cranberry Juice on the Rocks
Ham Kebobs Madeira*

Instant Potato Balls* or
Whole Cooked Carrots

Buttered Broccoli   *Avocado and Grapefruit Salad*

Fresh Peach Ice Cream
Coffee   *Tea*

For Dieters

Carrot or Mixed Vegetable Juice
Calorie-Counters Side-Dish Salad with Fruit Kebobs*
Plain Burger Kebobs*
or
Spiced Burger Kebobs*
Black Coffee   Skim or Low-Fat Milk
Low-Calorie Carbonated Beverages

For Mixed-Drink Lovers

A Tropical Drink,* Irish Coffee, Brandy Milk Punch
or a Favorite Short or Tall Mixed Drink
Sausage Kebobs* of Your Choice
or
Trout Kebobs*
Steamed Rice
or
Buttered Pea Pods
Corn Muffins
Stinger Fruit Kebobs*
Coffee   Tea

For Tea Drinkers

An Assortment of Differently Spiced Tea Bags
Tea Kettles   Cups and Saucers
A Tray with:
Raisins, Nuts (Almonds, Cashews, Pistachios), Cherry
Tomatoes, Green Onions, Banana Chunks in Orange Juice
Seasoned with Cinnamon, Mango Slices, Halved Hard-cooked

Eggs Seasoned with Coriander or Chili Powder,
Pickles and Chutney

Indonesian Chicken Saté*

Indian Chicken Tikka*

EARLY EVENING MENUS

A BALKAN MENU

Anise-flavored Aperitif, Raki or Ouzo

Cooked Medium Shrimp in Hot Dill Butter   Cocktail Picks

or

Smoked Herring on Cocktail Rye

or

Flaked Salmon Salad*   Sesame Crackers

Lamb Kebobs, Turkish Accent*

Bulgur*

Lettuce and Tomato Wedges with Oil and Vinegar

Raspberry Sherbet

Pine Nuts   Raisins   Turkish Coffee

A DECEMBER HOLIDAY MENU

Dry Vermouth with Vodka

Taramasalata (Fish Roe Dip)*   Sesame Crackers

Tiganita Tirakia (Fried Cheeses)*

Shashlik, Russian Accent*

Wild Rice and Mushrooms*   Broiled Tomato Halves

Chilled Tangerine Sections with Coconut

or

Berries with Sour Cream

Brandy and Benedictine

A SPRING MENU

*Carbonated Vin Rosé   Skewered Feta Sandwiches**
Skewered Lamb with Zucchini Surprises (broiled)*
or
Skewered Lamb with Orange Overtones (braised)*
*Cooked Spinach Topped with Avgolemono Sauce**
Baked Potatoes
Citrus Fruit Sections and Pineapple with Kirsch
or
*Ice Cream Bake (Rum Variation)**

Serving ideas: For dinner you might prefer a still rosé wine. Another thought is to have a dry vermouth or the French Lillet aperitif with the cheese and serve a still rosé with the main course.

A PUB MENU

Scotch with Soda   or   Very Dry Sherry   or   Ale
Chilled Cooked Shrimp
*with Spicy Cocktail Dip Sauce**
*Skewered Beef, Lamb Kidney, and Pork Sausage Links**
Baked Acorn Squash
Parsleyed New Potatoes
or
Raw Spinach Salad with Hard-cooked Eggs
Toasted English Muffins   Butter
Tea with Milk and Sugar

ANY SEASON MENU I

Chilled Clam Juice Cocktail

A Plate of:
Crisp Lettuce Leaf, Green Onion Garnish

and a Whole Canned Pimiento
Stuffed with Red Salmon

Skewered Steak à la Sauce and Sauces (Sauce Chasseur)*
Mariam's Pilaf*
Whole Green Beans with Almonds
Tossed Boston Lettuce and Escarole

French Vanilla or
Dutch Chocolate Ice Cream

ANY SEASON MENU II

Guacamole (Version I)*   Corn Chips

Skewered Steak à la Sauce and Sauces (Slightly Hot Sauce)*
Wild Rice and Mushrooms*
Fried Zucchini Topped with Skordalia Sauce*
or
Chilled Cooked Endives with Lemon Juice

Fresh Pears   Camembert Cheese   Tawny Port

ANY SEASON MENU III

Red Crab Meat Tossed with
Parsley and Lemon Juice
Toast Triangles   Crackers

Flank Steak Kebobs Oriental*
Instant Potato Balls*
or
Creamed Potatoes
Gelatin Avocado Mold   Buttered Carrots

Apple Wedges   Caraway Cheese Spread

Suggestion: Serve a red Bordeaux or a California Cabernet
Sauvignon with the meat course as well as with the cheese and
fruit, or switch to a sweet Madeira or Marsala with the latter.

ANY SEASON MENU IV

*German Sauerbraten Kebobs**
Boiled Macaroni Shells   Buttered Broccoli
Cucumbers in Sour Cream
Coffee   Iced Tea

Spiced Crab Apples   Pitted Prunes
Münster Cheese on Rye Crackers
Domestic Sauterne (dry or sweet)   or   Imported Bavarian Beer

Suggestion: With the main course, you might want to serve a red table wine, perhaps a Beaujolais or a California Pinot Noir.

EARLY EVENING MENUS OF TOASTS TO YOUR HEALTH

SCANDINAVIAN MENU (TOAST: SKAL!)

Aquavit   Beer
*Pickled Herring   Dill Burger Kebobs** (appetizer size)*
Gjetost Cheese on Rye Bread Wafers

*Lamb Kebobs Scandinavian**
Buttered Asparagus Spears   or   Bibb Lettuce Salad

Lightly Sweetened Rhubarb

or
Cherry Heering Liqueur
Coffee

JAPANESE MENU (TOAST: KAMPAI!)

Sake (Rice Wine), Warmed
or
Japanese Beer

Skewered Chicken Livers with Sesame Bananas*
(use 6-inch skewers)
Flaked Salmon Salad*   *Crackers*

Japanese Kushi Yaki (Main-Dish Version)*
Steamed White Rice

Mandarin Orange Sections
or
Mandarino Liqueur
Green Tea

ITALIAN MENU (TOAST: ALLA SALUTE!)

Dry Table Wine:
Red Bardolino   or   White Soave   or   Dry Orvieto (Secco)
Spiedini Mozzarella Special*
Prosciutto Wrapped Around Melon Chunks

Veal Kebobs Italiano*
Buttered Green Noodles
Brussels Sprouts with Chestnuts

Spumoni
Galliano or Strega Liqueurs
Caffè Espresso

Note: Although a dry wine is suggested for the entire menu, a sweeter one such as Marsala on the rocks may be used as an aperitif if preferred.

ARMENIAN MENU (TOAST: GENATST!)

Anise-flavored Aperitif, Oghe or Ouzo
Relish Tray: Olives, Cheese, Pickled Peppers, and Tomatoes

Lamb Kebobs Outdoors for a Family of 8 to 10*
Mariam's Pilaf*
Tossed Green Salad

Fresh Fruit in Season   *Demitasse*

GREEK MENU I (TOAST: ISS IYIAN!)

Mezethakia or Orektikon
(An Assortment of Appetizers)

Roditys (Rosé Wine)   Retsina (Resin-flavored Wine)
Taramasalata (Red Caviar)* with Crackers
or
Fried Codfish Topped with Skordalia Sauce*

Tiganita Tirakia (Fried Cheeses)*
or
Tray of Greek Cheeses: Feta, Kefalotiri, Kasseri

Tray of Greek Olives:
Salona Black Round Olives; Calamata Black Oblong Olives;
Chios Black Wrinkled Olives; Agrinion Green Round
Olives; Naphilion Green Oblong Olives

Spanakopetakia:* Phyllo-Wrapped Appetizers with
Spinach Filling

Lamb Kebobs Latholemono* (using 6-inch skewers)

Keftethakia (Cocktail-size Meatballs)
Sikotakia Tiganita (Fried Liver Pieces)

Almonds   Pistachio Nuts   Pecans
Platter of Fresh Fruits
Dried Figs on a String

GREEK MENU II (TOAST: ISS IYIAN!)

Fayeton
(A Main Meal)
Ouzo (or the French aperitif Pernod,
which is also anise-flavored)

Crock of Feta Cheese   Crusty Bread
Dolmathes (Stuffed Grape Leaves)*
or

*Chicken Soup Avgolemono**

*Lamb Kebobs Latholemono** *(using 10-inch skewers)*
or
*Greek Orange Beef Kebobs**
*Spanakopetes (Spinach Squares)**

*Cucumbers and Tomatoes or Greek Salad**

Phyllo-Wrapped Pastries:
Galatoboureko (custard-filled) or
Baklava (nut-filled)
or
Oranges   Apples   Grapes   Mavrodaphne (red sweet wine)
Tea with Honey and Lemon   or   Demitasse

Note: Mt. Ambelos (red) or Castel Danielis table wines may be
served with dinner. If you decide on the Greek Salad, omit the
crock of feta cheese. If desired, serve it with the fruit for the
telos (end). If you decide on the Greek Orange Beef Kebobs for
this menu, double the recipe.

GREEK MENU III (TOAST: ISS IYIAN OR YASUS!)

Fayeton
(A Main Meal)

*Chicken Soup Avgolemono**

*Greek Salad (Salata)**

*My Mother's Pastitsio**

*Special Beef Souvlakia**   *Sliced Beets with Celery and Onions*

Platter of Fresh Fruits
or
Partitioned Plate of Preserves:
Quince, Watermelon and Grapefruit Rinds
Cocktail Spoons   Small Plates

Metaxa Brandy in Snifters
Mavrodaphne on the Rocks, Lemon Twist

Note: Pendeli (red table wine) may be served with the Pastitsio course as well as with the Souvlakia. If you wish to omit the soup, instead serve appetizers of yogurt with caviar or smoked herring canapés.

HELP YOURSELF TO
TWO MAIN ITEMS

SOUP WITH SOMETHING SKEWERED

*Chicken Soup Avgolemono**
(Cold or Hot)
*Kefte Burger Kebobs**
with
*Greek Fondue Dip**

Serving idea: To serve more than 5 or 6, double the fondue and burger kebob recipes. If you wish, have two fondue pots, one on each side of the platter with the mugs of soup. At one corner of the table have a broiler for the burger kebobs or place them on platters when ready from the oven broiler. If a cool dessert is desired, consider the Chocolate-Bourbon Ice Cream Bake.*

SPINACH WITH SOMETHING SKEWERED

*Spanakopetes (Spinach Squares)**
*Lamb Kebobs Cosmopolitan**
or
*Ham Kebobs Madeira**

Serving idea: To serve 6 to 8, double the above kebob recipe of your choice; if your buffet skillet isn't large enough to accommodate 8 8-inch skewers, use two smaller ones.

STUFFED GRAPE LEAVES WITH SOMETHING SKEWERED

Dolmathes (Stuffed Grape Leaves)*
Skewered Shellfish Trio*
or
Jumbo Shrimp Kebobs*
Fresh Crusty Bread

Serving idea: The best way to serve Dolmathes is right from the pot immediately after they're cooked. Thus, if you think no one would object to helping himself from the kitchen range, by all means, direct the traffic pattern in that direction. The Dolmathes and Jumbo Shrimp Kebobs will serve 6 to 8, but if you decide on the Skewered Shellfish Trio, double that recipe.

LAYERS OF MACARONI AND MEAT WITH SOMETHING SKEWERED

My Mother's Pastitsio*
Chicken Kebobs Sicilian*
and
Chicken Kebobs Spartan*

Serving idea: This should satisfy 10 to 12 persons. If desired, include also a Greek Salad.* Depending on the hour and size of appetites, you might feel safer doubling the amount of one of the kebob recipes. A favorite dry wine—either red or white—would make a perfect beverage accompaniment.

STRICTLY SKEWERED MENUS

A Menu Served at Continuous Intervals

·

(7 to 8 P.M.*)*
Oyster Kebobs Parmesan*

·

(8 to 9:30 P.M.*)*
Chicken and Pimiento Kebobs*
(braised version)

·

(9:30 to 11 P.M.*)*
Skewered Beef Duo*   *Instant Potato Balls**
Cucumber and Tomato Kebobs*

·

(After Midnight)
Skewered Dessert: Sweet Cherry and Cake à la Mode*

Serving ideas: Serve the oysters and chicken in lap-style fashion on skewer-sampler plates and accompany with a very dry sherry or a Moselle. Set the third course at a table. And select a red table wine, either a Pinot Noir or a Cabernet Sauvignon. Serve dessert lap style with coffee or tea while relaxing in front of a fireplace or under the stars or just in another room.

(Remember, for this kind of a menu, it's best to serve only one kebob per person per course.

A Menu Served at Four Intervals

·

(Very Early in Evening)
Oyster Kebobs Parmesan*

or
Wooden Cheese Board with:
Hunks of Mild Cheddar and Münster
Crackers

•

(Early in Evening)
Indian Chicken Tikka*

•

(Peak of Evening)
Japanese Kushi Yaki*
(appetizer version)
Tray of:
Pickles   Hard-cooked Eggs   Crisp Noodles

•

(Later in Evening)
Skewered Dessert: Slightly Sweet, Fresh Fruit Delight*
or
Melon Wedges

Serving ideas: Serve dry Madeira (Sercial) or Lillet as an aperitif with the oysters, or if you decide on the cheese board, perhaps you'd prefer a dry white wine such as a Riesling. Serve the Chicken Tikka with tea and the Kushi Yaki with warmed sake (Japanese rice wine). Note, for a lighter menu and one served at only two intervals, first serve either the oysters or the chicken kebobs with the cheese selection, and then when serving the Kushi Yaki, also include a tray of melon wedges.

A Menu Served at Three Intervals

•

(Early Evening)
Cocktails of Choice
A Speared Centerpiece of Cheese*
and/or
Skewered Chicken, Japanese Accent*

•

(Peak of Evening)
Korean San Juk*
A Basket of Assorted Light and Dark Breads
Celery Sticks   Potato Chips   Carrots

·

(Later in the Evening)
Stinger Fruit Kebobs*
or
Stinger Beverages

Serving ideas: Rather than serve the Speared Centerpiece of Cheese, you might want to take cold cooked foods for threading on 6-inch skewers and spear them into various Styrofoam shapes. For kebob ideas, refer to Kebobs of Cheese and Sausage Tidbits, Cold Version* as well as the cold versions of Ham Slices on Skewers* and Ham Chunks on Skewers.* If serving at the above intervals does not seem desirable for a particular occasion, you might prefer to co-feature two skewered items (or three if desired) during the peak of the evening. Serve kebobs one at a time for the sampling, preferably the braised version before the broiled.

A Roman Menu

Dry Orvieto (Secco)   Red Chianti
Antipasto:
Cherry Tomatoes   Celery Sticks   Radishes
Hard-cooked Eggs   Sautéed Chicken Livers

·

Skewered Artichokes*

·

Lamb, Veal, and Pepperoni Kebobs*

·

Continental Fruit Kebobs*
Mediterranean Mists (Dry)*
or
Sweet Marsala

Serving idea: Here you might want to cook the meat kebobs from a buffet skillet which is placed on a cocktail table. When the kebobs are ready to eat, garnish them with topping mixture, place on plates next to the skillet and serve.

A Hellenic Menu

Santa Helena (Greek Dry White Wine) or Pinot Chardonnay
or
Roditys (Greek Rosé) or a California Grenache Rosé

Mezethakia:

Green Onions	*Tomato Wedges*	*Cucumber Sticks*
Yogurt	*Smoked Salmon on Crackers*	
Salt Shaker	*Pepper Grinder*	*Peppercorns*

·

Eggplant Kebobs Avgolemono*

·

Pork Kebobs Portokali*
or
Lamb Kebobs Mediterranean*

·

Sweet Potato Kebobs, Nonsweet Version*

·

Continental Fruit Kebobs*
Mediterranean Mists (Sweet)*
or
Metaxa in Brandy Snifters

Sea Fare Menu

Dry White Wine:
Pouilly Fuissé or Pinot Chardonnay or Johannisberg Riesling
Skewered Wrapped Oysters*
or
Oyster Kebobs Parmesan*

·

Shrimp Selection*
(Sweet-Sour, Spiced, or Spiked)
Skewered Shellfish Trio*

·

Wicker Basket of Fried Onion Rings
or
Spinach-Leaf-Bordered Bowl of Hot Fluffy Rice

·

Iced Cantaloupe or Honeydew with Strawberries

Serving ideas: If you wish to include fish in this menu, substitute either Skewered Fish Plaki* or Skewered Salmon* for the shrimp selection. Consider this menu only when you know all your guests love seafood.

Safari Menu

Pecan Burger Kebobs*
(appetizer size, 6-inch skewers)

A Cranberry Gelatin Mold
or
Cucumber and Tomato Kebobs*

·

South African Sosaties*

·

Sweet Potato Kebobs*

·

Tea   Lemon Sherbet   Coffee
Tray of Assorted Nuts

Champagne, Cheese and Chicken Menu

Ice Buckets and Bottles of Champagne:
Extra Dry   Pink   Sparkling Burgundy   Cold Duck
Tray of Cheeses:
Cheddar   Provolone   Brick   Gruyère   Nokkelost

Gouda   *Celery Stuffed with Roquefort*   *Brie*
Crackers
Thin Pumpernickel Slices

·

Indonesian Chicken Saté*
(Broiled)

·

Chicken Kebobs Confetti*
(Braised)

·

Chicken Kebobs Sicilian*
(Baked)

Serving ideas: Arrange champagne and the tray of cheeses on separate side or cocktail tables. Serve the chicken kebobs lap-style, one recipe at a time at desired intervals. If you don't have special cups for the dip sauce for the Indonesian Saté, use small egg cups.

Just a Bite with Beer

Keg of Beer
Assortment of Mugs
Bavarian-Style Pretzels   Crab Apples

·

Chicken Kebobs à la Sauce and Crumbs*

·

Beer Burger Kebobs*
or
Ham Slices or Chunks on Skewers (Version II)*
or
Skewered Mixed Sausages*

A Japanese-Style Evening

Platters of Assorted Miniature Muffins
Wine or Fruit Punch

·

Mushrooms en Brochette*

·

Skewered Scallops and Shrimp*
(appetizer version)

·

Japanese Kushi Yaki*
(appetizer version)

Serving ideas: Arrange large pillows on floor to form a circle for sitting. In center, position the punch bowl with cups. Off to the side, place a few platters of sweet and nonsweet varieties of muffins. Serve kebobs on small platters and pace the serving of each recipe at half-hour or hour intervals, as preferred.

A variation—International Style Evening: A more casual combination of foods, starting with Spiedini Mozzarella Special,* followed by the Indian Chicken Tikka* and then Skewered Greek Sausages.* Conclude the meal with fresh fruits. Fill oil and vinegar cruets, one with crème de menthe and the other with Cointreau, and serve for seasoning fruit to taste.

A Splendid Splurge

Bottles of:
Domestic or Imported Spring and Mineral Waters
or
Bottles of:
Pinot Chardonnay   *Tavel Rosé*   *Red Bordeaux*

·

Tray of:
Smoked Salmon   *Cooked Tiny Shrimp*   *Smoked Herring*
Thin Raw Onion Slices   *Crackers*

·

Skewered Feta Sandwiches*
(baked)

·

Skewered Chicken Livers, Georgia's Style*
(braised)

·

Beef Rib Eye and Oyster Kebobs*
(broiled)

·

Haute Sauterne   Port du Salut Cheese   Apple Slices

A Menu with a Confectionary Conclusion

Mushrooms en Brochette*

·

Platter of:
Thin Slices of Pastrami Rolled and Speared with Cocktail Picks
Poppy-Seed Rolls   Butter

·

Zucchini and Eggplant Kebobs*
or
Cucumber and Tomato Kebobs*

·

Chicken Kebobs Spartan*

·

Coffee

A Tray of Assorted Dried Fruits:
Dates Stuffed with Almonds and Rolled in Confectioners' Sugar
Figs   Apricots   Prunes   Peaches

Simple Sundaes:
French Vanilla Ice Cream   Molded or Break-up Chocolate
Maraschino Cherries   Freshly Ground Walnuts   Sliced Bananas

Serving idea: The Confectionery Side Table. Place chocolate on marble slab or counter-top tray in center of table. In advance, scoop ice cream into dishes and put in freezer until needed. At the table melt the chocolate in a chafing dish or in a double boiler over a buffet heating burner. Stir constantly with wooden spoon. When melted, pour over ice cream and let everyone garnish sundaes to taste.

A SNACK BUFFET

Chicken Consommé in Mugs

Cold Kebobs:

Roast Beef Slices on a Skewer*
Ham Slices on Skewers (Version 1: Served Cold)*
Kebobs of Cheese and Sausage Tidbits (Cold Version)*

Warmed Apple Sauce in Custard Cups
Corn on the Cob   Chive Butter

Hot Kebobs:

Snack Tray of Mixed Meat Kebobs*
Wiener and Burger Kebobs*

Halved Hard-cooked Eggs
Platter of Potato Chips   Corn Chips   Pretzels
Iced Tea

Serving ideas: Serve either the cold or the hot kebobs, or arrange the accompaniments in the center of a large table and place your selection of cold kebobs on one side of table and the hot on the other. Note: If you decide on both cold and hot, omit the cheese topping sauce and use only one sauce with the Snack Tray of Mixed Meat Kebobs.*

COME FOR A DRINK AND A SNACK OF SOMETHING SKEWERED

Champagne . . . and Beef Rib-Eye and Oyster Kebobs*
or
Decanters of Pouilly Fuissé (French white Burgundy) . . . and Spiedini Mozzarella Special* or Skewered Feta Sandwiches*
or
Decanters of Pinot Noir (California red Burgundy) . . . and Burgundy Burger Kebobs* or Parmesan Burger Kebobs*
or
Extra Dry or Medium Dry Spanish Sherry (Fino or Amontillado) . . . and Spanish Pinchos*

or

Sake (Japanese Rice Wine) . . . *and Skewered Chicken, Japanese Accent* or Korean San Juk**

or

Rum Coolers . . . *and Lamb Kebobs Caribbean**

or

Cocktails . . . *and Skewered Chicken Livers, Georgia's Style**

or

Moselle Wine . . . *and Pork, Ham, and Salami Kebobs* or Mixed Meat Kebobs, German Accent**

or

Keg of Light Beer . . . *and Beef Kebobs, Loaf Style**

or

Ale . . . *and Sparerib Kebobs**

or

Root Beer or Cola . . . *and Frank Kebobs in Seasoned Buns**

or

Pitchers of Milk or Fruit Punch . . . *and Ham Slices on Skewers* or Ham Chunks on Skewers, Sandwich Style**

or

Tea . . . *and Skewered Dessert: Slightly Sweet, Fresh Fruit Delight**

FOR OUTDOOR ENTHUSIASTS ON THE WEEKEND

Stuffed Vegetables and Fruits, Picnic Style*

Beef Kebobs, Individual Style*

Wicker Baskets of:
Dark and Light Breads

Bowl of Assorted Nut- and Coconut-coated Ice Cream Balls
Molasses Oatmeal Cookies*

or

Watermelon Soaked with Ruby Port
Wedges of Cheese: Port du Salut or Bel Paese

Note: As a beverage, you might want kegs of draft beer, gallon dispensers of red Chianti, or pitchers of iced tea.

18 · PARTIES

WHAT TO CONSIDER BEFORE PLANNING A PARTY

The purpose of a party is—fun. When planning a party, you might concentrate primarily on food—the menu, method of serving, and table setting—or you might even carry through a theme idea with invitations, room decorations, music, favors, and games. For the most part, the type of party you give will depend not only on your resources (such as money, time, and space) but also on your guests' ideas of fun, which vary widely.

A party is a sharing kind of event with extensive opportunities to explore. It can evoke expressions of emotion, exchanges of thought, physical exercise (from dancing, games, and the like), culinary experimentation; in short, sensory stimulation. What's more, all this exploration is nothing more and nothing less than play. And playing off life's tensions is very relaxing and very healthy.

If you're giving a party, it seems to me that above everything you should plan it in a way that will help everyone to open up easily. The key to a successful party is you. You're the catalyst, the leader, the organizer. As such, you must put your heart into it. If you don't, if you get caught up in following rules to the point where they control you and not you them, more than likely your party will be stiff. For certain, then, you'll have missed the whole purpose.

A great party doesn't just happen. Contrary to all the instant, effortless kinds of party plans you read about, a party does require organized and concerted effort, if you want the occasion to be memorable in a meaningful way to everyone who shared in it. You must manage your time well by planning ahead and by preparing in advance as many items as possible plus carefully tailoring the menu and activities to suit your guests. And what will probably more than compensate for all your exertion is the satisfaction you'll feel as you observe everyone having fun. If need be, have fewer but much better parties.

Now let's review some parties that feature kebobs on the menu. Adapt the following suggestions to your aims and ambitions, adding a little here or perhaps omitting a great deal there.

STRICTLY SKEWERED:
For a Small Group

Informal and refreshingly interesting, this party in my opinion is most appropriate when certain prerequisites are met. First, you should be entertaining 4 or 6 people who know each other quite well. Second, these friends should have a genuine liking for food. And third, you should feel no qualms about displacing the conventional menu for another with a new twist: to have course after course served from skewers and to have these skewered courses served sporadically throughout the evening—in different rooms and in different styles of serving . . . lap style, serve yourself, and table service.

The best time to serve each course must be determined by keeping alert to what appears a general readiness for food and to what makes a timely break in conversation. For this menu, you'll need plenty of skewers and, if you're going to mix sauces and thread skewers in advance, you'll also need plenty of room in your refrigerator.

SUGGESTED MENU

A SAMPLING OF SKEWERED FOODS

(Very Early Evening)
A Choice of Cocktail or Wine
Skewered Feta Sandwiches*
or
A Speared Centerpiece of Cheese*

(Early Evening)
Skewered Chicken Livers, Georgia's Style* and either Skewered
Chicken, Japanese Accent* or the braised version of
Chicken and Pimiento Kebobs*

(Peak of Evening)
Jumbo Shrimp Kebobs*
or
Pepper Steak Kebobs*
Choice of Chilled Vegetable Kebobs* and/or
Mushroom en Brochette* or Skewered Artichokes*

(Later in Evening)
Skewered Desserts (Slightly Sweet, Sweet, or Very Sweet)*
Coffee   Tea   Mediterranean Mists*

Serving ideas: With the menu above, serve the braised kebobs lap style on skewer-sampler plates. Serve the shrimp or pepper steak course at the table. If you decide on beef, place the portable broiler on a cart next to the table so that everyone can supervise the timing of his or her kebobs. If you've selected shrimp, broil the kebobs in oven broiler and place on individual dinner plates before bringing to the table. Place the skewered vegetables on side dishes. When the time comes for considering a final course, it might be just coffee, perhaps an after-dinner drink, and a survey: Do friends want dessert now? . . . Do they want to skip it? . . . Delay it? You might want to linger at the table awhile with the beverage and then later in another room serve dessert, lap style.

Note that the beginning courses of this kind of menu aren't to be considered appetizers to sustain one until the traditionally served heavier main course, which is usually eaten at the table. The course served midway in the progression of this meal could feature a lighter dish such as fish; thus, the course preceding it would be more substantial. Actually, how much (or little) to include in this kind of menu is gauged by having observed guests' general consumption and interest in specific foods. (Even my recipe for chicken livers won't excite the person who abhors liver.) As a guide, count on one kebob per person for each course. Surprisingly, dessert is not always skipped. Please don't feel confined to these suggestions. By all means, leaf through the pages of this book and pick others that perhaps seem more appealing to you, or select recipes that you've created (and, of course, tested before serving, even to friends).

STRICTLY SKEWERED:
For a Large Group

Set the stage for an indoor party of an international theme with a motif of travel, discovery, adventure. Design the invitations to communicate the concept of a kebob-tasting event with a sampling of both foreign and familiar flavors. Basically, concentrate your planning on the selection of kebobs. To serve the menu, arrange the table in such a way that the various courses can be presented at one time for self-helpings. Place the platters of broiled and baked kebobs on food warmers. Serve the braised kebobs either from decorative skillet appliances or from platters. Possibly you'd want someone by the table to serve these with decorative tongs. If the guest list isn't too large, off in the corner arrange a table with portable griddles and broilers for guests inclined to enjoy creating and cooking their own kebobs. Here place 6- and 10-inch skewers plus platters of raw and precooked foods and a selection of bastes, topping sauces, and dips. If your guests will be dropping in and out, plan on having a small table off to the corner or in the middle of a room. On this, include nothing but skewers of cold cooked foods speared into several decorative holders made of glass, wood, wax, plastic, or fruit. Also provide for a few skewer stands or decorative tumblers for the disposal of used skewers. Periodically check to make certain this table is replenished as needed for all-night snacking.

Variations:

Secure the names (and pronunciation) of the skewered foods found everywhere in the seven continents, photographs of kebob vendors, their titles, and all about the kebobs they sell. If desired, use this information to prepare an animated vignette, a wall grouping, or a table centerpiece.

Synchronize the selection of tunes from foreign lands with a sampling of kebobs adapted from those countries.

SUGGESTED MENU

A SELECTION OF STRICTLY SKEWERED ITEMS

*Here the menu is strictly up to you and if you want
adapted rather than authentic versions of foreign
recipes, consider the use of this book. In addition to a
selection of national cuisines such as Indian, Greek, Mexican,
South African, Italian, German, Korean and others, also
include a sampling of variously cooked kebobs—broiled,
braised, and baked—as well as the cold foods speared
into skewer holders.*

MORE IDEAS FOR STRICTLY SKEWERED PARTIES

A Block or Village Party Outdoors

Here's an idea for neighbors who want once or twice a year to block off the street or park area early in the evening to get together for fun and perhaps also fund-raising. Recruit volunteers in advance to make carts or stalls similar to those used by the saté sellers in Indonesia, by the currasquinho vendors in Brazil, or by the souvlakia peddlers in Greece. These carts could be stored and used through the years for special skewered snack gatherings.

An Unexpected Surprise Party

Consider this idea when you want to add a new dimension to the traditional holiday party. Introduce an expectation for a surprise when everyone arrives but don't reveal the surprise until the menu is served. At that time, point to the More Surprise Burger Kebobs.* (When preparing these, take a 1½-inch-square piece of paper and write the word "You" on it and then fold three to four times. Remove the pimiento from one jumbo stuffed olive and insert note.) The person whose kebob has the note might receive a gift, fetch a friend or relative who hasn't been seen for years, make an announcement, or whatever might be of interest and timely. If desired, double-feature the Burger Kebobs with either a Snack Tray of Mixed Meat Kebobs* or Skewers of Coated Mixed Meats.*

A Sausage Sampling Party

For this party, your guests must like sausages enough to taste a wide array of them grilled and broiled or served cold with dip sauces. And, of course, the greater variety you provide, the better the chance for guests to create sausage kebobs to their satisfaction. You might want to play on the word "serendipity" to develop the party theme, particularly since the menu features the idea of discovering new flavors from the combination of many different sausages and dip sauces.

TRAYS and TRAYS and TRAYS

Trays of sausages: *canned cocktail wieners, Vienna sausages, packaged cocktail sausages, sliced and cubed luncheon meats, smoked links, summer sausage, Bratwurst, liver sausage, bologna chunks, bologna slices folded in quarters, knackwurst, franks, and whatever else may appeal to you while selecting meats in the sausage shop. Perhaps the chapter on Sausage, page 153, will stimulate a few more thoughts.*

Trays of vegetables and fruits to thread on skewers with the sausages: *pickles . . . sweet, dill, cucumber slices; olives . . . black pitted, pimiento- or anchovy-stuffed; vegetables, raw and cooked . . . chunks of green peppers, zucchini, tiny onions, carrots, mushrooms, cherry tomatoes; sweets . . . canned and fresh fruit slices or chunks; dried pitted fruits stuffed with cheese, cheese balls rolled in nuts.*

Trays of skewers: *6- and 10-inch skewers for cooking indoors, and if cooking outdoors over large grills, the long-handled skewers, too.*

Skewer disposal containers

Cups of dip sauces: *Horseradish Dip Sauce, the lemon highlight variation, page 268; Sweet-Sour Dip Sauce, page 269; Sour Cream Dip Sauces, the Cheddar, anchovy and sweet accents, pages 272–73; Guacamole, pages 270–71; Spicy Cocktail Dip Sauces, pages 267–68. For those who might prefer basting their sausage kebobs, include a few sauces such as Tomato Barbecue Sauce, pages 265–66; Vinaigrette, page 263; and Thin Sweet-Sour Sauce, page 264.*

Baskets of bread: *frankfurter rolls, raisin muffins, crackers, cocktail ryes, pumpernickel, unsliced miniature bread loaves.*

Bottles of beverages: *soda pop, beer and wine.*

Cooking equipment: *for indoors, table broilers; and for outdoors, small hibachis or large grills.*

SKEWERS AND STEINS

Instead of a wine-tasting party, why not make it beer tasting. In fact, make this a come-with-something party where each guest is asked to bring a different beer. Plan on an assortment of beers imported from different countries and of types such as Pilsner, dark, ale, bock, malt, porter, stout, lager, pasteurized, and draft. Send packaged invitations of empty twelve-ounce beer bottles or cans with notes of party details taped on as labels. When guests arrive with their one, two, or three selections, they'll quickly learn that you've actually intended a double feature beer-tasting event, that is, not only sipping beverages from steins but also sampling beer-seasoned bites from skewers. And if you've requested guests to bring a beverage, think about making some favors, something derived from the theme "Skewers and Steins."

Depending on the specific climate you want to achieve, you can accessorize the party in one of many ways. Take music, for example. If you're aiming for a boisterous, chug-a-lug blast, then list on your agenda vocal tunes, a piano, and as many small instruments as you can gather. If, on the other hand, you're after the lively yet low-keyed beer garden atmosphere that's conducive, let's say, to the exchange of great philosophies, instead keep to the recorded instrumental sounds and play them only for a background effect. Lighting, obviously, is another way to capture a certain party feeling. Also, consider the spatial effect from the design, shape and size relationship of tables and chairs. You might want to paint beer barrels and cushion their tops for seating, or refinish a wooden picnic table, or . . . better yet, before you firm up your plans, visit a few novelty and junk shops and with an open mind search for ideas and items to carry out just the skewer and stein party appropriate to your needs.

SUGGESTED MENU

An Assortment of Beers Brought by Guests
A Tray of Various-Shaped Steins

Flaked Salmon Salad*　　　　　*Cocktail Ryes*

A Selection of Beer-Seasoned Kebobs:
Skewered Mixed Sausages*

Sparerib Kebobs*

Beer Burger Kebobs*   *or*   *Beef and Beer Kebobs**

Corn on the Cob

Carrot Sticks   *Deviled Eggs*

Chocolate Cup Cakes

SKEWERS AND A GREEK ISLAND FEAST

Admittedly, Greek cuisine—unsophisticated and limited—can't compare with the classical culinary art and variety of the French, Italian or Oriental food. So it's not the menu but the mood that really makes giving and going to a Greek party something unparalleled. It is very much alive.

Introduce the feeling for such a party with packaged invitations—"Your Passport to a Greek Island Party." Enclose a simulated passport with a small card entitled "Password." When guests arrive at the Customs Gate and give the password *"souvla,"* present them with a handkerchief and two skewers, which means you intend for guests to cook their own kebobs (souvlakia). But, if the password is *Komboloi,* present them with a handkerchief and Greek worry beads, which means you want guests to help themselves to souvlakia ready-to-eat.

For an in-out setting, arrange a buffet table indoors and on the patio or by a pool place several small tables for eating outdoors. For outdoor cooking, have guests select their choice of meat—beef, veal, lamb, pork, or mixed—and cook the kebobs themselves over coals on small grills. Or, have them get their kebobs from a large grill where a chef attends to cooking details using a long stick with a rag tied to the end. But, if you want to omit cooking outdoors, then serve the braised, baked or broiled kebobs on the buffet table.

There are many national customs, foods, and crafts to help you establish the Greek Island motif. For instance, as a food centerpiece for each of the tables outdoors, arrange a sampling of Greek wines (just beware of retsina, which requires

an acquired taste), Greek olives and cheeses and a small loaf
of homemade bread. If you wish, adopt the concept of Vas-
silopeta (Greek New Year's bread), which means the person
whose slice has a coin in it is to have good luck (add a quarter to each loaf while making the dough). To emphasize the
villagelike casualness of the gathering, you could have
guests leave their shoes at the Customs Gate for a banquet
in barefeet, or invite them to come in sandals. And above all,
to ignite the Greek Island fiery mood, the one essential—
whether recorded or live—is music. Recruit a few friends
who can lead and instruct various Greek folk dances where
everyone joins handkerchiefs to dance in a circle. Include
tunes ranging from a slow and moderate tempo to the vigor-
ous "Hasapico Horo," the butcher-style dance where everyone places hands on each others' shoulders and goes around
and around, steadily increasing speed with very fast, short,
choppy steps. *Opa!*

Variations:

Skip the passport and Customs Gate idea and simply start
the party on water. If you live on either coast, the gulf area
or lake region, you might want to go sailing with the group
for part of the day and return to a party indoors for a menu
of souvlakia—and more fun.

For a simpler and more formal party climate, change the
Greek Island feast to a Greek dinner and accessorize with a
few modern design symbols suggestive of the ancient cities.

SUGGESTED MENU

Ouzo Aperitif

*Taramasalata (Fish Roe Dip)**
*Dolmathes (Stuffed Grape Leaves)**
Greek Salad   Spanakopetes (Spinach Squares)**

Choice of Souvlakia
(1) Souvlakia ready to cook:
*Grilled Pork, Lamb (or veal) Kebobs Latholemono**
or

(2) Souvlakia ready to eat:
*Cooked Outdoors: Lamb Kebobs Latholemono**
Cooked Indoors: Choice of broiled
Chicken Kebobs Spartan, or Greek Orange Beef Kebobs,* or*
Skewered Greek Sausages or baked Skewered*
Fish Plaki or braised Pork Kebobs Portokali**

Table Centerpieces of Cheese, Bread and Wine

| *Phyllo Pastries* | *Fresh Fruits* |
| *Greek Coffee* | *Metaxa in Snifters* |

Note: For dessert, you may want to serve only fresh fruit and package the extremely rich phyllo pastries for take-home treats.

SKEWERS AND A PICNIC AWAY FROM HOME

As the coordinator for this picnic, you'll probably find it more convenient to prepare the meat and cookies for the menu, but allocate the remaining items to your guests according to who wants to bring what. Center this picnic around a "picking" theme. When all arrive at the picnic site—a park, forest preserve, canyon or lake—have them reach into a small box and pick a folded piece of paper which should be tucked away until just before eating. When it's time to eat, if desired, have those whose slips have matching numbers not only grill their food together but eat together as well. When it's time to call it a day, have another picking from a box. All the slips should be blank except the one with the next month's calendar marked "The Next Picnic."

Variations:
  More Picking . . . At about eating time, invite everyone to dip into a basket and pick one of the many numbered rolled packages which correspond with the numbers on the folded pieces of paper picked earlier. These packages might contain big, bright bibs which you've made (or made to order) with a bold design of the number . . . or select what-

ever picking item seems in key with the general interest and cooperation of the group.

A Picnic Play-All-Day . . . If your objective is to get everyone pleasantly all pooped out, carry out the subtheme of "Dawn, Daylight, Dusk, and Dark." Assemble everyone for a light breakfast and use only the cars necessary for packing picnic paraphernalia and passengers to travel together. Return home for a dance or a fireside chat.

SUGGESTED MENU

Chilled Sour Cream Fruit Salad
Picnic Potato Salad*   *Kidney Bean Salad*
Lamb and Beef Kebobs, Picnic Style*

or

Beef Kebobs, Individual Style*
Sliced Tomatoes and Cucumbers
Assorted Pickled Relishes

Hard Rolls

An Array of Chilled Melons and Other Fresh Fruits
Molasses Oatmeal Cookies*   *Coconut Crunch Cake*
Coffee   *Soda Pop*   *Beer*

SKEWERS AND CHEESE SAMPLING

> *Smile and the world smiles with you,*
> *Kick and you kick alone;*
> *For a pleasant smile will let you in,*
> *Where a kicker is never known.*
> ANONYMOUS

One way to communicate the party idea—sampling food and smiling—is with a skewer-and-cheese-designed invitation that includes the above quote. Basically, the sampling of food cofeatures an assortment of cheeses and two or three versions of braised kebobs. As for the selection of cheeses, plan a representative sampling, and for one kind of cheese, you might want to compare the taste of the imported version to that of the domestic. To serve the food, invite guests to sample the kebobs—at least one variety—first, and then to sample the assortment of cheeses. The skewers from the kebobs will function as picks to spear and eat the cheese (use only the 6-inch skewers). Thus, depending on your selection of braised kebobs, you may not need knives for this menu, which could be served lap style, very conveniently, if desired.

Variation:

To expand on the "smiling" idea, you might have someone take Polaroid pictures and attach them to a cheesecloth hung on the wall . . . and at the end of party have a judging and prizes, one to the most expressive smiler and one to the frowner as well.

SUGGESTED MENU

An Assortment of Cheeses
Crackers   Biscuits
A Selection of Chilled White and Rosé Wines
A Pair or Trio of Braised Kebobs
(recipes using your favorite meats)
Radish Buds, Celery and Cucumber Sticks
Apples Soaked in Sweet Vermouth   Pears Soaked in Citrus Juice
Cookies

INDEX

Almond(s):
  Franks in a Bun, Almond
    Version, 156
Anchovy(ies):
  Bean Stuffing, 220
  Butters, 43, 157
  Crunch Topping Mixture, 239
  Skewered Feta Sandwiches, 237
  Sour Cream with Anchovy
    Sauce, 272
  Stuffed Burger Kebobs, 82–83
  Topping Sauce, 236
  Veal and Salty Accents, 93–94
Angouro Salata (Cucumber
    Salad), 292–93
Appetizers:
  Dolmathes (Stuffed Grape
    Leaves), 277–79
  Feta and Cream Cheese Balls,
    275
  Flaked Kippered Herring
    Salad, 280–81
  Flaked Salmon Salad, 280
  Fried Cheeses, 275–76
  Grape Leaves, Stuffed, 277–79
  Griddled Cheese and Rye
    Kebobs, 235
  Indian Chicken Tikka, 179–80

  Indonesian Chicken Saté, 178–
    179
  Japanese Kushi Yaki, 45
  Lamb Kebobs Latholemono, 101
  Oyster Kebobs Parmesan, 198
  Skewered Chicken, Japanese
    Accent, 177–78
  Skewered Feta Sandwiches, 237
  Speared Centerpiece of Cheese,
    A, 233–34
  Spiedini Mozzarella Special,
    235–36
  Taramasalata (Fish Roe Dip),
    277
  Tiganita Tirakia (Fried
    Cheeses), 275–76
  See also Ground Beef recipes
Apple(s):
  Broiled Ham Kebob Snacks,
    141–42
  Pork and Apple Kebobs, 128
  and Poultry Kebobs, 185–86
  skewer cooking methods, 209
  Skewered Sausage, Viennese
    Accent, 166
Apricot(s):
  Skewered Veal with, 91–92
  Skillet Sauces, 91, 139

Artichoke(s):
  Fish Kebobs: Lemon and
    Riganato Accent, 200–01
  Minted Lamb Kebobs
    Avgolemono, 99–100
  Skewered, 212
  Skewered Sirloin with Stuffed
    Artichoke Bottoms, 49–50
  Tarragon Chicken Kebobs,
    175–76
Avgolemono:
  Chicken Soup, 281–82
  Eggplant Kebobs, 217
  Minted Lamb Kebobs, 99–100
  Sauces, 262–63, 278
Avocado:
  Dressing, 225
  Guacamole, Golden, 270
  Guacamole, Traditional, 270

baking, 24
Bamboo Shoots and Poultry
    Kebobs, 185
Banana(s):
  Broiled Ham Kebob Snacks,
    141–42
  Franks in a Bun, Banana
    Version, 155–56
  Ham Slices: Cold, 134–35
  Hawaiian Ham Kebobs, 139–40
  Pecan Beef Kebobs, 81
  Porkburger Kebobs, 130
  Poultry Kebobs: Honey-Rum
    Accent, 186
  skewer cooking methods,
    208–09
  Skewered Chicken Livers with
    Sesame Bananas, 147
  topping sauce, 48
Barbecue sauces:
  Tomato Basic, 266–67
  Tomato Cooked, 265–66
  Tomato Herbed variation, 267
  Tomato Hot variation, 267
  Tomato Sweet Glaze variation,
    267

  Tomato Sweet-Sour variations,
    67, 267
Bastes, 28–29
  dill, 115
  for lamb, 100, 116, 117
  for lamb kidneys, 151
  for mushrooms, 210
  for pork, 130, 142
  Roquefort, 41, 83
  for sausages, 154
  for sweet potatoes, 213
  See also Baste–Toppings;
    Butters; Coatings and
    Toppings; Dips; Marinades;
    Marinade–Bastes, Marinade–
    Baste–Toppings; Marinade–
    Topping; Marinade–Top-
    ping–Sauce; Sauces; Skillet
    Sauces; Topping Sauces
Baste–Toppings, 78, 107, 131,
    186, 187, 198, 248
Bean(s):
  Salad Bed, 225–26
  Stuffing, 220
Béarnaise Sauce, 262
Béchamel Sauce, 258–59
Beef:
  and Beer Kebobs, 59–60
  and Bourbon Kebobs, 60
  and Burgundy Kebobs, 58–59
  Cheese-Coated Kebobs, 70
  cuts for kebobs, 37–38
  Enchilada Kebobs, 71–72
  Flank Steak Kebobs, Oriental,
    61–62
  German Sauerbraten Kebobs,
    46–48
  Greek Orange Beef Kebobs,
    39–40
  Japanese Kushi Yaki, 44–46
  Kebobs, Individual Style, 66–67
  Kebobs, Loaf Style, 67–69
  Korean San Juk, 43–44
  Lamb and Beef Kebobs,
    Picnic Style, 249–50
  and Madeira Kebobs, 57–58
  Outdoor Kebobing with, 66–69
  Pepper Steak Kebobs, 40–41

Pronto Broiler Kebobs, 62–63
Pronto Skillet and Baking-Pan
Kebobs, 63–64
Rib-Eye and Oyster Kebobs,
248–49
Roast Beef Slices on a Skewer,
69–70
skewer cooking methods, 37–39
Skewered Beef with Canned
Fruit, 55
Skewered Beef Duo, 48–49
Skewered Beef with Fresh
Fruit, 56
Skewered Beef with Hearts of
Palm, 41–42
Skewered Beef, Lamb Kidney,
and Pork Sausage Links,
247–48
Skewered Sirloin with
Artichoke Bottoms, 49–50
Skewered Sirloin with
Cucumber, 52–53
Skewered Sirloin with
Eggplant, 53
Skewered Sirloin with
Mushrooms, 51–52
Skewered Sirloin with Onions,
54–55
Skewered Steak a la Sauce,
64–66
Special Souvlakia, 42–43
Sweet-Tangy Kebobs, 71
Taco Garnish Rolls, 226–27
See also Ground Beef
Beer:
and Beef Kebobs, 59–60
Burger Kebobs, 84
Beverages, 293–94
Biscuit-Ringed Knackwurst
Kebobs, 156
Blue Cheese:
baste, 41
Bread, French, 68
Bologna:
Mixed Meat Kebobs, German
Accent, 240
Pepperoni-Accented Kebobs,
157–58

Sweet and Cordial Triangles,
162–63
Bordelaise Sauce, 261
braising, 24–25
Bratwurst:
Skewered Greek Sausage, 164
Skewered Mixed Sausages, 167
Breads:
French Blue Cheese, 68
German, Reuben Style, 67
Italian Eggplant, 68
Broiled Ham Kebob Snacks,
141–42
broiling, 22–24
Brown Sauce I, 260
Brown Sauce II (Bordelaise),
261
Brown Sauce, Quick, 260
Brunch Kebobs, 250–51
Bulgur, 290
Burgundy:
and Beef Kebobs, 58–59
Burger Kebobs, 85
skillet sauce, 232
Butter(s):
Anchovy, 43
Clarified, 265
Garlic, 43
Lemon, 49
Tomato, 49
See also Bastes; Baste-Top-
pings; Dips; Marinades;
Marinade–Bastes; Sauces;
Skillet Sauces

Calorie Counter's Side-Dish
Salad, 227–28
Caribbean, Lamb Kebobs, 111
Carrot and Poultry Kebobs,
184–85
Chasseur Sauce, 65
Cheddar Cheese:
Pepperoni-Accented Kebobs,
157–58
Pineapple and Eggplant
Kebobs, 216–17

Cheddar Cheese (*Continued*)
  Sour Cream with Cheddar
    Sauce, 272
  topping, 166
Cheese(s):
  Coated Kebobs, 71
  Cucumber and Tomato Kebobs,
    211
  Fried, 275–76
  Griddled Cheese and Rye
    Kebobs, 235
  and Sausage Balls, 158–59
  and Sausage Chunks, 159–60
  skewer cooking methods, 209
  Speared Centerpiece of, 233–
    234
  topping sauce, 254
  See also individual listings
Cherry(ies):
  and Cake à la Mode, 231–34
  marinade–baste, 163
  Sweet and Cordial Triangles,
    162–63
Chicken and Poultry:
  Apple and Poultry Kebobs,
    185–86
  Bamboo Shoots and Poultry
    Kebobs, 185
  breasts, how to bone, 168–69
  Carrot and Poultry Kebobs,
    184–85
  Cumin Chicken Kebobs, 175,
    176
  Ginger Chicken, Skewered,
    174, 176
  and Ham Kebobs, Mediter-
    ranean Style, 243–44
  Indian Chicken Tikka, 179–80
  Indonesian Chicken Saté,
    178–79
  Kebobs a la Sauces and
    Crumbs, 183–84
  Kebobs Sicilian, 180
  Kebobs Spartan, 181
  Midwestern Chicken Kebobs,
    171
  and Pimiento Kebobs, 170–71

Polynesian Chicken Kebobs,
    173–74
Polynesian-Style Chicken and
    Ham Kebobs, 242–43
Pork and Sausage Kebobs,
    245–46
Poultry Kebobs: Honey-Rum
    Accent, 186
Poultry Kebobs: Northern
    Style, 186–87
Poultry Kebobs: Southern
    Style, 186–87
Rosemary Chicken Kebobs,
    174–75, 176
skewer cooking methods, 168–
    169
Skewered Chicken, Japanese
    Accent, 177–78
Skewered Chicken, Soup-
    Inspired, 176–77
Skewers of Coated Mixed
    Meats, 244–45
Soup Avgolemono, 281–82
Tarragon Chicken Kebobs,
    175–76
White Wine Poultry Kebobs,
    181–83
Chick-pea Dip, 271
Children's Favorite Cold Beef
    Liver Kebobs, 148–49
Chocolate:
  Bourbon Ice Cream Bake,
    295–97
  Mint Ice Cream Bake, 297
Citrus Burger Kebobs, 85–86
City Chicken, 90
Clarified Butter, 265
Coated Burger Kebobs, 81–82
Coated Chicken Liver Kebobs,
    148
Coatings and Toppings, 61, 101,
    104, 109, 166, 172, 193, 205,
    239, 244, 246
Cocktail Dip Sauces, 267–68
Cointreau Veal Kebobs, 92
Confetti Coating, 172
Continental Fruit Kebobs, 229

Cottage Cheese:
  Calorie Counter's Side-Dish
    Salad, 227–28
Cucumber(s) :
  Chunks of Vegetables and
    Fruits, 221–22
  Coated Chicken Liver Kebobs,
    148
  Salad, 292–93
  Shashlik, Russian Accent,
    106–07
  Skewered Sirloin with, 52–53
  Stuffed Red Onion and
    Cucumber Shells, 218
  and Tomato Kebobs, 211
Cumin Chicken Kebobs, 175–76
Curry(ied) :
  Fish Kebobs: Lemon and
    Curry Accent, 201–02
  Lamburger Kebobs, 117–18
  marinade, 179
  topping sauce, 117

Date Balls, 232–33
Desserts:
  Cherry and Cake à la Mode,
    231–32
  Chocolate-Bourbon Ice Cream
    Bake, 295–97
  Chocolate-Mint Ice Cream
    Bake, 297
  Confection from the Skillet, A,
    232–33
  Date Balls, 232–33
  Fresh Fruit Delight, 230–31
  Ice Cream Bake variations,
    297–98
  Molasses Oatmeal Cookies,
    294–95
  Rum Ice Cream Bake, 297
Dill(ed) :
  baste, 115
  Burger Kebobs, 79
  Lamburger Kebobs, 115
  sour cream sauces, 79, 95
  topping sauce, 79
  Veal Kebobs, 95–96

Dips, 31, 267–74
Dolmathes (Stuffed Grape
    Leaves), 277–79

Eggplant:
  Bread, Italian, 68
  Chunks of Vegetables and
    Fruits, 221–22
  Kebobs Avgolemono, 217
  Kebobs Mornay, 217
  Kebobs Skordalia, 217
  marinades for, 53, 104, 133,
    216, 221
  Pineapple and Eggplant
    Kebobs, 216–17
  Skewered Ham with, 132–33
  Skewered Lamb with, 103–04
  Skewered Salmon, 204
  Skewered Sirloin with, 53
  Zucchini and Eggplant
    Kebobs, 215–16
Enchilada Kebobs, 71–72

Feta (cheese) :
  brine for, 275
  and Cream Cheese Balls, 275
  Greek Salad, 291–92
  Skewered Feta Sandwiches,
    237
  Sour Cream Dip, 273
Figs:
  with Cheese Centerpiece,
    233–34
  Confection from the Skillet, A,
    232–33
Fish:
  Kebobs: Lemon and Curry
    Accent, 200
  Kebobs: Lemon and Domata
    Accent, 201–02
  Kebobs: Lemon and Riganato
    Accent, 200–01
  Kebobs Skordalia, 202
  skewer cooking methods,
    188–90
  Skewered Fish Plaki, 203
  See also individual listings

Flaked Kippered Herring Salad, 280–81
Flaked Salmon Salad, 280
Flank Steak Kebobs Oriental, 61–62
Fondue Dip, Greek, 273–74
Frankfurters:
  in a Bun, Almond Version, 156
  in a Bun, Banana Version, 155–56
  Tropicana Frank Kebobs, 154–55
French Blue Cheese Bread, 68
Fresh Fruit Delight, 230–31
Fried Cheeses, 275–76
Fruits:
  Chunks of Vegetables and, 221–22
  Confection from the Skillet, A, 232–33
  Continental Fruit Kebobs, 229
  Fresh Fruit Delight, 230–31
  skewer cooking methods, 208–09
  Skewered Beef with, 55–56
  Stinger Fruit Kebobs, 228
  Vegetables and Fruit Kebob Cookout, 218–22
  See also individual listings

Garlic:
  Butter, 43
  Fish Kebobs Skordalia, 202
  Sauce (Skordalia), 264
German:
  Bread, Reuben Style, 67
  Mixed Meat Kebobs, German Accent, 240
  Sauerbraten Kebobs, 46–48
Ginger, Skewered Chicken, 174, 175–76
Grains. *See* Pastas and Grains
Grape Leaves, Stuffed, 277–79
Greek:
  Chicken Kebobs Spartan, 181
  Dolmathes (Stuffed Grape Leaves), 277–79

Fondue Dip, 273–74
Kefte Burger Kebobs, 76
Lamb Kebobs Latholemono, 100–01
Lamb Kebobs Mediterranean, 112–13
Orange Beef Kebobs, 39–40
Pastitsio, 287–88
Pork Kebobs Portokali, 127–28
Salad, 291–92
Skewered Feta Sandwiches, 237
Skewered Sausages, 164
Souvlakia, Special, 42–43
Spanakopetes (Spinach Squares), 284–85
Spiced Burger Kebobs, 75–76
Taramasalata (Fish Roe Dip), 277
Griddled Cheese and Rye Kebobs, 235
Griddled Ham Kebob Snacks, 141
grilling, 25–27
Ground Beef:
  Anchovy-Stuffed Burger Kebobs, 82–83
  Beer Burger Kebobs, 84
  Burgundy Burger Kebobs, 85
  Citrus Burger Kebobs, 85–86
  Coated Burger Kebobs, 81–82
  Dill Burger Kebobs, 79
  Kefte Burger Kebobs, 76
  Mexicali Burger Kebobs, 77
  Parmesan Burger Kebobs, 77–78
  Pecan Burger Kebobs, 81
  Pineapple Burger Kebobs, 78–79
  Pizza Burger Kebobs, 80–81
  Plain Burger Kebobs, 74–75
  Roquefort Burger Kebobs, 85
  skewer cooking method, 73–74
  Spiced Burger Kebobs, 75–76
  with Surprise Centers, 86–87
  Texas Burger Kebobs, 83–84
  Wiener and Burger Kebobs, 252–53
Gruyère, Fried, 276

Guacamole:
  Golden, 271
  Traditional, 270

Ham:
  Apricot Ham Kebobs, 139
  Broiled Ham Kebob Snacks,
    141–42
  Chicken and Ham Kebobs,
    Mediterranean Style, 243–44
  Chilled Ham Kebobs, 142–43
  Chunks on Skewers, Cold,
    135–36
  Chunks on Skewers, Hot,
    136–37
  Griddled Ham Kebob Snacks,
    141
  Hawaiian Ham Kebobs, 139–40
  Kebobs Madeira, 132
  Mixed Meat Kebobs, German
    Accent, 240
  Orange Ham Kebobs, 137–38
  Pineapple Ham Kebobs, 138
  Plain Chicken Liver and Ham
    Kebobs, 242
  Polynesian Baked Kebobs,
    224–25
  Polynesian-Style Chicken and
    Ham Kebobs, 242–43
  Pork, Ham, and Salami
    Kebobs, 246–47
  skewer cooking methods,
    121–23
  Skewered Ham with Eggplant,
    132–33
  Skewered Ham and Lamb, 249
  Skewered Veal and Ham
    Wraparounds, 241
  Skewers of Coated Mixed
    Meats, 244–45
  Slices on Skewers, Cold, 134–35
  Slices on Skewers, Hot, 135
Hawaiian Ham Kebobs, 139–40
Hearts of Palm:
  Skewered, 211
  Skewered Beef with, 41–42
Herb sauces, 65, 67, 267

Hollandaise Sauce, 261–62
Horseradish sauces:
  Lemon Highlight, 268
  Tangy, 269
  Touch of Tomato, 268
Hot Sauce, 226

Ice Cream Bakes:
  Chocolate-Bourbon, 295–97
  Chocolate-Mint, 297
  Rum, 297
  variations, 297–98
Indian Chicken Tikka, 179–80
Indonesian Chicken Saté, 178–79
Instant Potato Balls, 286–87
Italian:
  Chicken Kebobs Sicilian, 180
  Eggplant Bread, 68
  Skewered Sausages, 165
  Spiedini Mozzarella Special,
    235–36
  Veal Kebobs, 94–95

Japanese:
  Kushi Yaki, 44–46
  Skewered Chicken, Japanese
    Accent, 177–78
Jumbo Shrimp Kebobs, 191

Kebobs:
  estimating portions of, 19
  history of, 17–18
  seasonings for, 28–33
  serving of, 17–21
  skewer cooking methods, 22–27
Kefte Burger Kebobs, 76
Kidneys, Lamb:
  Skewered, 151–52
  Skewered Beef, Lamb Kidneys,
    and Pork Sausage Links,
    247–48
Kippered Herring Salad, Flaked,
  280–81

Knackwurst:
  Biscuit-Ringed Knackwurst
    Kebobs, 156–57
  Skewered Mixed Sausages, 167
  Skewered Sausages, Viennese
    Accent, 166
  Tropicana Frank Kebobs,
    154–55
Korean San Juk, 43–44
Kümmel Pork Kebobs, 126

Lamb:
  and Beef Kebobs, Picnic Style,
    249–50
  Curried Lamburger Kebobs,
    117–18
  Dilled Lamburger Kebobs, 115
  Kebobs Caribbean, 111–12
  Kebobs Cosmopolitan, 104–05
  Kebobs Latholemono, 100–01
  Kebobs Mediterranean, 112–13
  Kebobs with Onion, 105
  Kebobs Scandinavian, 113–14
  Kebobs, Turkish Accent, 106
  Minted Lamb Kebobs
    Avgolemono, 99–100
  Minted Lamburger Kebobs, 116
  Moroccan-Inspired Lamb
    Kebobs, 109–11
  Outdoor Kebobing with, 118–19
  Roast Lamb Kebobs, Sweet
    Version, 119–20
  Roast Lamb Kebobs, Tart
    Version, 120
  Shashlik, Russian Accent,
    106–07
  skewer cooking methods, 97–99
  Skewered Ham and, 249
  Skewered Lamb with Eggplant,
    103–04
  Skewered Lamb with Orange
    Overtones, 101–02
  Skewered Lamb with Zucchini
    Surprises, 102–03
  South African Sosaties, 107–08
  Spanish Pinchos, 108–09

  Spur-of-the-Moment Lamb
    Kebobs, 114
  Veal and Pepperoni Kebobs,
    239–40
Leftover Roast Meats:
  Beef, 70–71
  Chicken, 184–87
  Ham and Pork, 140–42
  Lamb, 119–20
  Mixed Meats, 245, 257
Lemon(s):
  Butter, 49
  Fish Kebobs: Lemon and
    Curry Accent, 201–02
  Fish Kebobs: Lemon and
    Domata (Tomato) Accent,
    200
  Fish Kebobs: Lemon and
    Riganato (Oregano) Accent,
    200–01
  Latholemono Marinade–Baste,
    101
  and Oranges, Stuffed, 219–20
Lingonberry:
  Dressing, 223
  topping sauce, 251
Liquors. See Spirits.
Liver, Beef:
  Children's Favorite Cold Beef
    Liver Kebobs, 148–49
  and Onion Kebobs, 149–50
Liver, Calf's, Skewered, 150–51
Livers, Chicken:
  Coated Chicken Liver Kebobs,
    148
  Plain Chicken Liver and Ham
    Kebobs, 243
  Skewered, Georgia's Style, 146
  Skewered, and Pork Sausage
    Links, 251–52
  Skewered, with Sesame
    Bananas, 147
Liver Sausage:
  Cheese and Sausage Balls,
    158–59
  Cubed Luncheon Meat Kebobs,
    162
Lobster en Brochette, 190

Low-Calorie Dip Sauce, 273
Low-calorie menu, 304
Luncheon meats:
  Chopped Luncheon Meat
    Kebobs, 161
  Cubed Luncheon Meat Kebobs,
    162
  Pepperoni-Accented Kebobs,
    157–58

Madeira:
  baste–topping, 198
  and Beef Kebobs, 57–58
  Continental Fruit Kebobs, 229
  Ham Kebobs, 132
  marinade–bastes, 57, 150
  mushroom sauce, 64
  sauce, 63
  skillet sauce, 132
  Topped Potato Mounds, 286
Marinades, 28, 29–30, 55
  for artichokes, 99
  for beef, 39, 41, 52, 55, 61, 67
  for chicken, 179, 244
  for chicken and ham, 243
  for crab, 194
  for eggplant, 53, 104, 133, 216,
    221
  for lamb, 99, 102, 103, 105, 107
  for lobster, 190, 195
  for mixed meats, 247
  for mushrooms, 51
  orange, 138
  for oranges, 221
  for pineapple, 216
  for pork, 127, 138
  for red snapper, 206
  sesame-seed, 44
  for shrimp, 193, 194
  for sirloin, 51, 52, 53, 54
  for sweet potatoes, 214
Marinade–Bastes, 40, 45, 147,
    165, 249, 252
  beer, 59
  bourbon, 60
  Burgundy, 58
  cherry, 163

  for chicken, 170, 174, 175, 176,
    178, 180, 181, 182
  for fish, 200, 201
  Latholemono, 100
  Madeira, 57, 150
  for pork, 125, 126, 128, 140
  for salmon, 204
  for shrimp, 191, 192
Marinade–Baste–Toppings, 46,
    56, 89, 108
  pineapple, 173, 192
Marinade–Topping, 47
Marinade–Topping–Sauce, 164
Mediterranean Mists, 293–94
Menus, 301–23, 326, 328, 331–36
Mexicali Burger Kebobs, 77
Mexican:
  Bean Salad Bed, 225–26
  Braised Vegetable Kebobs, 226
  Enchilada Kebobs, 71–72
  Main Course Salad, 225–27
Midwestern Chicken Kebobs, 171
Minted:
  Lamb Kebobs Avgolemono,
    99–100
  Lamburger Kebobs, 116
Mixed Meat(s), 238, 255–57
  Brunch Kebobs, 250–51
  Kebobs, German Accent, 240
  Mixed Pork Kebobs, 130
  Snack Tray of Mixed Meat
    Kebobs, 253–54
  See also individual listings
Molasses Oatmeal Cookies,
    294–95
Mornay Sauce, 259
Moroccan-Inspired Lamb
    Kebobs:
  Mild, 109–10
  Nippy, 110–11
Mozzarella Cheese:
  Anchovy Crunch Topping, 239
  Spiedini Mozzarella Special,
    235–36
  topping mixture, 205
Mushroom(s):
  en Brochette, 210
  Chicken Kebobs Sicilian, 180

Mushroom(s) (*Continued*)
  Madeira Sauce, 64
  Onion and Green Pepper,
    Sautéed, 282
  Skewered Sirloin with, 51–52
  Wild Rice and, 290–91
Mustard sauces:
  Mild, 270
  Sweet-Sour, 269–70

Nonsweet Sweet Potato Kebobs,
    214
Nonsweet Triangles, 163

Olive(s):
  Cheese and Sausage Balls,
    158–59
  Cheese and Sausage Chunks,
    159–60
  Chicken Kebobs Confetti,
    172–73
  Chicken Kebobs Sicilian, 180
  Jumbo Shrimp Kebobs, 191
  Nonsweet Triangles, 163
  Poultry Kebobs, Northern
    Style, 186–87
Onion(s):
  Beef Liver and Onion Kebobs,
    149–50
  Lamb Kebobs with, 105–06
  Mushrooms and Green Pepper,
    Sautéed, 282
  Skewered Sirloin with, 54
  Stuffed Red Onion and
    Cucumber Shells, 218
On-the-Range Pork Kebobs,
    123–24
Orange(s):
  Chunks of Vegetables and
    Fruits, 221–22
  Greek Beef Kebobs, 39–40
  Ham Kebobs, 137–38
  Ham Slices: Hot, 135
  Polynesian Baked Kebobs,
    224–25

Polynesian Chicken Kebobs,
    173–74
Pork Kebobs Portokali, 127–28
Skewered Lamb with Orange
    Overtones, 101–02
Skewered Scallops with Fruit,
    195–97
Stuffed Lemons and, 219–20
Sweet-Sour Shrimp Kebobs,
    192–93
Tropical Salad Bed, 224–25
Oregano:
  Fish Kebobs: Lemon and
    Riganato Accent, 200–01
  marinade–baste, 176
Oyster(s):
  Beef Rib-Eye and Oyster
    Kebobs, 248–49
  Kebobs Parmesan, 198
  Skewered Wrapped, 198

Paprika marinade–baste, 176
Parmesan Cheese:
  Biscuit-Ringed Knackwurst
    Kebobs, 156–57
  Burger Kebobs, 77–78
  Confetti Coating, 172
  Fried, 276
  Oyster Kebobs Parmesan, 198
  Pronto Broiler Kebobs, 62–63
  Veal Kebobs, 93
  Zucchini and Eggplant Kebobs,
    215–16
Party ideas, 324–36
  large group, 327–28
  small group, 325–27
  themes, 328–36
Pastas and Grains:
  Bulgur, 290
  Miriam's Pilaf, 289
  Pastitsio, 287–89
  Wild Rice and Mushrooms,
    290–91
Pastitsio, My Mother's, 287–89
Peanut Dip Sauce, 178
Pea Pods, Water Chestnuts and
    Bamboo Shoots, Sautéed, 283

Pecan Burger Kebobs, 81
Pepper(s):
    Chunks of Vegetables and
        Fruits, 221–22
    Pork Kebobs, 124–25
    Skewered Mixed Sausages, 167
    Steak Kebobs, 40–41
    Stuffed Sweet Red, 218–19
Pepperoni:
    Accented Kebobs, 157–58
    Lamb, Veal, and Pepperoni
        Kebobs, 239–40
Pilaf, Miriam's, 289
Pimiento:
    Chicken and Pimiento Kebobs,
        170
    Poultry Kebobs, Northern
        Style, 186–87
    Tarragon Chicken Kebobs,
        175–76
Pineapple:
    Burger Kebobs, 78–79
    and Eggplant Kebobs, 216–17
    Franks in a Bun, Banana
        Version, 155–56
    Ham Kebobs, 138
    Ham Slices: Hot, 135
    Lamb Kebobs Caribbean,
        111–12
    marinade–baste–toppings, 192
    Polynesian Chicken Kebobs,
        173–74
    Pork and Apple Kebobs, 128–29
    Porkburger Kebobs, 139
    Skewered Pork and, 140–41
    Skewered Red Snapper, 206–07
    Skewered Scallops with Fruit,
        195–97
    Sweet-and-Sour Skewered
        Pork, 124–25
    Tropicana Frank Kebobs,
        154–55
Pizza Burger Kebobs, 80–81
Plain Burger Kebobs, 74–75
Plain Chicken Livers and Ham
    Kebobs, 242
Plaki Topping Sauce, 203

Polynesian:
    Chicken Kebobs, 173–74
    Salad, 224–25
    -Style Chicken and Ham
        Kebobs, 242
Pork:
    and Apple Kebobs, 128–29
    Chicken, Pork, and Sausage
        Kebobs, 245–46
    Ham and Salami Kebobs,
        246–47
    Kebobs Portokali, 127–28
    Kümmel Pork Kebobs, 126
    Latholemono style, 100–01, 122
    Mixed Pork Kebobs, 129
    On-the-Range Pork Kebobs,
        123–24
    Peppery Pork Kebobs, 125–26
    Porkburger Kebobs, 130
    Sage Skewered, 127
    skewer cooking methods,
        121–23
    Skewered Pork and Pineapple,
        140–41
    Sparerib Kebobs, 131
    Sweet-and-Sour Skewered
        Pork, 124–25
    See also Ham; Pork Sausage;
        Salami; Sausages
Pork Sausage:
    Skewered Beef, Lamb Kidneys,
        and Pork Sausage Links,
        247–48
    Skewered Chicken Livers and
        Pork Sausage Links, 251–52
    Skewered Sausages, Viennese
        Accent, 166
Potato(es):
    Balls, Instant, 286–87
    Mounds, Madeira-Topped, 286
    Salad, Picnic, 287
    Stuffing, 218
Poultry. See Chicken and Poultry
Pronto Broiler Kebobs, 62–63
Pronto Skillet and Baking-Pan
    Kebobs, 63–64

Red Snapper, Skewered, 206–07
Roast Beef:
  Cheese-Coated Kebobs, 70–71
  Cold or Warm Slices on a
    Skewer, 69–70
  Enchilada Kebobs, 71–72
  Sweet-Tangy Kebobs, 71
Roast Lamb:
  Kebobs, Sweet Version, 119–20
  Kebobs, Tart Version, 120
Roquefort:
  bastes, 41, 83
  Burger Kebobs, 85
Rosemary Chicken Kebobs,
  174–75, 176
Rum Ice Cream Bake, 297

Sage Skewered Pork, 127
Salads:
  Calorie Counter's Side-Dish,
    227–28
  Cucumber, 292–93
  Greek, 291–92
  Main Course, 222–27
  Mexican Main Course, 225–27
  Picnic Potato, 287
  Polynesian Main Course,
    224–25
  Scandinavian Main Course,
    223–24
Salami:
  Nonsweet Triangles, 163
  Pork, Ham, and Salami Kebobs,
    246–47
Salmon:
  Salad, Flaked, 280
  Skewered, 204
Salt, use of, 31–32, 188
Sandwiches:
  Beef Kebobs, Loaf Style, 67–68
  Broiled Kebob Ideas, 256
  Chilled Ham, 142–43
  Franks in Bun, Banana or
    Almond version, 155–56
  Griddled Cheese and Rye
    Kebobs, 235
  Ham Chunks, Cold or Hot, 136–
    137

Ham Slices, Cold, 134
Lamb Kebobs, Mild and Nippy,
  109–11
Pizza Burger Kebobs, 80–81
Plain Burger Kebobs, 74–75
Sandwich on a Stick Idea, 160
serving methods, 18
Skewered Feta Sandwiches, 237
Skewered Italian Sausages, 165
Texas Burger Kebobs, 83–84
Sauces:
  for artichokes, 212
  Avgolemono, 262–63, 278
  Béarnaise, 262
  Béchamel, 258–59
  Bordelaise, 261
  Brown I, 260
  Brown II (Bordelaise), 261
  Brown, Quick, 260
  Butter, Clarified, 265
  Chasseur, 65
  Chick-pea, 271
  Clarified Butter, 265
  Garlic, 264
  Greek Fondue, 273–74
  Guacamole, Golden, 271
  Guacamole, Traditional, 270
  Herb, 65
  Hollandaise, 261
  Horseradish, with Lemon, 268
  Horseradish, Tangy, 269
  Horseradish, with Tomato, 268
  Hot, 226
  Low-Calorie, 273
  Madeira, 63
  Mornay, 259
  Mushroom-Madeira, 64
  Mustard Dip, chilled, 269–70
  Mustard Dip, warm, 270
  for scallops, 197
  Skordalia (garlic), 264
  Slightly Hot, 65
  Sour Cream with Anchovy,
    272
  Sour Cream with Cheddar, 272
  Sour Cream, Mild, 273
  Sour Cream, Sweet, 272–73

Spicy Cocktail, I, 267
Spicy Cocktail, II, 268
Supreme, 259
Sweet-Sour, 269
Sweet-Sour, Thin, 264
Tomato Barbecue I, 265–66
Tomato Barbecue II, 266–67
Tomato Barbecue variations,
67, 267
Tomato Horseradish, 268
Vinaigrette, Basic, 263
Vinaigrette, Variation, 263–64
See also Bastes
Sauerbraten Kebobs, 46–48
Sausages:
Biscuit-Ringed Knackwurst
Kebobs, 156–57
Cheese and Sausage Balls:
Cold, 158–59
Cheese and Sausage Chunks:
Hot, 159–60
Chicken, Pork, and Sausage
Kebobs, 245–46
Chopped Luncheon Meat
Kebobs, 161
Cubed Luncheon Meat
Kebobs, 162
Franks in a Bun, Almond
Version, 156
Franks in a Bun, Banana
Version, 155–56
Nonsweet Triangles, 163
Pepperoni-Accented Kebobs,
157–58
skewer cooking methods, 153–
154
Skewered Greek, 164–65
Skewered Italian, 165
Skewered Luncheon Meats,
160–61
Skewered Mixed, 167
Skewered Sausages, Viennese
Accent, 166
Sweet and Cordial Triangles,
162–63
Tropicana Frank Kebobs,
154–55
See also individual listings

Scallops, 189
Skewered Scallops and Shrimp,
197
Skewered Scallops with Fruits,
195–97
Skewered Scallops with
Vegetables, 195–97
Scandinavian:
Ham Rolls, 223–24
Lamb Kebobs, 113–14
Lingonberry Dressing, 223
Main Course Salad, 223–24
Seafood Salad Bed, 223
Seafood:
Salad Bed, 223
See also Fish; Shellfish;
individual listings
Sesame seed (s) :
Continental Fruit Kebobs, 229
marinade, 44
Skewered Chicken Livers with
Sesame Bananas, 147
Shashlik, Russian Accent, 106–07
Shellfish:
Cooking methods, 188–89
See also individual listings
Shrimp, 188–89
Jumbo Shrimp Kebobs, 191
Skewered Scallops and, 197
Skewered Shellfish Trio, 194–95
Spiced Shrimp Kebobs, 191–92
Spiked Shrimp Kebobs, 193–94
Sweet-Sour Shrimp Kebobs,
192–93
Single-Spiced Chicken Kebobs,
174–76
Skara (grill), 118
Skewered Artichokes, 212
Skewered Beef Duo, 48–49
Skewered Beef with Hearts of
Palm, 41–42
Skewered Beef, Lamb Kidney,
and Pork Sausage Links,
247–48
Skewered Beef Sirloin with
Single Vegetable, 49–55
Skewered Beef Steak a la Sauce,
64–66

Skewered Calf's Liver, 150–51
Skewered Cheese Canapes, 233–36
Skewered Chicken Livers,
    Georgia's Style, 146
Skewered Chicken Livers and
    Pork Sausage Links, 251–52
Skewered Chicken Livers with
    Sesame Bananas, 147
Skewered Feta Sandwiches, 237
Skewered Fish Plaki, 203
Skewered Ginger Chicken, 174,
    175–76
Skewered Greek Sausages, 164
Skewered Ham with Eggplant,
    132–33
Skewered Ham and Lamb, 249
Skewered Italian Sausages, 165
Skewered Lamb with Eggplant,
    103–04
Skewered Lamb Kidneys, 151–52
Skewered Lamb with Orange
    Overtones, 101–02
Skewered Lamb with Zucchini
    Surprises, 102–03
Skewered Mixed Sausages, 167
Skewered Pork with Pineapple,
    140–41
Skewered Sausages, Viennese
    Accent, 166
Skewered Scallops with Fruits,
    195–97
Skewered Scallops and Shrimp,
    197
Skewered Scallops with
    Vegetables, 195–97
Skewered Shellfish Trio, 194
Skewered Sirloin with Single
    Vegetable, 49–55
Skewered Steak a la Sauce, 64–66
Skewered Veal with Apricots,
    91–92
Skewered Veal and Ham
    Wraparounds, 241
Skewered Veal with Vermouth,
    90–91
Skewered Wrapped Oysters, 198
Skewers, 17–19

Skewers of Coated Mixed Meats,
    244–45
Skillet Sauces, 31, 146, 163, 167,
    216, 227, 239, 240, 241, 244,
    246
    apricot, 91, 139
    Burgundy, 232
    for chicken, 170, 171, 172
    Cointreau, 92
    for lamb, 104, 106, 112
    orange, 102
    for pork, 124, 129, 132
    for veal, 90, 94, 95
    See also Bastes
Skordalia Sauce, 264
Slightly Hot Sauce, 65
Snack Tray of Mixed Meat
    Kebobs, 253–54
Soup:
    Chicken Soup Avgolemono,
        281–82
Sour Cream sauces:
    Anchovy Accent, 272
    Cheddar Accent, 272
    Dill, 79, 95
    Mild, 273
    Sweet Accent, 272
South African Sosaties, 107–08
Spanakopetes (Spinach Squares),
    284–85
Spanish Pinchos, 108–09
Sparerib Kebobs, 131
Speared Centerpiece of Cheese,
    A, 233–34
Special Beef Souvlakia, 42–43
Spice:
    Use of, 32–33
    See also individual listings of
        herbs and spices
Spiced Burger Kebobs, 75–76
Spiced Shrimp Kebobs, 191–92
Spiedini Mozzarella Special,
    235–36
Spiked Shrimp Kebobs, 193–94
Spinach Squares, 284–85
Spirits, use of, 33
    See also Beverages, Burgundy,
        Madeira

Spur-of-the-Moment Lamb
  Kebobs, 114
Stinger Fruit Kebobs, 228
Stuffed:
  Grape Leaves, 277–79
  Lemons and Oranges, 219–20
  Red Onion and Cucumber
    Shells, 218
  Sweet Peppers, 218–19
  Tomatoes, 219
Stuffings:
  Bean, 220
  Potato, 218
  Sweet Potato, 220
  Zucchini, 219
Supreme Sauce, 259
Surprise Burger Kebobs, 86–87
Sweet Potato:
  Kebobs, 213–14
  Stuffing, 220
  See also Yams
Sweet-Sour Sauces:
  Dip, 269
  Mustard, 269–70
  Thin, 264
  Tomato Barbecue, 267
Sweet-Sour Shrimp Kebobs,
  192–93
Sweet-and-Sour Skewered Pork,
  124–25
Sweet-Tangy Kebobs, 71
Swiss Cheese:
  Ham Chunks: Cold, 136
  Ham Chunks: Hot, 136–37

Taco Garnish Rolls, Beef, 226–27
Tangy Skewered Veal, 89
Taramasalata (Fish Roe Dip),
  277
Tarragon Chicken Kebobs,
  175–76
Texas Burger Kebobs, 83–84
Tomato(es):
  Barbecue Sauces, 265–67
  Butter, 49
  Cucumber and Tomato
    Kebobs, 211

Fish: Lemon and Domata
    (tomato) Accent, 200
  Horseradish Sauce, 268
  skewer cooking methods, 209
  Stuffed, 219
Topping Sauces, 30–31, 45, 47,
  50, 54, 61, 162, 177
  anchovy, 236
  avgolemono, 262–63
  banana, 48
  cheese, 254
  curry, 117
  dill, 79
  for fruit, 230
  lingonberry, 251
  pizza, 80
  Plaki, 203
  for pork, 137
  Scandinavian, 113
  See also Bastes
Tropical Drink, 293
Trout Kebobs, 204–05

Variety Meats:
  skewer cooking methods,
    144–45
  See also Kidneys; Liver, Beef;
    Liver, Calf's; Liver, Chicken
Veal:
  City Chicken, 90
  Cointreau Veal Kebobs, 92
  Dilled Veal Kebobs, 95–96
  Kebobs Italiano, 94–95
  Kebobs Parmesan, 93
  Lamb, Veal, and Pepperoni
    Kebobs, 239–40
  Mixed Meat Kebobs, German
    Accent, 240
  and Salty Accents, 93–94
  skewer cooking methods, 88–89
  Skewered Veal with Apricots,
    91–92
  Skewered Veal and Ham
    Wraparounds, 241
  Skewered Veal Vermouth,
    90–91
  Tangy Skewered, 89

Vegetable(s):
  Braised Mexican Kebobs, 226
  Chilled Vegetable Kebobs,
    210–12
  Chunks of Vegetables and
    Fruits, 221–22
  and Fruit Kebob Cookout,
    218–22
  Hearts of Palm, Skewered,
    211
  Onions, Mushrooms, and Green
    Peppers, Sautéed, 282
  Pea Pods, Water Chestnuts,
    and Bamboo Shoots, Sautéed,
    283
  skewer cooking methods, 208–09
  Stuffed, 218–20
  Sweet and Sour, 284
  Verve, 283–84
  See also Salads; individual
    listings
Vermouth Skewered Veal, 90–91
Vinaigrette Sauce:
  basic, 263
  variation, 263–64

White Wine Poultry Kebobs,
  181–82
Wiener and Burger Kebobs,
  252–53
Wild Rice and Mushrooms,
  290–91
Wine, use of, 33, 209

Yam(s):
  Tropicana Frank Kebobs,
    154–55
  See also Sweet Potatoes
Yogurt:
  curry marinade, 179
  curry topping sauce, 117

Zucchini:
  Braised Mexican Kebobs, 226
  Chunks of Vegetables and
    Fruits, 221–22
  and Eggplant Kebobs, 215–16
  Skewered Calf's Liver, 150–51
  Skewered Lamb with Zucchini
    Surprises, 102–03
  Stuffing, 219